Response Set
in
Personality
Assessment

Modern Applications in Psychology

under the editorship of

Joseph D. Matarazzo
UNIVERSITY OF OREGON MEDICAL SCHOOL

Judson S. Brown
UNIVERSITY OF IOWA

Response Set
in
Personality
Assessment

edited by

IRWIN A. BERG

ALDINE PUBLISHING COMPANY / *Chicago*

First published 1967 by
ALDINE Publishing Company
320 West Adams Street
Chicago, Illinois 60606

Library of Congress Catalog Card Number 66-28342
Designed by Bernard Schleifer
Printed in the United States of America

Preface

The central concern of this book is with response sets and their relationship to personality assessment. "Sets" are tendencies to respond in a particular direction and there is nothing particularly new about them. It has been known for many decades that response sets or biases occur in many everyday situations. On the first toss of a coin, for example, about 80 per cent of the people responding will call "heads" instead of the 50 per cent chance would lead us to expect. When entering a theater or a museum, it is often possible to turn either left or right to reach a main staircase; however, 75 per cent of those entering will bear right and only 25 per cent left. To consider another example, in taking tests, the correct answer may be unknown or there may be no obviously correct answer; yet chance does not operate to provide an equal distribution of responses among the available options. Where the choice is *true-false* or *agree-disagree,* about 75 to 80 per cent of the subjects will choose *true* or *agree.* Similarly, in a situation where the subject must choose either 1, 2, 3, or 4 to indicate his preference, about 60 per cent will select "3" and only 5 per cent will choose "1," when there is no correct or clearly appropriate answer. Chance expectancy, of course, would be 25 per cent for each option.

For more than sixty years it has been suspected that these sets or response biases were related to personality characteristics. In 1902, for example, Goddard mused over the fact that he found a preponderance of left-handers among mental retardates which was a form of reverse bias since about 75 per cent of normal persons are right-handed. Subsequent writers related neuroticism to hand preference as well as to other response biases. However, while over the years a number of persons studied various sets in relation to personality, the relationship was elusive. A relationship was definitely present but it was not clear enough to be particularly useful for assessment purposes.

The problem of the meaning and usefulness of set is old, but there is something new in the spate of published research that has recently shed considerable light on the problem. This renewed research activity was probably triggered by Lee J. Cronbach's 1946 article on response sets in test-taking behavior. Cronbach described a number of response sets as they occurred in tests, and he noted that they seemed to be related to personality traits. But he regarded sets as a nuisance in psychological testing and wished to get rid of them. Cronbach's succinct statement seemed to crystallize reactions among a number of social scientists who appreciated his position but who wanted to use rather than get rid of response sets. They did use them, chiefly for identifying aberrant personality characteristics; however, most researchers used only a few stimuli which produced only a few biased responses. As a result, their findings were somewhat better in predictive power than the old, pre-World War II studies but not much better.

Other researchers worked with a particular class of response sets but used many stimuli and the many responses such stimuli produced. The outgrowth of their efforts has been one of the liveliest research areas in psychology during the past fifteen years. Virtually all of these research efforts may be placed in one of three groups which have been labeled the *Social Desirability Variable,* the *Acquiescence Set,* and the *Deviation Hypothesis.* The present book is devoted to a statement of these three approaches and the evidence that supports each.

The Social Desirability Variable is focused on the set to

endorse favorable traits. Allen L. Edwards developed this approach, and he and his students have published most of the evidence that demonstrates the operation and significance of the variable. As a result of their studies, there seems little doubt that a consistent tendency to present oneself in a favorable light when taking tests does exist and that this is fraught with meaning for personality testing. Of the three approaches to research on personality and response sets, Edwards's is the least cluttered, the most sanitary in design, and the most systematic in adhering to a program of research. It is also the narrowest in application and in the range of behavior with which it is concerned. The Social Desirability Variable is centered on test-taking behavior, which is indeed behavior but obviously limited in scope.

The Acquiescence Set approach is concerned with tendencies to give responses such as *agree, yes, like,* and *true* to a variety of stimulus conditions. A number of different researchers over the years have used this approach in their studies; however, Douglas N. Jackson and Samuel J. Messick have been more closely identified with acquiescence set studies than others. The research in this area is relatively more scattered than that done on the Social Desirability Variable; this is understandable, since the behavior dealt with is considerably broader. The import of acquiescence set research goes far beyond the superficial tendency to express agreement. The authoritarian personality, the noncritical thinker, the conformist, and other similar persons may eventually be better understood in terms of the operation of what seems to be a basic trait, namely, the set to acquiesce. In addition, deeper knowledge of this set may provide a means of understanding the behavior of a particular person in a particular situation. This would lead, in turn, to a more effective means of predicting behavior.

The Deviation Hypothesis, the third approach, utilizes deviant sets or responses which *go counter to* a popular expression of bias. Thus, if most people turn right at some particular point, this approach demands a close look at those who turn left. Where most people acquiesce, the Deviation Hypothesis is not interested in them but rather in those who say *no*. The hypothesis was formulated by Irwin A. Berg, and most of the supporting evidence has been published by him and his students. Of the three approaches, the Deviation Hypothesis is by far the broadest but also the least specific. It is broadest in that it seeks to encompass all behavior, and it is least specific in that it is not thoroughly nailed down by research data. Like the other two approaches, a large number of studies dealing with the Deviation Hypothesis have been published, but with such a vast territory staked out for investigation, many areas remain to be explored. Nevertheless it is quite clear that the application of the Deviation Hypothesis can serve to identify and predict response characteristics for a wide variety of deviant groups.

As set forth in the present book, the three approaches to response set in personality assessment are offered in order of tidiness and ambitiousness. The Social Desirability Variable is the neatest of the three as well as the most limited in the behavioral range covered. Accordingly, following an orientation chapter by Richard K. McGee, it is the first presented. Next, by these criteria of neatness and scope, is the Acquiescence Set approach, and last is the Deviation Hypothesis. A summarizing chapter by Harold B. Pepinsky follows.

Response Set and Personality Assessment began as a symposium held at Louisiana State University in Baton Rouge on February 25 and 26, 1965. The papers read at that symposium were later expanded, updated, and revised for the present book. In such a venture there are always antecedents in the form of institutions and persons who helped make it a success. It is a pleasure to acknowledge the assistance of the Louisiana State Department of Hospitals. This state agency gives the LSU Department of Psychology an annual grant, which assisted materially in defraying the symposium expenses. I should like to thank the Department of Hospitals officers for their interest and support: the late Director, R. Butler Walden; the present Director, Lee Agerton; the former Commissioner of Mental Health, J. Paul Pratt, M.D.; the present Commissioner, William Addison, M.D.; and Assistant

Commissioner H. J. Walters. Cecil G. Taylor, Chancellor of Louisiana State University, cut much red tape for us in preparing the symposium and then gave a welcoming address which was both gracious and warmly effective. Finally, I wish to thank my patient, tender-and-true wife, Sylvia, who was hostess to guests during the symposium, who put up with a curtailed social life while I wrote and later edited this book, and who then helped with the indexing.

Irwin A. Berg

Contents

Response Set in Relation to Personality: An Orientation

In clinical work we sometimes ask, "Who counsels the counselor?" or we are concerned about whether therapists can follow the ancient dictum, "Heal thyself." This dilemma is brought to mind inasmuch as this chapter is supposed to produce a set in a group of set experts, to help the reader become *eingestellt* for what the following papers present. To accomplish this, I will focus first on the whole concept of "set" in psychology, which has been done quite adequately, although not too recently (Dashiell, 1940; Gibson, 1941; Gibson and McCarvey, 1937). Second, I will review briefly the specific set area that has received a major portion of research attention in the field of personality and assessment.

An adequate review of the men, events, and ideas that have influenced the development of the study of response set would almost be a comprehensive history of psychology in the twentieth century. Nearly all areas of scientific or professional psychology in some way base their theories or technical procedures on the assumption that the subject, whether animal or human, always displays in behavior some predisposing tendency that in part, predetermines or *biases* the response or responses he is about to make to a stimulus.[1] Psychologists

1. It will be recalled that Pavlov recorded widely variant pretesting behavior in his dogs, which seemed to indicate that some entered the laboratory and submitted to the apparatus harness much more willingly than others. This has led Professor Kimble to observe that even animals have attitudes toward experiments that need to be taken into account.

believe that "all behavior is motivated" to the extent that when they cannot explain behavior simply by an imbalance in homeostatic processes, they then consider it quite legitimate to think of curiosity and investigative and exploratory drives (Rethlingshafer, 1963). Thus, if a psychologist began to investigate an area in which motivation were not a factor, he would immediately find himself in an awkward position. Since without motivation there can be no behavior, the psychologist would have nothing within his realm of scientific competence to study.

A quick overview of the science suggests that set is in the same situation. Allport (1955), Dashiell (1940), and Hefferline (1962) have pointed out that set is ubiquitous to all forms of behavior. In Gibson's words, "The concept of set or attitude is a nearly universal one in psychological thinking, despite the fact that the underlying meaning is indefinite, the terminology chaotic, and the usage by psychologists highly individualistic" (1941, p. 781). Gibson lists 34 terms and phrases used in the literature as variants of the set concept.

One cannot talk about responses to stimuli in the area of learning, perception, problem solving, or social attitudes without invoking the concept of set as a mediating influence operating somewhere between stimulus and response. Set seems to have become a universal hypothetical construct constituting a major portion of the "O" in the S-O-R paradigm. Thus, Stagner (1948) has made personality and set nearly equivalent concepts. He identifies a personality trait as an elaborate mental set which is demonstrated in a readiness to respond to a variety of stimuli in more or less consistent ways. Allport's (1937) definition of trait is so close to the concept of set, at least as it is used in response set work, that it makes trait and set two identical concepts, specifically when he refers to the capacity to render many stimuli functionally equivalent and to initiate consistent forms of expressive behavior. To return to personality assessment, what better examples are to be found of "many stimuli being made functionally equivalent" than the operation of a set; or of a factor "consistently guiding adaptive and expressive behavior" than the presence of the social desirability set?

I. "SET" IN THE SCIENCE OF PSYCHOLOGY

In the Würzburg School at the turn of the century, Marbe, Watt, Ach, and Külpe initiated the controversy surrounding "imageless thought." Just as their predecessors in the German branch of the new science of psychology had done, these men attempted to lay open the conscious mind to the scrutiny of external observers. They became convinced that the images and sensations reported by introspective subjects could not alone account for the totality of consciousness.

Watt divided consciousness into four separate periods and instructed his observers to concentrate on each of them independently. Using an association task, he attempted to study what transpired at various points throughout the experience. Whereas others had been emphasizing the interval immediately following the stimulus word, when the observer was searching for a response word, Watt concentrated his attention on the preparatory period that preceded the stimulus. In this way, he introduced the *Aufgabe* as a crucial element—that is, the subject's conscious awareness of the task he is to perform while it is being transmitted to him through the instructions for the procedure. It is as though, in contemplating the task, the subject begins to think about and solve the problem —to respond—before the problem is actually presented. Thus, the *Aufgabe* sets up within the subject a "set" or *Einstellung*.

This initial work was soon elaborated and extended by Ach, who attempted to account for the manner in which the initial *Aufgabe* is unconsciously perpetuated and continues to exercise its influence throughout an extended task. To explain this, Ach named, or invented, a new concept, *the determining tendency,* which identified a trend in the stream of consciousness that focused the observer's attention on the overall task without interruption by each new stimulus. In his discussion of this phenomena, Boring gives the following example:

The concept of the determining tendency implies that the

tendency operates superiorly to reinforce associative tendencies. Thus, given a 5 with a 2 below it printed on paper, the
most usual associates would be 7, 3, and 10. If the subject
has been instructed to add, one association will be strength-
ened so that 7 will almost inevitably occur; or, if the *Aufgabe*
has been to subtract, then another association is reinforced
and becomes the strongest (1950, p. 405).

It is possible to translate this Würzburg situation to the
response set problem encountered in personality assessment.
For example, when a subject is given a copy of the MMPI or
the Personal Preference Schedule, an *Aufgabe* is created
that connotes, in effect, "We want to know something about
you, we are asking that you contribute to our knowledge by
describing yourself with this list of phrases and adjectives."
The subject does not know exactly what will be asked of him,
but as he considers the task, he may modify the *Aufgabe* with
his own input: "I know that in addition to the information
they receive, I also stand to gain or lose something as a result
of what I tell them." In contemplating this total *Aufgabe*, he
becomes *eingestellt*, or set, to respond accordingly.

As he moves from test item to test item, his perception
of the impression to be gained from his responses may be
modified, but it likewise becomes increasingly apparent to
him that some important consequence will ensue. Although
he may have formed an erroneous conclusion about the
nature of the test he nevertheless has formed a conclusion
that becomes progressively refined, discriminated, and reinforced. In this way the determining tendency develops and
operates to influence the specific responses the subject will
give, even before he encounters many of the individual items.

It is a long way in time, if not in concept, from Würzburg
to personality assessment, and perhaps we should consider
the various aspects of *Einstellung* in general psychological
research, before we discuss its particular place in personality
assessment.

SET IN PERCEPTION

As Gibson (1941) pointed out in his critical review of set in experimental psychology, in no area has set been more frequently investigated than in perception. At Würzburg, Külpe showed that the tachistoscopic presentation of stimuli may yield perceptions strikingly different from the actual stimuli employed. In this demonstration of the *Aufgabe,* subjects were instructed to focus their attention on selective aspects of the stimulus; these then became "perceived," whereas other equally present but unattended components of the configuration did not. This demonstration was little more than a refinement of the earlier complication experiments performed in the Leipzig Laboratory, which Titchener perpetuated in America. But it was clearly evident that when a complex of stimuli occur simultaneously, the one for which the subject has a set is perceived more quickly than those for which he is not set.

As research and theory developed in the area of perception, two distinct positions tended to emerge, which Allport (1955) has identified as the "formal" and the "functional." The formal position emphasized the structural, or autochthonous, aspects of perception which include the stimulus, the afferent neurons, and the sensory-cortical areas of the central nervous system. The facts of psychophysics and the laws of perceptual organization from the Gestalt School are part of this position. On the other hand, the functional position, in the typical American tradition, has broadened its horizons to include needs, tensions, values, defenses, and general internal motivational factors related to the individual and his past experience. Thus formulated, the directive-state theory of perception has been the focal point of the "new look" in perception.

Allport discusses six propositions of the directive-state theory, citing experimental evidence from some now universally known investigations. For example, subjects tend to perceive food objects in ambiguous pictures in proportion to the number of hours they have been deprived of food (Levine, Chein, and Murphy, 1942). When rewards or punishments are selectively associated with stimuli, those that are rewarded are more frequently perceived and those that are punished are perceived less frequently (Proshansky and Murphy, 1942; Schafer and Murphy, 1943). An individual's personal values will determine which words he perceives in tachistoscopic presentation (Postman, Bruner, and McGinnies, 1948), or the magnitude of an object will be perceived in proportion to the value that object has to the perceiver (Bruner and Goodman, 1947; Bruner and Postman, 1948). Finally, misperceptions have been studied as indicators of an individual's personality characteristics as he has revealed them by telling "projective" stories about ambiguous pictures (Cattell and Wenig, 1953). Other studies of misperception relate to the emotionally disturbing or threatening properties of socially undesirable or taboo topics (McCleary and Lazarus, see Bruner and Krech, 1950; McGinnies, 1949).

Out of these investigations of the directive-state theory, the concept of "perceptual defense" emerged as something of a two-headed monster. Allport pointed out the dilemma produced by a type of manikin-theory, which reduces psychology to a homunculus situation. As Bruner and Postman (see Bruner and Krech, 1950) indicated, this notion also suggests an image of some super-ego function that peers through a Judas window and scans incoming stimuli in order to pass judgment and permit only selected ones to enter the consciousness. Not only have the directive-statists had to face this dilemma, they have received impressive challenges to and criticisms of their experimental procedures as well as the always dangerous and difficult threat of nonconfirming replications by other investigators.

A period of growing divergence between the formal and the functional groups was intensified by the tendency to include the directive-state theory as a central support to the crystallization of theory in social psychology and the development of both theory and practice in clinical psychology. Allport (1955) suggests that during this divergence, the directive-state position, attacked from many sides, tended to drop into disrepute.

However, the significance of these developments in perceptual theory for the concept of set lies in the reformulation of the directive-state theory, primarily by Bruner (*see* Blake and Ramsey, 1951) and Postman (*see* Rohrer and Sherif, 1951), in such a way as to bring it into line with the earlier "formal" position and, at the same time, broaden the potential for new experimental directions. The central theme of the Bruner-Postman reformulation is that people seldom perceive anything "out of the blue." Rather, the observer operates from a set or a hypothesis that tells him what objects to look for and how to expect them to appear. Subsequently, the occurrence of the stimulus events tends either to confirm or to "infirm" the hypothesis or—to state it an equivalent way— to strengthen or to weaken the set. Allport suggests that while Bruner and Postman have not gone further than their reformulation to develop an extended set theory beyond the area of perception, this does not reflect on the central position of their reformulation in perception. In fact, the way was left open for Allport to offer the Structural Theory of Set Dynamics as a final resolution of old problems. The important role of set in perception becomes unmistakably clear in Allport's words:

> The pursuit of the elusive perceptual process into the interior of the organism has been like a long and perplexing dream. Some may feel a little disappointed on waking to find that those remarkable mechanisms that were thought to direct perceptions and to limit our phenomenological horizons according to our personal needs and values seem no longer necessary. It may be disillusioning to find that the heralded revolution in perceptual theory and the new "laws" that were to maximize the individual perceiver are already being modified in accordance with a unifying principle that is more universal and more revealing (1955, pp. 435–36).

SET IN THINKING AND PROBLEM SOLVING

Pratt's (1936) review of the literature on problem solving noted the unanimity of opinion regarding the positive influence of *Einstellung*, and no one has disagreed with his observation. Gibson and McCarvey stated the issue this way: "Since the classical experiments of the Würzburg School, virtually all investigators have recognized implicitly, if not explicitly, that a major feature of all thinking processes is their directed character" (1937, p. 327).

A set induced by the premises of a syllogism tends to determine the conclusion derived, independent of the logical validity of the conclusion (Sells, 1936). An attitude of affirmation or negation, once established, favors a particular conclusion that "sounds like" the premises. Syllogism experiments showed that this "atmosphere-effect" can be a very effective determinant of thinking errors, even though it is involuntary and not present in the subject's awareness.

At this point it is relevant to comment that set variables are significant in understanding psychopathological states. One aspect of thinking disorder found in schizophrenia may be interpreted as an inability to maintain a set. Rosenthal, Lawlor, Zahn, and Shakow (1960) have discussed this primarily in terms of motor sets in reaction time studies. On the other hand, a psychological deficit in set maintenance may also explain logical errors.

Perhaps the most popular method of observing set in problem solving has been the classic experiment by Luchins (1942). His studies, corroborated many times since, demonstrated clearly that solving a series of problems by a specific method tends to trap the subject into using the same method on later problems, even where it is actually inappropriate to do so. The concept of "functional fixity"—set as a barrier to problem solving—was originally introduced by Duncker in the 1930's, but Adamson (1952) investigated it more thoroughly. These studies have shown that the function of an object can become a set in such a way that the problem solver is unable to divorce himself from one object-function relationship and use the object effectively in a totally different way. Hence, once a light bulb is used as a source of heat, the subject becomes functionally fixed, or *set,* and is unable to see the bulb as a means of providing buoyancy to suspend a weight a constant distance below the surface of water.

A twenty-minute lecture incorporating general hints on how to reason and warnings against becoming stuck with a single method of attack has been shown to facilitate the performance of college students attempting to solve the string problem and similar reasoning problems (Maier, 1933).

This brief review of the problem-solving literature also indicates that a number of investigators have incorporated a recognition of and concern for the *Einstellung* variable in an area traditionally distinct from personality and personality assessment.

SET IN LEARNING

A similar picture may be found in the area of learning. Hilgard (1956) has attributed to set the role of providing functionalism's supplement to the traditional associationism and traces the roots of this development back to the imageless-thought controversy stimulated at Würzburg. Woodworth (1906) and Angell (1906), who usually take opposing positions on such theoretical matters, were in close agreement, as were others in the functionalist camp, on the dynamic significance of predisposing sets. As a result, Woodworth's early motivational theory of learning included set as a major component, a factor that later led him to expand his position by introducing two new concepts; *situation-set* and *goal-set* (Woodworth, 1937). The situation-set concept called attention to aspects of the task environment, which may be only indirectly related to the stimulus-response sequence. The goal-set concept refers to the inner steering process that gives unity to a series of goal-directed activities, thus guiding the organism through the task. The close similarity between goal-set and Hull's (1952) fractional anticipatory goal response (r_G) is evident. In fact, Hull has explicitly accounted for mental sets and other types of directing ideas by saying that they are conditioned responses, ultimately reducible to fractional anticipatory goal responses. Thus, the concept of set has been utilized as a postulate in the systematic mathematico-deductive theory of learning.

Hull is not alone in his use of anticipation as a factor in learning. We find similar notions included, although somewhat less seriously, in Contiguity Theory. Guthrie (Smith and Guthrie, 1921) called attention to the significance of precurrent or preparatory responses in the total behavior sequence. These responses place the organism in a state of readiness for the consequences to follow and are said to be conditioned stimuli encountered while the organism is moving toward the goal. In his use of readiness or anticipation, Guthrie is very close to the position of other learning theorists, and perhaps the only unique aspect of his position is that the readinesses consist in tensions of the muscles. It is noteworthy that Hefferline (1962) begins his treatment of set with a discussion of the electromyographic demonstrations of the relationship between muscular tension produced by ready signals and simple reaction time (Davis, 1940; Freeman, 1948). Much of his review is devoted to physiological studies of posture-regulating mechanisms (Sherrington, 1952), high level cerebral activity (Sperry, 1955), and "the postural substrate" (Freeman, 1948).

Mention should also be made, at least in passing, of the use of set as one of five laws subordinate to the major laws of readiness, exercise, and effect in Thorndike's Connectionism (1913). Here, Thorndike called attention to the principle that learning may be guided by a total attitude or set of the organism and documented his position with the observation that responses are in part determined by "enduring adjustments" that develop as a result of exposure to a given culture.

Another significant use of the set concept in learning theory is found in relation to expectancy. The most systematic formulation of expectancy theory is primarily in Tolman's Sign

Learning. According to Tolman (1934), a learner follows signs, or expectancies, which lead him to the goal. The expectation is that a particular event will follow pertinent behavior. Thus, an organism "learns what leads to what"; if the anticipated consequence follows, the expectation is confirmed. There is a striking resemblance between this notion and the previously referred to Bruner-Postman hypothesis-theory of perception. It is also evident from Tolman that expectancy and habit are very much alike. The variables that control expectancy for Tolman are nearly identical to those Hull uses to explain the process of habit growth. MacCorquodale and Meehl (1954), in their reformulation of Tolman's theory, have more closely identified expectancy with the universal concept of habit. On the other hand, Dashiell (1940) has related set to motivation. He says that the animal raring to go in the apparatus is really demonstrating a set. Thus, whether it is a partial response, a habit, or a motivational component, set has been very much involved in learning theory construction.

Without taking the time for an extensive review of set in conditioning studies, one parallel between that field and response set in personality assessment is especially interesting. Schlosberg (1932) became concerned with the difficulty of producing conditioned responses in human subjects and suggested that the experimenter must isolate the task from the obscuring effects of attitudes and volition. Razran (1936) took an extreme point of view when he found that salivary conditioning was absent, or greatly diminished, when he instructed his subjects not to form associations. Razran suggested that pure conditioning is exclusively an animal form of learning that is present in human subjects only when their attitudinal behavior is weakened or absent. This approach to set as something disadvantageous, to be eliminated or avoided where possible, is reminiscent of Cronbach's (1946, 1950) warnings about the invalidating effect of noncontent variance in test scores.

Clearly, set has been well represented in the experimental and theoretical endeavors of the leaders in the psychology of learning.

The majority of phenomena, or processes, encountered in

the study of learning may be considered special circumstances of the basic concept—variations on the set theme. For example, sensory preconditioning, latent learning, stimulus generalization, transfer of training, reminiscence, and spontaneous recovery all seem to occur because the organism, as a result of its experience, is inclined, predetermined, or *eingestellt* to carry its past into a new situation and to modify its behavior vis-à-vis new stimulus in-puts. The most discernable instance of this manifestation of set is the "learning-how-to-learn" phenomena, investigated and developed under the title of "Learning Sets" (Harlow, 1949; Reese, 1964).

Finally, a discussion of learning is only partially complete without a simultaneous concern for the other side of the same coin—retention or forgetting. Bugelski (1956) has observed that the role of set in determining retention is largely speculative, because it has received relatively little attention. However, McGeoch (1942) included set as the second psychological condition of forgetting. The Zeigarnik (1927) and related studies (Lewis and Franklin, 1944) on retention of interrupted tasks offer other examples of a type of set-controlled behavior.

SET IN SOCIAL ATTITUDES

One more major area of psychological theory and research endeavor deserves attention as an extension of the *Einstellung* concept—the concept of attitude, the great forte of the social psychologist and, to some extent, the clinical psychologist. Allport (1935) described attitude as "probably the most distinctive and indispensible concept in contemporary American social psychology."

While the social area has expanded in many directions since the publication of Murchison's *Handbook*, the concept of attitude is apparently no less important in the present time. In his classic discussion of attitudes, Allport cited sixteen separate definitions of the concept and identified the common thread running through them. "In one way or another, each regards the essential feature of attitude as a *preparation or readiness for response.* The attitude is incipient and preparatory rather than overt and consummatory. It is not behavior, but the precondition of behavior" (Allport, 1935, p. 805). In his own definition, it is evident that he means the same process we have been calling set. "An attitude is a mental and neural state of readiness, organized through experience, exerting a directive or dynamic influence upon the individual's responses to all objects in a situation with which it is related" (p. 810). It is interesting that in his 1935 discussion, Allport found (just as we are doing here) that perception, judgment, learning, memory, and thought have frequently been reduced to the operation of attitude.

Earlier I noted that Allport's definition of personality trait is very similar to set, but he also uses the term attitude to explain the process whereby many stimuli become functionally equivalent. Although it appears that he considers trait and attitude interchangeable terms, he reserves for attitude the essence of a narrowly limited state of readiness, such as the determining tendency or *Aufgabe* when specific behaviors are involved. On the other hand, where more widely extended or generalized behavior is involved, he makes no meaningful distinction between attitude and trait.

SUMMARY

The foregoing discussion has attempted to highlight the extent to which the concept of set has become incorporated, sometimes unwittingly and almost always under some other name, in the theory and experimental investigations carried on in four distinct research areas from the era of the Würzburg School to the present time. At first glance, it is difficult to understand from such a broad survey what Dashiell (1940) was attempting to communicate when he called set the neglected fourth dimension in psychological research. The area appears to be anything but neglected. At the same time, the very fact that it has been used so extensively by so many different individuals under so many different synonyms indicates a need for a unifying system of theoretical postulates and empirical studies related to a *psychology of set*. This would be a gigantic task, one that is not likely to be undertaken soon.

This review has not attempted to present new information or to reorganize existing background material in order to focus on new directions for response set inquiry.[2] What has been attempted, however, is a survey that would demonstrate, as clearly and emphatically as possible, both the breadth of the set phenomena in relation to behavior and the exceedingly large number of individual investigators who, in one way or another, have been concerned with set as a hypothetical construct.

II. RESPONSE SET IN PERSONALITY ASSESSMENT

A very disturbing question arises out of such a demonstration, particularly for those concerned with response set in personality assessment. Much of the work performed on the MMPI, the California F Scale, and similar instruments has been devoted to demonstrating that a set exists. Yet, why, in the face of reports from our colleagues, should we have any doubt that a set exists? Why should we expect that the behavior involved in taking a test is in any way unique and therefore immune from set influence? Imagine for a moment an individual whose perception of ambiguous pictures, judgment of the size of coins, method of solving verbal reasoning problems, rate of learning a serial discrimination, or reaction to a social movement is influenced by some "determining tendency." It seems highly improbable that he should suddenly and mysteriously be free to respond to stimuli *qua* stimuli when he begins to take a personality inventory. Why,

2. Likewise, this review is not intended to be taken as exhaustive. Surely the reader will think of many more examples than have been discussed in these pages. This will only further make the point that "set" has many faces and many proponents within the science of psychology.

then, do investigators persist in this search for the obvious? Why are there reports that almost gleefully refute the influence of set with such labels as "the response-style myth," "response set paralysis," or "the vanishing variance component"? Why, on the other hand, are there still new reports that enthusiastically reconfirm the original insight that the major common factors in personality inventories are interpretable in terms other than those related to specific item content?

To attempt an answer to these questions, the rest of this orientation will focus on some of the milestones in the response set movement generally, in hopes of coming to grips with some of the crucial issues that have concerned all investigators.

The short history of response set has had four distinct phases or stages. The first, "The Era of Discovery," occurred prior to and terminated with the second publication by Cronbach (1950), in which he reaffirmed his earlier statement of the probability that response sets interfere with accurate measurement and restated his position that such influence should be eliminated where possible. Cronbach added the somewhat tentative suggestion that some response sets might be psychologically similar to personality traits, in which case they might be capitalized upon.

In so doing, he ushered in the second major stage— "The Era of Elaboration." During this period in the 1950's, the first significant work in the major response set areas began to appear. For example, the Deviation Hypothesis was formulated (Berg, 1955, 1957), the relationship between item desirability and the probability of endorsement was identified and measured (Edwards, 1953, 1957a) and the California F Scale was discovered to measure acquiescence instead of authoritarianism (Bass, 1955; Cohn, 1953; Gage, Leavitt, and Stone, 1957; Leavitt, Hax, and Roche, 1955).

The next major stage—"The Era of Enchantment"— developed during the late 1950's and early 1960's. It was then that the noncontent variance of test scores acquired new meaning as a potentially useful tool for assessing individual personality traits or life styles. Numerous papers appeared that suggested that the various sets were related to psychologically meaningful dimensions of personality (Couch and Keniston, 1960; Crowne and Marlowe, 1960; Frederiksen and Messick, 1958; Jackson and Messick, 1958).

Finally, stemming largely from the third stage and partially overlapping it, is the fourth and current period—"The Era of Challenge and Defense." During recent years, the proponents of the major response sets have been challenged, sometimes vigorously attacked, and required to defend their positions with more careful enunciation and with new data. Some of these challenges have been the result of specific studies designed to test the assumptions of a position, with nonconfirming results. Others have been critical reviews of the field in general (Block, 1962; Foster, 1961; McGee, 1962d; Rorer, 1963; Rorer and Goldberg, 1964a, 1964b; Siller and Chipman, 1963). Sometimes the leading investigators have challenged one another (Berg, 1963; Couch and Keniston, 1961; Edwards and Walker, 1961; Sechrest and Jackson, 1962, 1963).

A comprehensive review of the literature characterizing the current period has been collected and organized in the monograph by Rorer (1963). However, in spite of his apparent doubts of the value of response set, the field continues to produce new studies and rebuttals to former challenges. The papers that follow will focus on the crucial issues that have concerned and continue to concern investigators in the area of response set.

WHAT DETERMINES RESPONSE?

Several general issues, each subsuming lesser, more specific problem areas, may be identified in individual studies and general reviews of the field. The first is: "What determines the response that is made to any single item?"—a question with at least six possible answers.

1. *Chance.* For each item response, the alternative always exists that the response is entirely random behavior. Of all the possible explanations, the chance factor appears least

likely to explain effectively the responses to test items that have been used to study response set. Primarily because investigators are continually cognizant of the problem of reliability, they have either computed the reliability of their instruments or employed instruments for which adequate reliability has been demonstrated. To be sure, some random error exists in all tests, but it is safe to look elsewhere for the determinants of test responses.

2. *Stimulus Variables.* Most psychological research expects the stimulus to play an important role in the response elicited, as Dashiell (1940) indicated when he denoted this as the first dimension to psychological research. However, some people have been so enthusiastic about set that they have denied stimulus properties, or would like to do so, when it comes to personality tests. In assessment techniques, the stimulus corresponds to the item content. Obviously, the more a response is determined by item content, the less it can be influenced by set. It is as though a "War between the Variance Components" were being fought with *set* and *content* the opposing armies.

How important is content? Certain elements of confusion have been injected through a tendency to misconstrue Berg's (1959) discussion of the importance of item content. What Berg said—very clearly—was that it makes no difference what *type* of content is used as stimuli, that ambiguous pictures, musical sounds, and verbal statements can be equally effective in observing biased responses. This is not the same as saying that whatever content is, in fact, present has little or nothing to do with the response that is given.

A number of studies have specifically attempted to partition the total variance of test scores into components related to content, set, and error (Chapman and Bock, 1958; Helmstadter, 1957; Rorer and Goldberg, 1964b). All of these models for mathematically dividing set and content into separate units have necessarily employed item reversals; this has created another important issue: Can test items be psychologically reversed without increasing grammatical complexity or decreasing reliability?

Most of the earlier attempts to reverse items were made

with the California F Scale and are reviewed by Christie, Havel, and Seidenberg (1958). A recent ambitious undertaking by Rorer and Goldberg (1964b) produced reversals of all items in the MMPI. People who have approached the question seriously have generally felt that adequate reversals could be written, but only with great difficulty. However, when this is accomplished, the evidence for a significant response set component is shown to be quite limited. In effect, then, it has been claimed that, in a reliable test, the error component approaches zero, the set component is minimal, and the content component is the major response determinant.

3. *Response Alternative Available.* It may be somewhat pedantic to include this alternative, but it is clearly important for conceptual reasons, if for no other. Cronbach's (1946) early definition of set included a reference to the form in which the item was presented, and much of the work on response set has been because of the true-false or agree-disagree format. Needless to say, no one has been concerned with an acquiescence set component in the total variance of the Personal Preference Schedule, nor is it meaningful to study polarization (O'Donovan, 1965) in the MMPI.

4. *"Fractional Antedating Responses."* This term may be borrowed from Hullian Learning Theory to identify another possible determinant of an individual item response. The question is: "How many responses are made to an item? It is generally assumed that one or, at most, two responses are made to any item. One is a cognitive reaction to the content, which in turn stimulates a second or motor response on the answer sheet.

However, response set theorists must assume that more responses than these are given. For example, in addition to his cognitive response to the content, the individual may make an emotional response as he considers the meaning of the content for him personally. Perhaps another cognition follows, in which he contrasts the traces of the emotional response to his interpretation of some reference group. Additional emotional responses may follow, ultimately stimulating the final motor response, which is always used as the basis of the data. Hence, in producing the data, a person may respond not to the printed stimulus directly but rather to one or more fractional responses within himself. Something of this process is obviously involved in social desirability responding and perhaps even in acquiescent responding.

5. *Subject Variables.* Closely related to point 4 is behavior that occurs when people are asked to respond to nonexistent or nonsense items (Berg and Rapaport, 1954; McGee, 1961, 1962b, 1962c; Nunnally and Husek, 1958). In such cases, the individual must respond only to himself because, presumably, no other stimulus is present. How much help subjects have had from the structure of these "tests" has varied considerably, but when responses do occur, the assumption is that they are solely subject determined.

The major aspect of the subject variable consideration is the personality trait assumption. A number of traits—including need for approval (Marlowe and Crowne, 1961), anxiety (Stricker, 1963), acceptance versus rejection (Couch and Keniston, 1960; McGee and Land, 1963), cognitive strength (Jackson, 1958, 1959), and authoritarianism—have been proposed as the basic response determinant.

An additional response determinant that may be considered a subject variable is group membership. Evidence suggests that an individual may respond in a particular way to an item if he is a modal member of a particular criterion group or if he is a deviant in a group whose modal response is to some other alternative.

6. *Artifacts of Tests.* One final factor that may determine responses to test items can be identified as certain artifacts in the tests themselves. These may be uncovered by asking: "What manipulations can be performed on objective tests that will increase or decrease the frequency of certain types of responses?" Three such intratest variables—item sequence, item context, and time limit—were investigated in the Moccasin Bend studies on acquiescence (McGee and Komorita, 1963).

The first study was concerned with item sequence. It had previously been observed (McGee, 1962a) that the agreement of averaged scores of a group of subjects tended to decrease markedly through the course of the 30-item F Scale. This raised questions concerning the pattern of acquiescence scores that might be observed in other tests. Former records from two independent samples of college students were analyzed by dividing the test into three equal parts and plotting the mean agreement score for each block of items. Figure 1 shows

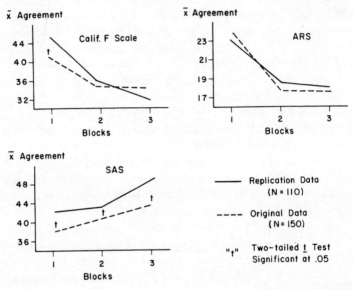

FIG. 1. Stability of sequence effects over two independent samples.

the performance of the two samples on three measures of acquiescence. A remarkable agreement between the two samples, in terms of the pattern of responses from block to block, is obvious. If the set to make agreement responses is stronger at the beginning of a test and tends to dissipate, as is evident in the F Scale and the Agreement Response Scale (ARS), and if the items are reversed so that item 1 becomes item k, item 2 becomes $k - 1$, and so forth, then the same pattern of agreement scores should be found again.

Therefore, three forms of each test were administered to

similar groups of college students. Form I contained the items in the original order; Form II, in the reversed sequence; and Form III, in a sequence established by a table of random numbers. The results are shown in Figure 2. These lines were

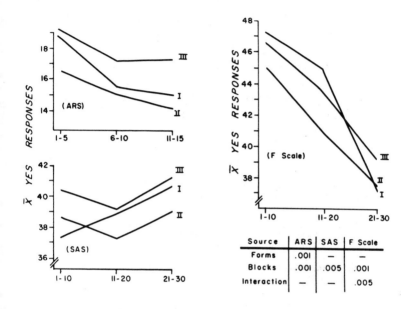

FIG. 2. Agreement responses by blocks of trials as a function of the sequence in which items appear in three acquiescence measures.

plotted so that the abscissa points represent identical blocks of items, irrespective of the position of those items in the individual forms. Hence, it may be seen that in the ARS, for example, the greatest amount of agreement occurred to items 1 through 5, no matter if they came first or last or were scattered randomly throughout the test.

The data were analyzed according to Lindquist's (1953) Type I analysis of variance design. The ARS was the only one of the three scales that revealed a significant difference between forms, but all three revealed significant between-

blocks differences. Only the F Scale showed a significant interaction effect.

These data suggest that reversing the sequence in which
items are presented has little or no effect on the agreement
responses produced to them. However disappointing it may
be, the conclusion is rather inescapable that the most likely
explanation of these response patterns is the verbal content
of the item.

The second study of this series focused on how the context within which items are presented acts as a possible influence on agreement responses. In this study, three lists of
MMPI items were prepared according to the probability of
endorsement values reported by Hathaway and McKinley
(1940). Figure 3 shows, diagramatically, how these lists were
prepared. Each list contained thirty items drawn from the
MMPI so that one list was composed of items with an endorsement probability of 85 to 95 per cent; items in the second

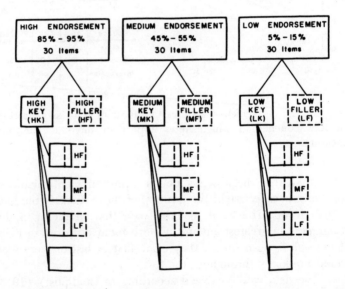

FIG. 3. Construction of twelve item pools containing items of
varying endorsement probability used to study the effects of context upon agreement tendency.

list had an endorsement probability of 45 to 55 per cent; and items in the third list had from 5 to 15 per cent endorsement. Fifteen items from each separate list were randomly selected and designated as "Key" items, while the remaining fifteen were designated "Filler" items. These lists were then intermixed so that each list of Key items was presented in a random arrangement with each list of Filler items. The Key lists were also presented separately. This gave a total of twelve different tests, each presented to an independent sample of college students (N = 30 in each case).

The number of agreement responses made to the list of Key items in each Filler condition was recorded and analyzed by a simple randomized analysis of variance procedure, and a separate test was run for each endorsement level.

The results of these analyses are seen in Table 1, which shows clearly that none of the *F* ratios was significant. Altering the context within which the items occurred also had no effect on the agreement scores made, apparently, to the verbal content. It is especially noteworthy that the medium endorsement items, which should be expected to be affected most because they were most ambiguous (Cronbach, 1946), were not affected at all by the presence of high or low agreement context.

TABLE 1. Agreement Responses to Key Lists of Fifteen Items as a Function of Context in Which Items Were Presented

		FILLER CONTEXT			
KEY LISTS	*None*	*High Endorsement*	*Medium Endorsement*	*Low Endorsement*	*F Ratio*
High Endorsement					
Mean	13.20	13.97	13.97	13.40	2.50
S.D.	3.66	1.05	1.22	1.52	$p<.10$
Medium Endorsement					
Mean	7.83	8.13	8.33	7.63	0.83
S.D.	1.93	1.71	1.64	2.02	$p>.20$
Low Endorsement					
Mean	1.73	1.60	2.17	1.50	0.71
S.D.	1.73	1.47	2.53	1.50	$p>.20$

In the third analysis of a potential test artifact, we manipulated the amount of time available for responding to each item. The items of the F scale, ARS, and Social Acquiescence Scale (SAS) were individually photographed and reproduced on 2″ x 2″ transparencies so they could be administered with a standard slide projector in a group session. The slides were then shown to two groups of the same college student population used previously. The slides were exposed for thirty seconds each to the first group. The subjects in this group were instructed to read the item over carefully and consider it as long as necessary before responding. The second group was shown the items in the ARS and SAS for five seconds apiece and the F Scale items, because they are generally longer, for eight seconds. The number of agreement responses made under such conditions was determined and compared with the number of agreements made to the same items in the regular paper-and-pencil form by similar subjects in the sequence analysis study described earlier.

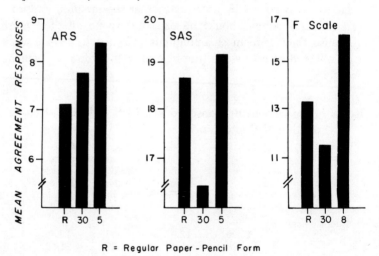

FIG. 4. Relationship of agreement responses to available desion time.

As the results (Figure 4) show, the tendency to make agreement responses varies inversely with the amount of time available to the subject for considering the item. The mean agreement scores were compared between presentation conditions by use of t tests. Both the F Scale and the SAS show a statistically significant difference in agreement when the five-second or eight-second condition is compared with the thirty-second condition. Likewise, significantly less agreement is recorded in the thirty-second condition than in the regular paper-and-pencil form of the test. This suggests that where the administration procedures of a test emphasize or promote speeded responses, the proportion of agreement responses will be increased.

These factors can be said to be test variables, as opposed to subject variables, which might function as determinants of item responses. In two of the three studies, it appeared that agreement tendency is a function of item content and could not be modified by manipulating the sequence or the context within which the individual items occur. The third investigation demonstrated that the effects of speed can overcome the influence of content and alter the agreement tendency.

THE INFAMOUS PERSONALITY VARIABLE

The second major issue in the field of response set has arisen from the first. In answering the question, "What determines the response to a test item?" many investigators have contended that subject variables, specifically "underlying personality syndromes," account for response set variance. Is response set or style a manifestation of a subject's personality? If a personality trait is "enhanced and capitalized upon," does it have any meaning or utility in personality assessment? If it does, it·should fit the personality trait concept and fulfill at least two essential expectations.

First, it should appear *consistently* in similar situations. A number of available studies are consistent in their finding of low correlations of agreement scores across several tests.

Siller and Chipman (1963) and Stricker (1963) have recently reported low-to-modest correlations between acquiescence measures. These findings provide support for similar data reported in two studies by McGee (1962b, 1962c) and one by Foster (1961).

Iwawaki (personal communication) has replicated the first study by McGee by administering the same acquiescence measures to students at the Japanese Defense Academy. His correlation matrix was very similar to the original one. This finding has two explanations: either the Japanese culture yields a basic personality type very similar to that found in American students or the content of the test items is such that, even when translated into Japanese, it leads all educated people to respond in a uniform manner. Iwawaki also found that only two of the five measures correlated with the number of agreement responses made to the MMPI. These were the ARS and the F Scale which correlated .42 and .34 respectively ($N = 102$).

While it has also been reported that the major social desirability scales have only moderate correlations with one another, this is not surprising, since the two scales were designed with markedly different rationales and do not purport to be comparable instruments.

Second, a personality trait should *predict independent behavior* not related to taking another pencil-and-paper test. This expectation has been raised previously as a request for independent validity criteria (McGee, 1962d). Subsequent to the early critical review of methodology, a number of studies have appeared in which the investigators compared set scores with independent behavioral measures. Foster (1961), for example, correlated set scores with conformity performance in an Asch-like situation and with two compliance tasks and found zero-order correlations between these measures. He concluded that there was no evidence that the response set score could be used to predict behavior in situations that should be psychologically relevant to the personality trait the set score is purported to measure. Foster's findings were identical in every respect to the data collected by similar methods independently, and almost simultaneously, by McGee (1961, 1962c). Stricker (1963) also failed to support a conceptualization of response styles as measures of conformity, but he recognized the need to use behavioral measures in a direct test of the matter. He also reported that all tests to date had been negative.

On the other hand, Quinn (1963) has stated rather emphatically that response sets represent stable, consistent individual response tendences, which have their independent behavioral correlates. He based his conclusion on data from agreement responses and from three nonpsychometric conformity tasks.

Kuethe (1960) used a classroom drama to analyze the acquiescence set as a predictor. He found a relationship between acquiescence as a personality variable, measured by the MMPI *Pt* scale, and psychasthenia. He concluded that the acquiescence set had demonstrated its usefulness in identifying two distinct behavior patterns and had earned the right to be regarded as a personality variable. On the other hand, Kuethe pointed out that it is improper to assume that acquiescence is measured by most personality inventories, just because of the number of true-keyed items in the scale.

Klein and Solomon (1961) studied game-playing behavior among schizophrenics and found no reliable relationships between this task and response set scores. In another study, they (Solomon and Klein, 1961) reasoned that naysaying, the opposite of the acquiescence set, is associated with efficient impulse control. They applied this reasoning to hospitalized schizophrenics and found that the naysaying tendency is predictive of discharge and obtaining privileges in chronic schizophrenics. Rosenhan (1963) found no relationships between hypnosis, conformity, and measures of acquiescence.

And still the search goes on. It is difficult to make a general statement about all of these studies; the results are equivocal. Data appear on both sides of the issue, and the arguments are about equally divided in favor of and opposed to the acceptance of acquiescence scores as predictors of independent behavior.

It is evident, however, that little agreement exists on the definition of essential terms. To a number of investigators, "acquiescence" means the number of *yes, true,* or *agree* responses made on the answer sheet of an objective inventory. To some, it even means the number of *like* and *like much* responses to the Perceptual Reaction Test (Zuckerman, Oppenheimer, and Gershowitz, 1965). To others, "acquiescence" is a conceptual personality trait, descriptive of a person who is easy to persuade or influence or who readily accepts external direction, no matter what he does on a true-false answer sheet. Kuethe (1960) clearly indicated this confusion when he pointed out that a person does not get a high score in the positively keyed *Pt* scale because he is acquiescent, but rather that he is acquiescent because this trait is characteristic of people who earn high *Pt* scores. At the same time, he predicted, and found, that people who could be "led" in a mock courtroom testimony situation would have a strong acquiescent response set and would therefore have low *Pt* scores. Hence, the situation is one of deciding when to expect the acquiescent person to respond *no* to his test items and when to conclude that he has overcome his acquiescence as evidenced by having answered *yes* to them.

SET, STYLE, AND BIAS

Closely related to this definitional dilemma is a third issue. This is the confusion that seems to arise from the terms *set, style,* and *bias,* which many people use as equivalent or interchangable terms. Jackson and Messick (1958) proposed the term *style* in order to underscore the "personal mode" for responding which they expected to have utility in personality assessment. This position leads to the conclusion that response "set" is the general term, whereas response "style" is a specific manifestation, when it may denote a personal mode of expression that has interpretative significance as a personality trait. If this interpretation is correct, it is reminiscent of Allport's (1937) distinction between attitude and trait.

Rorer (1963) has proposed a conceptual distinction between sets and styles. He uses set in a more orthodox manner, like *Einstellung,* as a frame of reference against which a subject evaluates the stimulus before making a response. He uses style to refer to the manner or mode by which the responses are made. In this sense, sets operate in relation to the meaningful item content whereas styles operate in relationship to nonstimulus-intrasubject personality syndromes. Part of the confusion, as Rorer has identified it, is due to the fact that acquiescence has been conceptualized as a generalized set, although it has been operationally defined in terms of the disproportionate tendency to select *yes* responses, which is a style.

Wiggins (1962) has used the term "method variance" instead of set and reserves style for the variance in scores characteristic of subjects independent of the test. In this sense, it may be concluded that the Moccasin Bend studies of test artifacts were investigating method variance, not stylistic variance.

There has been little effort to crystallize a definition for Berg's favorite term, response *bias.* It may be concluded however, that bias is a general term used to denote the results of any noncontent influence on a response. Thus, both sets and styles, as well as extraneous factors that contribute to error variance, tend to bias the response. To whatever extent the total variance is not 100 per cent stimulus-determined, response bias is operative.

III. SUMMARY STATEMENT

It seems that measurement psychologists can assert unhesitatingly and unequivocally that response bias accounts for a significant component of variance in personality assessment methods. This conclusion may be asserted because not to do so would be to deny the presence of a phenomena as ubiquitous to psychology as behavior itself. We can see that it is as absurd to think of test responses without set as it would be to think of learning without motivation or perception without organization. Yet, the response set field has become enmeshed with its own conceptualization problems. Because response styles have not consistently demonstrated personality trait characteristics, the tendency has been to throw the set out with the style.

It is precisely this problem of conceptual confusion that has led to and perpetuated the intense interest in response set research. There is no common consensus about what to expect from the data, because there is no consensus about what sort of criteria to use in establishing that a set exists in the first place. Investigators are striving independently to find some clarification of these areas. Renner (1964) identifies the response set interest as an example of a current emphasis on a "super-nomothetic" model of statistical and hyperobjective test scores. He sees this development as a further symptom of the general dissatisfaction of psychologists with traditional clinical assessment techniques. This may well be part of the motivation, but it also seems that a search continues for the solution to some basic semantic and definitional problems.

There appear to be two groups of people with opinions about the acquiescent set. The first group are those who have defined acquiescence as a test response. They tend to investigate the set through multivariate procedures, by correlating and factoring agreement responses and finding that they cluster in such a way that they can only meaningfully be labeled as an "acquiescence" factor. These people have data that reflect acquiescence. The other group has been concerned with the personality variable. They have expected to find consistent item-response behavior across tests and predictive efficiency of scores for nontest behavior. Because this group has been disappointed, they have been led to consider the whole business as a big myth (McGee, 1962a; Rorer, 1963). If I may be permitted an observation about the "state of the art," I am inclined to believe that the "sets" have it over the "styles." It is possible to assert set influence, but the personality variable issue is far from being clearly established.

Most papers conclude with remarks similar to those of Struening and Spilka (1964): "It appears that . . . response style in general is difficult to isolate in a pure form. . . . Rather, any attempt to measure them seems to include a complex of influences and their interactions. Needless to say, much further research is necessary to adequately conceptualize, measure, and control the influence of various response styles and sets."

On the other hand, maybe there have been too many investigations already. In the last fifteen years, psychologists concerned with problems of measurement have been "further researching" to the point where they have apparently jumped on the response set horse and ridden off in all directions simultaneously. The time has come to make a searching assessment of the data as they now exist and then begin an organized attack on some basic definitional issues. One clear and unmistakable conclusion will come from this approach: Set is set, wherever it is found.

T W O / ALLEN L. EDWARDS

The Social Desirability Variable: A Broad Statement [1]

I

I am particularly concerned, as indeed many other psychologists are, with the description of personality and with all of those behaviors and characteristics of the person that are subsumed under this quite vague concept. I shall take the not unusual position that describing an individual's personality involves the making of statements about the individual. These statements may refer to specific acts of behavior, that is, the statements may describe what an individual does, how he does it, when and where he does it, and the specific conditions under which he behaves in a specific way. The statements may also refer to the broad categories of behavior that many psychologists describe as traits. Thus, we may use the following statement to describe a person: "He has a strong degree of dominance." Or we may be more specific and use a series of statements to describe the particular instances of dominant behavior that characterize the individual.

In describing an individual's personality we may also make use of statements that refer to his desires, his ambitions, his likes and dislikes, his needs, the things he daydreams about, his fears and anxieties, the things that irritate him and those that please him, and how he feels about competition,

1. The preparation of this paper was supported in part by Research Grant MH-04075 from the National Institute of Mental Health, United States Public Health Service.

success, and failure. The point is, we are in no way limited in the kinds of statements we may use in describing an individual's personality, although we may consider some statements to be more relevant or of greater significance than others. Thus we may consider the statement, "He weighs 160 pounds," to be of less relevance or of less significance than such statements as, "He has an IQ of 175," or, "He experiences a great deal of anxiety when he has to compete with others."

Exactly what kinds of statements are, in general, considered to have the greatest significance in the description of personality is not known with any degree of certainty. I suggest, however, that it may be that statements that can be described as representing *desirable* and *undesirable* characteristics would, in general, also be considered the kinds of statements that are of the most importance in describing personality. Most of the letters I have received recommending candidates for positions or appointments tend to stress either the desirable or undesirable characteristics of the person, and sometimes both. Relatively few of the statements made in these letters can be considered neutral.

In evaluating statements made about another person as desirable or undesirable, I am, of course, making a personal judgment in terms of standards I have acquired. As Sherif (1936) pointed out many years ago, we do not arrive in this world fully equipped with a set of norms of evaluation, but rather we acquire these standards primarily through interactions with others. The process by which a child acquires sensitivity to social stimuli and learns to behave in ways prescribed by society is often referred to as the socialization of the child. Social learning theorists, such as Bandura and Walters (1963), have emphasized the importance of social variables in accounting for the development and modification of human behavior. The precise nature of the process by which a child learns to behave in whatever ways he does eventually behave is not of importance to the topic of this chapter. We are all aware that many parents use techniques of reinforcement to reward behaviors they approve of or consider desirable and techniques of punishment to inhibit or extinguish behaviors they disapprove of or consider undesirable—with some degree of success. It is important, however, that we distinguish between the acquisition or learning of the specific behavior and the learning of the evaluation that society places upon that behavior. For example, although an individual may learn that an act is considered undesirable by others, this does not necessarily mean that he will learn to avoid performing that act. Similarly, despite the fact that we may have learned that certain acts are considered desirable by others, this does not insure that we will behave in accordance with these standards. Almost all college students will, if asked, tell you that cheating on an examination is undesirable, including those students who either occasionally or consistently engage in cheating. Almost all of us would agree that to perform an act of kindness toward another is desirable, and yet we may often avoid doing so. In other words, it is my contention that most individuals learn the evaluation others place upon various patterns of behavior regardless of whether they actually behave in accordance with these evaluations.

II

Consider the set of all possible statements that could be made in describing the personality of an individual. Whether there is some limited number of statements on which we might agree and which, in turn, could be used to describe every individual's personality has not been determined. Yet it seems reasonable to believe that there is probably some finite number of statements—whether it be one thousand, two thousand, three thousand, or more—that would be sufficient. By sufficient I mean such that any additional statements would provide no new information that could not be obtained from the statements in the finite set or from some combination of the statements in the the finite set.

Whatever the exact number of statements required to

describe personality completely, each of these statements can be assigned a number that I call the *social desirability scale value* (SDSV) of the statement. The SDSV of a statement provides an index of the location of the statement on what I call the *social desirability continuum*. When I say that each of these statements can be assigned a scale value, I am not stating an hypothesis but making a statement of fact. Anyone who is familiar with psychological scaling methods knows that it is possible to use these methods to obtain SDSVs of personality statements. In other words, the appropriate technology is available and merely needs to be applied if we wish to obtain SDSVs of personality statements.[2] One may, of course, question whether the SDSVs thus obtained make psychological sense or whether it is meaningful to obtain the SDSVs of personality statements, but this is another matter. The point is that we can obtain the SDSVs and, having obtained them, it then becomes necessary to demonstrate that they do provide meaningful and useful information. I shall try to show later that the SDSVs of personality statements can be used to make various predictions which can then be empirically tested.

I have used the term *social* desirability scale value of a statement to emphasize that I mean some consensus based upon group judgments as to the location of the statement on the social desirability continuum. The SDSV of a statement, in other words, is a normative value and reflects the typical or average judgment when a large number of different judges are involved. There are, of course, individual differences in judgments of desirability and, although these individual judgments provide the basis for obtaining the SDSV of a statement, the individual judgments should not be identified with the normative judgment or SDSV of the statement. I shall use the term *personal desirability* to refer to the judgments of desirability made by particular individuals. Personal desirability refers to the point where a given individual judges a statement to be located on the social desirability continuum,

2. Psychological scaling methods are described by Edwards (1957b), Guilford (1954), and Torgerson (1958).

whereas SDSV refers to the location of a statement on the same continuum as determined by the judgments of a group.

A question of some importance, and one to which I shall return later, is the degree to which an individual's judgments of desirability are in accord with the normative values based upon the judgments of a group. For the time being I merely wish to emphasize the distinction between an individual's judgments of desirability and the SDSV of a statement which refers to a normative value.

III

At this point I want to describe the method we have used most often in obtaining SDSVs of personality statements. Table 1 shows a 9-point rating scale on which 1 corresponds to extremely socially undesirable, 5 corresponds to neutral, and 9 corresponds to extremely socially desirable. The other

TABLE 1. Social Desirability Rating Scale

Rating	Meaning of Rating
1	Extremely Undesirable
2	Strongly Undesirable
3	Moderately Undesirable
4	Mildly Undesirable
5	NEUTRAL
6	Mildly Desirable
7	Moderately Desirable
8	Strongly Desirable
9	Extremely Desirable

points on the rating scale correspond to varying degrees of social undesirability and social desirability. Individuals are asked to rate personality statements, using this 9-point rating scale. The instructions given to the judges emphasize that they are to judge how socially desirable or undesirable they would consider the characteristic or content represented by the statement if it were used to describe another person. In other words, if a given statement were made by one person in describing another, would the person making the statement be saying something socially desirable or socially undesirable about the other person? It must be emphasized that the judges are not asked to rate the statement in terms of whether it does or does not describe them, but rather to judge whether the statement would be considered desirable or undesirable if applied to another person and to indicate how desirable or undesirable in terms of the 9-point rating scale.

For each personality statement we thus obtain a distribution of ratings. We may then apply the method of equal-appearing intervals, the method of successive intervals, or some other psychological scaling method to the distributions of ratings to obtain the SDSVs of each statement. Considerable evidence shows that the SDSVs derived from any one of the various psychological scaling techniques are highly correlated with the SDSVs derived by the other techniques and with the arithmetic means of the distributions of the ratings. In most of our research, therefore, we have simply found the mean rating assigned to a statement and called this the SDSV of the statement.

The mean rating or SDSV of a statement provides an index of the statement's location on the social desirability continuum. Statements with low scale values are statements that, on the average, are judged as representing socially undesirable characteristics, and statements with high scale values are statements that, on the average, are judged as representing socially desirable characteristics. Statements with scale values between the two extremes of the continuum represent statements with varying degrees of judged desirability or undesirability. Some statements have scale values that fall toward the center of the psychological continuum and are judged to represent neither very desirable nor very undesirable characteristics.

You will find it enlightening if you ask a group of judges to rate the following three statements for social desirability using the 9-point rating scale.

1. He is trusted by most of the people who know him. (7.9)

2. He likes to read science fiction. (5.3)

3. He tries to control others by getting them to feel sorry for him. (2.6)

If you then find the average rating of each statement, you should observe that these are fairly close to those reported in parentheses after each statement. The reported SDSVs of the statements are based upon the combined judgments of 47 male and 48 female college students.

When a large number of personality statements are judged for social desirability on a 9-point rating scale, statements with the same SDSVs may be found to have distributions of ratings that differ in their spread or dispersion. For example, two statements may both have a scale value of 6.0, but the ratings for one of the statements tend to be concentrated in the intervals close to 6.0, whereas the ratings for the other statement are spread over a larger range of intervals. The standard deviation of the distribution of ratings assigned to a statement is a measure of the spread or dispersion of the ratings. The dispersion or standard deviation of the social desirability ratings provides an index, therefore, of the degree to which the judges agree on the location of the statement on the social desirability continuum. Thus, if two statements both have scale values of 6.0 but one has a standard deviation of .8 and the other, one of 1.2, it means that there is greater agreement among the judges about the location of the first statement on the social desirability continuum than there is for the second statement.[3]

IV

Suppose that we have obtained the SDSVs of a set of statements and that we then present these same statements to another independent group of subjects with instructions

3. It has been found that statements with large standard deviations are those that tend to have a smaller probability of being answered consistently on two different occasions than statements with small standard deviations (Edwards and Walsh, 1963).

to describe themselves in terms of the statements by answering each one *true* or *false*. For this second, independent group of subjects, we can obtain the proportion of *true* responses given to each statement. This proportion is the *probability of item endorsement* in self-description under the standard instructions ordinarily used in administering personality scales and inventories. By having available the SDSVs of the statements as well as the probability of a *true* response—P(T)—we can determine whether these two variables are related. If we plot P(T) against SDSV for any large set of random or representative statements, we will find that P(T) increases linearly with SDSV. That is, if a statement has an extreme socially desirable scale value, it will also have a high probability of being answered *true*. Conversely, if it has a low or socially undesirable scale value, it will also have a low probability of being answered *true*.

It is, of course, possible that the correlation between P(T) and SDSV may be quite low for selected sets of statements. This may occur when the statements have either a restricted range in SDSVs or a restricted range in P(T)s. The available evidence, however, quite strongly supports the notion that in the population P(T) and SDSV are positively and highly correlated. Thus, for random and representative sets of statements drawn from the population, we may also expect to find P(T) and SDSV to be highly correlated.

If we know the SDSV of a personality statement, we may define the concept of a *socially desirable response* to the statement. A socially desirable response may be defined as a *true* response to a statement with a socially desirable scale value and as a *false* response to a statement with a socially undesirable scale value. The probability of a socially desirable response—P(SD)—to a statement is obtained by dividing the number of socially desirable responses given to the statement by the total number of responses given to the statement. We know that P(T) increases linearly with SDSV. The relationship between P(SD) and SDSV must, therefore, be V-shaped. Items with extreme socially desirable scale values have a high probability of eliciting *true* and socially desirable responses, and items with extreme socially undesirable scale values also have a high probability of eliciting *false* and socially desirable responses. Items with neutral SDSVs or scale values that deviate only moderately from the neutral point have relatively low probabilities of eliciting socially desirable responses.

V

In my monograph on the social desirability variable (Edwards, 1957a, p. 260), I emphasized that there were undoubtedly individual differences in the tendency to give socially desirable responses to personality statements. We might attempt to measure these individual differences in various ways. The one that I originally proposed was based upon *individual rates* of SD responding. I developed a Social Desirability *(SD)* Scale consisting of 39 Minnesota Multiphasic Personality Inventory (MMPI) items. All of the items in the *SD* Scale are keyed for socially desirable responses. Individuals who obtain high scores on the *SD* Scale have given a relatively large number of socially desirable responses, and individuals with low scores on the *SD* Scale have given relatively few socially desirable responses in self-description.

For comparative purposes it is convenient to transform the raw score—or the number of socially desirable responses given by individual subjects—into *rates* of SD responding. An individual's rate of SD responding is obtained by dividing the number of socially desirable responses he has given by the total number of responses or, in other words, by the total number of items he has answered. The mean rate of SD responding for a group of individuals can be obtained by averaging the individual rates or, equivalently, by dividing the mean score on a set of items keyed for socially desirable responses by the number of items in the set. I shall indicate individual rates of SD responding by p and the mean rate for a group of subjects by P.

VI

In a personality or trait scale, each item is keyed for a response that supposedly indicates the presence of the trait the scale was designed to measure. It seems reasonable to believe that if a given trait is itself socially desirable, many of the keyed responses to items in a scale designed to measure the trait will also be socially desirable responses. Similarly, if a given trait is itself socially undesirable, many of the keyed responses to the items in the scale designed to measure the trait will also be socially undesirable responses.

Consider a trait scale in which all of the trait-keyed responses are also socially desirable responses. If the mean rate of SD responding to the items in the trait scale is approximately the same as that estimated by the *SD* Scale, then the mean score on the trait scale should be approximately equal to

$$\overline{X} = nP$$

where n is the number of items in the scale and P is the estimated mean rate of SD responding provided by the *SD* Scale. For example, if the trait scale contains a total of sixty items keyed for trait *and* socially desirable responses and if the mean score on the *SD* Scale for a group of subjects is 31.0, then the mean rate of SD responding for the group will be estimated as

$$P = 31/39 = .79$$

If the same mean rate of SD responding applies to the sixty items in the trait scale, then the expected mean score on the trait scale will be

$$\overline{X} = 60(.79) = 47.4$$

If all of the keyed responses in a trait scale are also socially undesirable responses, then the mean trait score on the scale would be predicted to be

$$\bar{X} = n(1 - P)$$

Thus, if the same group of subjects were administered a 60-item trait scale in which all trait responses are socially undesirable responses, on the basis of their estimated mean rate of SD responding as given by the SD Scale, the predicted trait mean score will be

$$\bar{X} = 60(1 - .79) = 12.6$$

For trait scales that have some degree of balance in the number of items keyed for socially desirable and socially undesirable responses, the expected mean score on the trait scale will be given by

$$\bar{X} = n_1 P + n_2(1 - P)$$

where n_1 and n_2 are the number of items keyed for socially desirable and socially undesirable responses, respectively. Thus, for a 60-item trait scale with forty items keyed for socially desirable responses and twenty items keyed for socially undesirable responses, the predicted trait mean score for the same group of subjects would be

$$\bar{X} = 40(.79) + .20(1 - .79) = 35.8$$

VII

Some years ago, Jerald Walker and I (Edwards and Walker, 1961) published a short article in which we suggested that the SD Scale might be used as a short form of the MMPI. We now know that we were wrong. Although use of the mean probability of a socially desirable response may predict mean scores on trait scales fairly well, regardless of whether the trait keying of items in the scale is balanced for social desirability, this is not so for the individual case. In the first instance, we are using a mean rate of SD responding to predict a mean score on a trait scale. In the second instance, we would like to use an individual's rate of SD responding to predict his individual score on the trait scale. But it is obvious that, despite variability in individual rates of SD responding as measured by the *SD* Scale, if a trait scale has a balance in its social desirability keying—that is, if the scale contains an equal number of items for which the trait response is a socially desirable response and for which the trait response is a socially undesirable response—each subject's predicted score on the trait scale will be exactly the same. This will be so regardless of differences in rate of SD responding as measured by the *SD* Scale. In this case, the predicted individual trait scores cannot measure individual differences in the observed trait scores simply because the predicted trait scores will have no variability.

The fact that predicted trait scores on a trait scale with a balance in its social desirability keying are all the same does not necessarily mean that individual differences in rates of SD responding to items in the scale are nonexistent. For example, if we ignore the trait keying of items in the scale and simply count the number of socially desirable responses the subject has given, we would expect the individual rates of SD responding on the trait scale to be correlated with individual rates of responding on the *SD* Scale. The mean rate of SD responding on the trait scale may be higher or lower than the mean rate on the *SD* Scale, but this is unimportant provided there is variation in the individual rates of SD responding.

I do not say that the individual rates of SD responding on the two scales should be perfectly correlated but only that they should be positively correlated. Certain conditions can serve to lower the correlation. For example, if the trait scale contains a large proportion of items with scale values that deviate only moderately from the neutral point on the social desirability continuum, the correlation may prove to be lower than would be the case if the scale values of the items in the trait scale were more similar to those of the items in the *SD* Scale.

Whenever we correlate scores on the *SD* Scale with scores on some other trait scale, we should remember that we are correlating estimated individual rates of SD responding with the trait scores. Whether the rate of SD responding, as measured by the SD Scale, will correlate positively or negatively or not at all with the trait score should depend upon the nature of both the social desirability keying of the items in the trait scale and the SDSVs of the items. Obviously, if the trait score is obtained by adding together some number of socially desirable responses and some number of socially undesirable responses, the resulting total score will not, in general, reflect differences in individual rates of SD responding. Trait scores on such scales should, therefore, have lower correlations with scores on the SD Scale than they have with scores on trait scales that are consistently keyed for either socially desirable or socially undesirable responses.

There can be exceptions to this general case also. Suppose, for example, that a scale has a balance in its social desirability keying, but that the items keyed for socially desirable responses are such that almost every subject gives the socially desirable response to them. In this instance, individual differences in the trait scores would be primarily the result of responses to those items keyed for socially undesirable responses. Thus, despite the balance in the social desirability keying of items in the scale, scores on this scale would be predicted to have a negative correlation with scores on the SD Scale. Similar considerations would apply if the set of items keyed for socially undesirable responses were such that almost every subject gives the socially desirable and non-keyed trait response to them. Responses to these items would thus contribute very little to individual differences in the trait scores, and the trait scores, in turn, would reflect primarily individual differences in responses to the set of items keyed for socially desirable responses. Scores on this scale would thus be predicted to have a positive correlation with scores on the SD Scale.

The presence of a large number of items with relatively neutral scale values in a trait scale should also serve to lower the correlation between scores on the trait scale and scores on the SD Scale. Even though a scale may have either a large or a small proportion of items keyed for socially desirable responses, if these items all have relatively neutral SDSVs, the correlation between scores on the trait scale and scores on the *SD* Scale may be relatively low. This should be so because neutral items are relatively insensitive stimuli for eliciting socially desirable responses.

VIII

Consider a scale in which the trait-keyed response for some of the items is a socially desirable response and the trait-keyed response for other items is a socially undesirable response. Specifically, take the case of two items; for one item, the trait response is a socially desirable response, for the other, it is a socially undesirable response. If the trait is the primary determiner of responses to these two items, we would expect to find that individuals who give the trait and socially desirable response to one item tend to give the trait and socially undesirable response to the other item. The correlation between the two items should, in this instance, be positive.

Suppose, however, that the tendency to give socially desirable responses is also operating. In this case, we would expect individuals with strong tendencies to give socially desirable responses to follow their tendencies and give the socially desirable response to both items. But the socially desirable response to one item is the keyed response, whereas the socially desirable response to the other item is *not* the keyed response. Thus, if the tendency to give socially desirable responses is operating, the correlation between the trait responses to the two items should decrease from what it would be if the trait were the only important determiner of subjects' responses to the two items.

It can be shown that the maximum number of item correlations of the kind described occurs when a scale has an equal number of items keyed for socially desirable and socially undesirable responses. Since the correlations between these items contribute to the average intercorrelation of the items, social desirability considerations lead us to predict that the average intercorrelation of items in a scale will be highest when all items are keyed for either socially desirable or socially undesirable responses. For scales that have a balance in their social desirability keying, the average intercorrelation of the items should be low compared with the values obtained for scales that have an imbalance in their social desirability keying.

The average intercorrelation of the items in a scale is related to various indexes of the internal consistency or homogeneity of the items in a scale. Scales in which the items have a high degree of internal consistency or homogeneity are scales in which the items are generally assumed to be measuring a common factor or dimension. I mentioned previously that scales having an extreme imbalance in their social desirability keying would, on the basis of social desirability considerations, be predicted to have higher correlations with the SD Scale than would scales having a balance in their social desirability keying. If the argument I have made with respect to the relationship between the internal consistency of a scale and the nature of the social desirability keying of the items in the scale is correct, scales with an extreme imbalance in their social desirability keying should also have a higher degree of internal consistency than scales with a balance in their social desirability keying. Other things being equal, we would also predict that scales that have a high degree of internal consistency should have higher correlations with the SD Scale than those scales that have a low degree of internal consistency.

IX

I regard the tendency to give socially desirable responses in self-description as a general personality trait. If this is so, the tendency should not only operate with the particular items contained in the *SD* Scale but also with items in various other personality trait scales. I have tried in this chapter to give a broad statement of the implications of this trait in relation to performance on various personality scales and to psychometric properties of personality scales. In Chapter 3, I shall review some of the research studies designed specifically to test the validity of these implications.

THREE / ALLEN L. EDWARDS

The Social Desirability Variable: A Review of the Evidence[1]

I

The social desirability scale value (SDSV) of a personality statement would be a meaningless concept if the ratings of various statements by different individuals were made completely at random so that the ratings were independent. One of the first problems to be faced, therefore, is the reliability of SDSVs. Reliability is the degree to which the scale values derived from the ratings of one group of judges agree with those derived from the ratings of another group. I wish to emphasize that the problem of the reliability of SDSVs is in no sense different from the problem of reliability of any other kind of rating. For example, ten staff members of a graduate department may be asked to rate on a 9-point rating scale each of twenty graduate students with respect to some trait or ability. If we find the average rating assigned each of the twenty students we are, in essence, finding the scale value for each student. In such cases we are also interested in the reliability of the mean ratings assigned to the students.

A psychometrician might approach the problem of the

1. This work was supported in part by NIMH Research Grant MH-04075, United States Public Health Service.

reliability of ratings in several ways. For example, the judges might be divided at random into two groups and the scale values or mean ratings found separately for each group. The correlation between the two sets of scale values provides an index of the reliability of the scale values. The average intercorrelations of the ratings of all judges can also be used to obtain an index of the reliability of the scale values. No matter what procedures are used to determine the reliability of SDSVs, if the scale values are to be reliable, the ratings obtained from different judges must be correlated and not independent. This is turn means that different judges must exhibit some degree of agreement in the relative ordering of statements in relation to social desirability.

Considerable evidence demonstrates that SDSVs derived from different but comparable groups of judges are highly correlated and therefore highly reliable. We typically find product-moment correlations between the scale values derived from two different groups of judges to be .95 or higher. These results have been confirmed by other investigators. For example, Messick and Jackson (1916b) scaled the 566 items in the Minnesota Multiphasic Personality Inventory (MMPI) using a 9-point rating scale and the method of successive intervals to obtain the scale values of the statements. The judges consisted of 171 students at Pennsylvania State University. The scale values obtained by Messick and Jackson correlated .96 with the scale values of the same items as obtained by Heineman and given in Dahlstrom and Welsh (1960). Heineman obtained the scale values of the MMPI items by finding the mean rating assigned to the items on a 5-point rating scale by 108 students at the University of Iowa.

Comparable test-retest reliability coefficients are obtained when the same group of judges rates the same items on two different occasions. For example, Walsh and I (Edwards and Walsh, 1963) had a group of judges rate 2,824 personality statements for social desirability. The same judges rated a serial sample of 176 of these statements for social desirability approximately two weeks later. The product-moment correlation between the scale values derived from the two sets of ratings was .97 for 47 male judges and .98 for 48 female judges.

It is conceivable that, if one were to select two groups of judges in such a way that the two groups differed in some characteristic, the scale values derived from the two groups might not be related. It may seem quite reasonable, for example, to expect that if mental patients and normals are asked to judge the same set of personality statements, the scale values obtained from the judgments of these two groups would be quite unrelated. Reasonable as this hypothesis may seem, the facts do not support it. Taylor (1959), for example, had diagnosed schizophrenic patients and a group of normal controls judge the items in the Schizophrenic (Sc) Scale of the MMPI for social desirability. The scale values based upon the judgments of the schizophrenic patients correlated .98 with those obtained from the judgments of the normals. Klett (1957), using the 140 items in the Edwards Personal Preference Schedule (EPPS), had male neuropsychiatric patients judge the items for social desirability. The scale values based upon the judgments of the neuropsychiatric patients correlated .88 with scale values derived from the judgments of college students. In another study, Cowen, Staiman, and Wolitzky (1961) had forty male schizophrenics rate 139 trait-descriptive adjectives for social desirability. A control sample of forty patients drawn from the general medical wards of the same hospital also rated the 139 trait-descriptive terms for social desirability. The correlation between these two sets of scale values was .98. In an unpublished study by Kogan and Kogan, cited by Edwards (1957a), neuropsychiatric patients rated the 128 items in the Interpersonal Check List (ICL) for social desirability. The scale values derived from the judgments of the neuropsychiatric patients correlated .95 with those based upon the judgments of college students. These studies, each involving a different set of personality statements, demonstrate quite conclusively that the SDSVs derived from the judgments of mental patients are highly correlated with the SDSVs derived from the judgments of normal controls.

That SDSVs based upon the judgments of still other diverse groups are highly correlated with those based upon the judgments of normals has been shown by a number of other studies. For example, pedophiles (Cowen and Stricker, 1963), novice nuns (Zax, Cowen, and Peter, 1963), alcoholics (Zax, Cowen, Budin, and Biggs, 1962), and a geriatric sample (Cowen, Davol, Reimanis, and Stiller, 1962) have been used as judges in obtaining SDSVs of trait-descriptive terms. In all cases the scale values derived from the judgments of these various groups have been highly intercorrelated as well as highly correlated with the scale values of the same terms based upon the judgments of college students (Cowen and Budin, 1964).

Even when judgments of social desirability are obtained from groups in different cultures, the SDSVs of personality statements tend to be substantially correlated. Scale values based upon the judgments of Norwegian students were found to correlate .78 with those based upon the judgments of American college students (Lövaas, 1958); those of students at the University of Beirut correlated .86 with those of American college students (Klett and Yaukey, 1959); those of Japanese students correlated .90 with those of American college students (Iwawaki and Cowen, 1964); and those of French students correlated .95 with those of American college students (Cowen and Frankel, 1964). Finally, the scale values based upon the judgments of Japanese students correlated .85 with those based upon the judgments of French students.

There seems little doubt, on the basis of the evidence presented, that the SDSVs derived from the judgments of quite different groups are quite similar, provided the statements being judged have not been selected so that they have a restricted range on the social desirability continuum. Obviously, if statements are such that their scale values are concentrated in a narrow range on the social desirability continuum, we would expect the scale values derived from different groups to be less highly correlated.

The fact that scale values based upon the judgments of different groups are highly correlated does not mean, of course, that group differences may not exist for selected sets of statements. For example, if the statements in a large set can be classified in terms of content into several different classes, then it may be found that items with certain kinds of content may be rated higher or lower, on the average, by one group than another. The items in the EPPS, for example, can be classified in terms of fifteen different content areas. Klett (1957) found that, despite a correlation of .88 between the scale values based on the judgments of mental patients and those based on the judgments of college students, the mental patients assigned higher mean ratings to items referring to Deference, Order, and Nurturance and lower mean ratings to items referring to Affiliation, Change, and Heterosexuality than the college students did.

II

The reported correlations are between averages. Such correlations may be considerably higher than those between the ratings of individual judges. Although the high reliability of SDVS indicates that individual ratings must be correlated with each other and with the normative values, it is of some interest to examine the actual range and magnitude of the individual correlations. James Walsh and I (Edwards and Walsh, 1963) obtained normative SDSVs for a serial sample of 176 statements drawn from a larger set of 2,824 statements. Forty-seven male and 48 female students rated these statements for social desirability. The scale values derived from the male judges correlated .97 with those derived from the female judges, and we therefore combined the two sets of ratings to obtain the SDSVs of the 176 statements based upon 95 judges. I shall refer to these SDSVs as the normative SDSVs. Another independent sample of 103 females and 105 males rated the same statements, and each individual's rating was correlated with the normative SDSVs. The distribution of the correlation coefficients is shown in Figure 1; it is clear that the judgments of personal desirability—the individual ratings

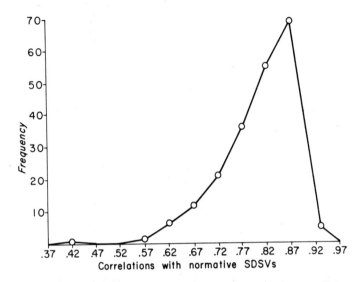

Fig. 1. Frequency distribution of the correlation coefficients between individual ratings of social desirability and the normative SDSVs for a sample of 105 males and 103 females.

of social desirability—are, for most of these individuals, substantially correlated with the normative values.

To find out the degree to which ratings of social desirability obtained from different individuals are correlated, we intercorrelated the ratings of 103 females and the ratings of 105 males for a set of 150 items.[2] In this analysis, we included the SDSVs of the same items based upon the judgments of another group. These SDSVs were treated as though they were obtained from one additional judge, so that we had one correlation matrix of order 104 x 104 for the females and another of order 106 x 106 for the males. These two correlation matrices were then factor analyzed by the method of principal components. Figure 2 shows the distribution of the first factor loadings for these two groups of subjects.

2. The 150 items were the first 150 items in a serial sample of 176 items. We had to eliminate the last 26 items because of restrictions in our computer program.

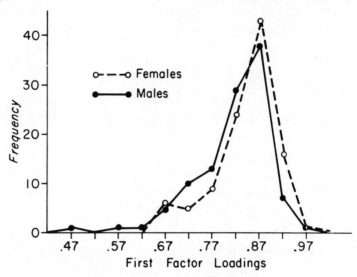

FIG. 2. Frequency distribution of first factor loadings of 105 males and 103 females. The last point on the right is the loading of the vector of normative SDSVs.

The normative SDSVs had the highest loadings in both analyses, the observed values being .98 for both the males and the females. It is also obvious, however, that each individual subject had a substantial loading on the first factor. Indeed, the first factor for the males accounted for 67 per cent of the total variance and the first for the females, for 71 per cent. If we extract a second factor, we find that for the males the second factor accounts for 21.9 per cent of the total variance and for the females, the second factor accounts for only 1.77 per cent.

The results obtained for the individual case are reassuring in that we may have some confidence that individual ratings of social desirability are not idiosyncratic but rather tend to agree with each other and with the normative SDSVs.

III

In my initial investigation of the relationship between P(T) and SDSV, I used a set of 140 statements from the EPPS (Edwards, 1953). The product-moment correlation between P(T) and SDSV for this set of statements was .87. Subsequent research has shown that this relationship holds for all of the random or representative sets of statements which have been investigated (Cowen and Tongas, 1959; Cruse, 1963; Edwards, 1957a, 1959a; Hanley, 1956; Kenny, 1956; Taylor, 1959). I shall describe only three of these studies. Two are of significance because they both involved large sets of personality statements. The other is significant because it shows that the relationship between P(T) and SDSV is also found with relatively young children.

In one of these studies, Cruse (1963) scaled the 1,575 items in Hilden's (1954, 1958) Universe of Personal Concepts for social desirability, using a group of 43 male and 52 female judges. These statements plus another 72 statements, which Cruse had previously scaled for social desirability, were administered as a personality inventory to another group of students, who were instructed to describe themselves by answering each statement *true* or *false*. The correlation coefficient between P(T) and SDSV for this set of 1,647 statements was .90.

In another large scale study, James Walsh and I (Edwards and Walsh, 1963) had 47 males and 48 females rate 2,824 personality statements for social desirability. The correlation between the male SDSVs and the female SDSVs was .986. We combined the two sets of ratings, obtaining the SDSVs of the statements based upon the judgments of 95 judges.

Another two groups of 110 males and 111 females, responded to the statements in self-description. Because the probabilities of item endorsement based upon the responses of males and females correlated .96, we combined the responses of these two groups to obtain probabilities of a *true* response based upon the responses of 221 subjects. The product-moment correlation between P(T) and SDSV for this set of statements was .892.

The linear relationship between P(T) and SDSV found with college students and adults has also been found with young children. Cruse (1963) obtained the SDSVs for a set of personality statements based upon the judgments of college students. He then selected a set of forty statements so that the SDSVs of the statements were spread across the complete social desirability continuum. These forty statements were administered orally to young children, who were asked to answer *yes* or *no* to each statement. The correlation between the proportion of *yes* responses and the SDSVs of the statements was .96.

IV

It will be recalled that a socially desirable response is defined as a true response to an item with a socially desirable scale value or as a false response to an item with a socially undesirable scale value. Because the relationship between P(T) and SDSV is linear, the relationship between P(SD) and SDSV must be V-shaped. Alan Klockars and I divided a serial sample of 176 personality statements drawn from a larger group of 2,824 statements into two sets: those with SDSVs greater than 5.0, the neutral point on the social desirability continuum, and those with SDSVs less than 5.0. There were eighty items in the set with socially desirable scale values and 96 items in the set with socially undesirable scale values. We found for each set separately the correlation coefficient between P(SD) and SDSV and the regression coefficient of P(SD) on SDSV. These correlation and regression coefficients are given in Table 1 and the regression lines are shown in Figure 3.

TABLE 1.   Relationship between the Probability of a False Response to 96 Items with Socially Undesirable Scale Values and the Probability of a True Response to 80 Items with Socially Desirable Scale Values

	False: SDSV $<$ 5.0	True: SDSV $>$ 5.0
P	.787	.750
^{s}P	.140	.182
^{s}SDSV	.610	.784
^{r}P-SDSV	−.721	.669
^{b}P.SDSV	−.165	.155

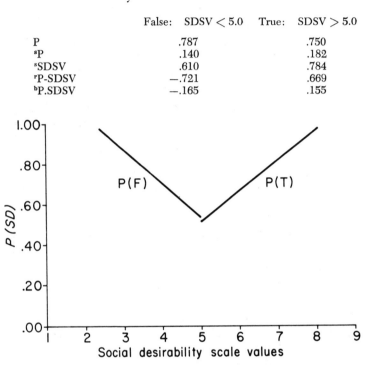

FIG. 3. Regression lines showing the relationship between P(F) and items with socially undesirable scale values and between P(T) and items with socially desirable scale values.

Except for sign, the two correlation coefficients and the two regression coefficients are fairly comparable. We note also that the mean probability of a socially desirable and *true* response to the items with SDSVs greater than 5.0 is .750, and that the mean probability of a socially desirable and *false* response to items with SDSVs less than 5.0 is .787. The difference between these two means is not large and indicates only a slightly greater tendency for items with socially undesirable scale values to elicit, on the average, socially desirable responses than the items with socially desirable scale values.

The two means, .787 and .750, represent *mean rates* of SD responding to these items. The weighted average is .77 and represents the *mean probability* of a socially desirable response when averaged over the complete social desirability continuum. Because P(SD) is a V-shaped function of SDSV, so that items at both extremes of the social desirability continuum have higher probabilities of eliciting socially desirable responses than items with scale values that depart only moderately from the neutral point, we can expect to obtain different mean rates of SD responding for selected sets of items. Thus, if we estimated mean rate of SD responding using only items with extreme SDSVs, we should obtain a higher estimate than we would if we used only items with relatively neutral SDSVs.

If the SDSVs of personality items are normally distributed, we would have many items with scale values in the central or neutral section of the social desirability continuum and relatively few items with extreme SDSVs. If items with a normal distribution of SDSVs were used to estimate the mean rate of SD responding, the mean rate thus obtained would be considerably lower than that based upon a bimodal or a rectangular distribution of SDSV. There is evidence to indicate, however, that the distribution of SDSVs is neither normal nor rectangular but rather bimodal. Figure 4 shows the distribution of SDSVs for a set of 2,824 personality statements. It is obvious that for this set of items the distribution of SDSVs is bimodal and that items with scale values in the neutral interval are relatively few in number compared with items on both sides of the neutral interval.

The distribution of SDSVs for another set of 1,647 items has been obtained by Cruse (1963) and is even more markedly bimodal than the distribution shown in Figure 4. It is also true that the SDSVs of the 566 items in the MMPI have a bimodal distribution.

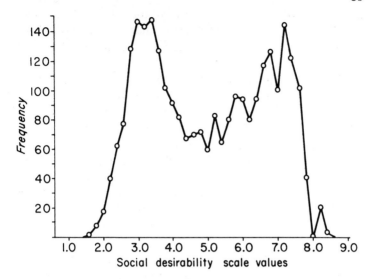

Fig. 4. Frequency distribution of SDSVs of 2,824 personality statements.

V

The MMPI Social Desirability (*SD*) Scale consists of 39 items. Nine of the items have socially desirable scale values and are keyed *true*, and the remaining thirty items have socially undesirable scale values and are keyed *false*, consistent with the definition of a socially desirable response. Since the mean score on the *SD* Scale is typically between 29 and 32 for college students, the mean or average rate of SD responding, as measured by these items, is between .74 and .82. In other words, about 75 to 82 per cent of the responses given by the average student to the items in the *SD* Scale are socially desirable responses. These two values, .74 and .82, are fairly realistic estimates of the limits within which we may expect the population mean rate of SD responding to fall. It will be recalled that the mean rate of SD responding to a serial sample of 176 items drawn from a larger set of 2,824 items was .77. For the set of 140 items contained in the EPPS, the mean rate of SD responding was found to be .81 (Edwards, 1962).

In general, the mean rate of SD responding, as measured by the SD Scale, has also been found to be a fairly good predictor of the mean rate of SD responding on a variety of MMPI trait scales. In two independent studies, predictions concerning mean scores on MMPI scales, based on the assumption that the mean rates of SD responding to the items in these scales would be approximately the same as the mean rate of SD responding on the SD Scale, were found to be, in general, fairly accurate (Edwards, 1962, 1964).

Table 2 shows the predicted and observed means on 57 MMPI scales based upon the responses of a sample of 150 male college students. The mean score on the SD Scale for this group of subjects was 30.81 and consequently the predicted mean rate of SD responding was

$$P = 30.81/39 = .79$$

This is the value of P that was used to obtain the predicted means on the MMPI scales.

It is obvious from values of the differences between the predicted and observed mean shown in Table 2 that there are cases where the predicted trait mean score over- or under-estimates the observed trait mean score. An example is the F Scale of the MMPI. All but one of the items in the F Scale are keyed for socially undesirable responses. Since $P = .79$ for this group of subjects, the predicted mean on the F Scale is

$$\bar{X} = 1(.79) + 63(1 - .79) = 14.02$$

whereas the observed mean is 5.71.

We can better understand why the F Scale mean is overestimated if we look at the relationship between the probability of a keyed response—$P(K)$—and SDSV for the 64 items in the F Scale, shown in Figure 5. The SDSVs of the items in the F Scale are based upon values reported by Messick and Jackson (1961b) and the $P(T)$s are based upon values re-

TABLE 2. Observed Means, $\bar{X}_O$, Predicted Means, $\bar{X}_P$, and Difference between the Two Means [a]

SCALE	$\bar{X}_O$	$\bar{X}_P$	D	SCALE	$\bar{X}_O$	$\bar{X}_P$	D
Ai	10.89	10.32	.57	Ma-O	7.09	5.99	1.10
A	13.42	9.35	4.07	Ma-S	11.27	12.37	−1.10
Ac	12.85	13.64	−.79	Mf	26.86	28.84	−1.98
Ad	5.82	6.72	−.90	Mp	11.60	22.59	−10.99
MAS	17.28	11.08	6.20	Ne	5.52	6.30	−.78
B	25.73	25.41	.32	No	5.52	3.78	1.74
Ca	11.93	8.72	3.21	Nu	12.75	9.83	2.92
Cn	27.57	25.00	2.57	Or	13.89	11.05	2.84
D	19.54	20.72	−1.18	Pa	9.55	14.20	4.65
Dn	15.19	17.64	−2.45	Pa-O	1.87	4.83	−2.96
Do	17.04	16.90	.14	Pa-S	7.53	9.37	−1.84
D-O	9.77	8.77	1.00	Pd	17.58	15.14	2.44
D-S	10.55	11.16	−.61	Pd-O	6.82	6.46	.36
Dy	20.15	17.68	2.45	Pd-S	10.60	8.68	1.92
Eo	11.79	10.05	1.74	Pn	13.37	8.67	4.70
Es	48.68	45.02	3.66	Pr	8.44	8.46	−.02
F	5.71	14.02	−8.31	Pt	13.30	10.66	2.64
Fm	14.09	16.10	−2.01	Pv	15.70	16.88	−1.18
Ho	18.05	13.40	4.65	R	15.74	14.20	1.54
Hs	5.08	6.93	−1.85	Re	20.34	19.48	.86
Hy	21.51	24.78	−3.27	Rp	20.58	21.80	−1.22
Hy-O	6.23	6.72	−.49	Sc	12.87	17.54	−4.67
Hy-S	15.70	18.06	−2.36	Si	26.46	17.60	8.86
Ie	31.21	28.49	2.72	Sp	17.80	19.17	−1.37
Im	8.79	7.31	1.48	St	21.40	22.22	−.82
K	14.93	19.64	−4.71	To	21.77	21.96	−.19
L	3.56	7.21	−3.65	Tt	12.67	19.38	−6.71
Lp	32.25	36.02	−3.77	Sd	13.22	27.54	−14.32
Ma	18.40	18.36	.04				

a. From Edwards (1964).

ported by Goldberg and Rorer (1963). As Figure 5 shows, the SDSVs of the items in the F Scale are, in general, extreme so that they have relatively high probabilities of eliciting socially desirable responses and, consequently, low probabilities of eliciting keyed responses.[3] The mean rate of SD responding to these items is approximately .91 rather than .79, as estimated by the SD Scale. As a result, the predicted mean trait

3. As Figure 5 shows, all but one of the items in the F Scale are keyed for socially undesirable responses.

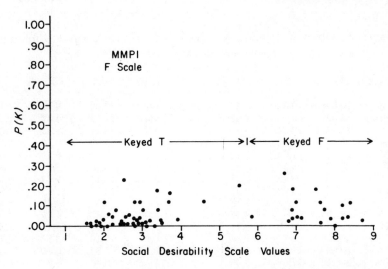

FIG. 5. The relationship between the probability of a keyed response, P(K), and the SDSVs of the items in the MMPI F scale.

score of 14.02 overestimates considerably the observed mean of 5.71. But this discrepancy between the predicted mean and the observed mean is not unexpected when one recalls that the items included in the F Scale were selected in such a way that less than 10 per cent of the normal subjects in the MMPI standardization group gave the keyed response.

It must be emphasized that the mean score on a trait scale will be accurately predicted only insofar as the mean rate of SD responding to the items in the scale is approximately the same as the mean rate of SD responding to the items in the SD Scale.

VI

If a trait scale has a large proportion of items keyed for socially desirable responses, the scores on the scale may reflect individual differences in rates of SD responding as well as possible individual differences in the trait itself. If the trait scores reflect individual differences in rates of SD responding, so that high trait scores are associated with high rates and low scores with low rates, the trait scores should be positively correlated with scores on the SD Scale. For example, the Leadership (*Lp*) Scale of the MMPI contains fifty items, 44 of which are keyed for socially desirable responses, and typically correlates about .77 with the SD Scale for college males.

On trait scales that have a small proportion of items keyed for socially desirable responses, individuals with high rates of SD responding should obtain relatively low scores, and scores on trait scales of this nature should be negatively correlated with scores on the SD Scale. An example is the Psychasthenia (*Pt*) Scale of the MMPI, which contains 48 items, of which 47 are keyed for socially undesirable responses. When college male students are used as subjects, the *Pt* Scale typically correlates about —.84 with the SD Scale.

Trait scores on scales balanced in their social desirability keying should be relatively uncorrelated with rates of SD responding and, therefore, relatively uncorrelated with scores on the SD Scale. The Masculinity (*Mf*) Scale of the MMPI contains sixty items, of which approximately half (28 items) are keyed for socially desirable responses and approximately half (32 items) are keyed for socially undesirable responses. Thus, scores on this scale should have a relatively low correlation with scores on the SD Scale, and, for college males, the typical correlation between scores on the *Mf* Scale and scores on the SD Scale is —.16.

The three MMPI scales cited are not isolated examples. In general, it has been found that the correlations of MMPI scales with the SD Scale are linearly related to the proportion of items in the scales keyed for socially desirable responses. Scales with a large proportion of items keyed for socially desirable responses tend to be positively correlated with the SD Scale; scales balanced in their social desirability keying tend to have low correlations with the SD Scale; and scales with a small proportion of items keyed for socially desirable responses and, consequently, a large proportion keyed for socially undesirable responses tend to have negative correlations with the SD Scale. In one study, the product-moment correlation between the proportion of items keyed for socially desirable responses in 43 MMPI scales and the corresponding correlations of the scales with the SD Scale was found to be .92 (Edwards, 1961). The magnitude of this correlation coefficient shows that the correlations of the scales with the SD Scale could be predicted quite accurately on the basis of the proportion of items keyed for socially desirable responses in the scales.

It was pointed out previously that the presence of a large number of items with relatively neutral scale values in a trait scale should serve to lower the correlation between scores on the trait scale and scores on the SD Scale. To test this hypothesis we (Edwards, Diers, and Walker, 1962) obtained for each of sixty personality scales the proportion of items with SDSVs in the neutral interval on the social desirability continuum and the correlations between the scores on each of the sixty scales and scores on the SD Scale. We then correlated the proportion of neutral items in the scales with the absolute values of the correlations with the SD Scale. The product-moment correlation between the two variables was —.52. The fact that this correlation is negative and of some magnitude, despite the quite restricted range in one variable, the proportion of neutral items in the scales, confirms the prediction that the presence of a large number of neutral items in a trait scale serves to lower the correlation of the scale with the SD Scale.

The results of this study provide one possible explanation of why trait scales that have either a large or a small proportion of items keyed for socially desirable response may occasionally be found to have relatively low correlations with the SD scale. Neutral items or items with SDSVs that depart only moderately from the neutral point on the social desirability continuum are not very sensitive stimuli for eliciting socially desirable responses. Thus, despite the fact that most of the items in a scale may be consistently keyed for either socially desirable or socially undesirable responses, if these are neutral items, then scores on the scale may have low correlations with scores on the SD Scale.[4]

VII

It is my position that scores on various personality trait scales are correlated with scores on the SD Scale to the degree to which they are measuring the same common personality trait I believe the SD Scale to be measuring: the tendency to give socially desirable responses in self-description. One way to examine the hypothesis that scales measure in varying degrees the same common trait or factor is to intercorrelate the scales and then to factor analyze the resulting correlation matrix. We have done this with MMPI scales.

In one study, Carol Diers and I (Edwards and Diers, 1962) administered the MMPI under standard instructions, under instructions to give socially desirable responses, and under instructions to give socially undesirable responses. For each set of instructions we obtained scores on 58 MMPI scales. Scores on these scales were intercorrelated and factor analyzed separately for each set of instructions. The first factor loadings under each set of instructions were highly correlated, the lowest correlation being .97. In all three analyses, the first factor loadings of the MMPI scale were linearly related to the correlations of the scales with the SD Scale, the lowest correlation being .96. Thus MMPI scales that have high positive correlations with the SD Scale have high loadings at one pole of the first factor, and scales that have high negative correlations with the SD Scale have high loadings at the opposite

4. It is now known that if all the items in a scale have SDSVs within the neutral interval of the social desirability continuum and if all of the items are keyed *true*, scores on the scale can be expected to have a negative correlation with scores on the SD Scale. The magnitude of the correlation should depend upon the actual distribution of the SDSVs within the neutral interval. For a more complete discussion of this point, see Edwards and Diers (1963).

pole of the first factor. The scales with relatively low loadings
on the first factor tend to be those scales with a balance in
their social desirability keying and/or a large proportion of
items with relatively neutral scale values. In view of the linear
relationship between the first factor loadings of the MMPI
scales and the correlations of the scales with the *SD* Scale, the
interpretation of the first MMPI factor as a social desirability
factor seems entirely plausible.

Even more compelling evidence that the first factor is a
social desirability factor, however, is that the first factor loadings of the MMPI scales can be predicted quite accurately
from the proportion of items in the scales keyed for socially
desirable responses. For standard instructions, instructions to
give socially desirable responses, and instructions to give
socially undesirable responses, the correlations between the
first factor that are opposite in sign to those scales consistently
cially desirable responses were .89, .92, and .94 respectively.
These results, of course, are precisely what would be predicted
on the basis of social desirability considerations.

For example, scores on the *SD* Scale are assumed to
measure rates of SD responding because all items in the *SD*
Scale are keyed for socially desirable responses. When an
MMPI trait scale also has all of its items keyed for socially
desirable responses, it is assumed that trait scores on the scale
also reflect individual differences in rates of SD responding.
Trait scores on such scales should be positively correlated with
scores on the *SD* Scale. These scales should also have loadings
with the same sign on the first MMPI factor as the sign of
the loading of the *SD* Scale.

When all items in an MMPI scale are keyed for socially
undesirable responses, high trait scores should be associated
with low rates of SD responding and low scores with high
rates of SD responding. Thus, trait scales consistently keyed
for socially undesirable responses should have negative correlations with the *SD* Scale as well as loadings on the MMPI
first factor that are opposite in sign to those scales consistently
keyed for socially desirable responses. As I have shown, the
obtained correlations between the first factor loadings of

MMPI scales and the proportion of items in the scales keyed for socially desirable responses is consistent with this prediction.

VIII

Reasons have been given why scales containing a balance in their social desirability keying should have lower average inter-item correlations than scales in which the items are more consistently keyed for either socially desirable or socially undesirable responses, provided the tendency to give socially desirable responses is operating. Subjects who have strong tendencies to give socially desirable responses should tend to give the trait response to those items for which the trait response is also a socially desirable response. But these same subjects should tend to give the nontrait response for items for which the trait response is a socially undesirable response. Thus the correlation between the trait responses to the two items, one a socially desirable response and the other a socially undesirable response, should be lower than it would be if both items were keyed for either socially desirable or socially undesirable responses.

To test this hypothesis we (Edwards, Walsh, and Diers, 1963) used the Kuder-Richardson Formula 21 (K-R 21) values of 61 personality scales as an index of the average intercorrelation of the items in the scales. For each we also obtained an index of the degree of imbalance in the social desirability keying of the items. Scales in which the proportion of items keyed for socially desirable responses is .50 have the maximum degree of balance in their social desirability keying, because in this instance they have the same number of items keyed for socially desirable and socially undesirable responses. These scales should, therefore, have relatively low K-R 21 values. On the other hand, scales with all of the items keyed for socially desirable responses or for socially undesirable responses have a maximum degree of imbalance in their social desirability keying; these scales should tend to have higher K-R 21 values than scales balanced in their social desirability keying.

When we correlated the index of imbalance in the social desirability keying with the K-R 21 values of the scales, we obtained a correlation coefficient of .62. The fact that this correlation is positive and of some magnitude is consistent with the prediction that scales containing an extreme imbalance in their social desirability keying should have a higher degree of internal consistency, as measured by the K-R 21 values, than scales more balanced in their social desirability keying.

IX

In this chapter I have reviewed some of the evidence concerning the social desirability variable, which has shown that:

1. The SDSVs of personality statements are highly reliable and highly correlated, even when based upon the judgments of quite diverse groups.

2. Individual ratings of social desirability of personality statements are positively correlated with each other and with the normative SDSVs of the statements.

3. The probability of a *true* response to personality statements is linearly related to the SDSVs of the statements. Statements with extreme socially desirable scale values have high probabilities of eliciting *true* responses, and statements with extreme socially undesirable scale values have low probabilities of eliciting *true* responses.

4. Because the relationship between P(T) and SDSV is linear, the relationship between the probability of a socially desirable response and SDSV is V-shaped. Items at both extremes of the social desirability continuum have high probabilities of eliciting socially desirable responses, and items with neutral SDSVs have relatively low probabilities of eliciting socially desirable responses.

5. In two large-scale studies, the SDSVs of personality statements were found to have a bimodal distribution. The distribution of SDSVs in the MMPI is also bimodal.

6. An estimate of the mean rate of SD responding based upon the *SD* Scale predicts quite accurately the mean score on a variety of MMPI trait scales.

7. Individual differences in the rate of SD responding, as measured by the *SD* Scale, are correlated with trait scores on various personality scales. The proportion of items keyed for socially desirable responses in the trait scales predicts quite accurately the correlation of the scale with the *SD* Scale.

8. As the proportion of neutral items in a scale increases, the absolute magnitude of the correlation of the scale with the *SD* Scale decreases. In other words, the larger the proportion of neutral items in a scale, the lower the absolute value of the correlation of the scale with the *SD* Scale.

9. The first factor loadings of MMPI scales are highly correlated with the correlations of the scales with the *SD* Scale and also with the proportion of items keyed for socially desirable responses in the scales.

10. The internal consistency of MMPI scales, as measured by the K-R 21 values of the scales, is related to the degree of imbalance in the social desirability keying of the items in the scales. Scales consistently keyed for either socially desirable or for socially undesirable responses tend to have higher K-R 21 values than scales better balanced in their social desirability keying. Scales with a high degree of internal consistency are also scales that tend to have the highest, either positive or negative, correlations with the *SD* Scale.

X

The various hypotheses I have presented and the evidence relevant to these hypotheses refer to a general trait I have defined as the tendency to give socially desirable responses in self-description. I hope that you will not identify this trait with another trait, which might be defined as the tendency to falsify responses in self-description. Whether a subject's answer to a personality item is dishonest or inaccurate can be determined only by means of some criterion by which the truthfulness of the response may be evaluated. Thus, if a subject answers *true* to the statement; "My grades are better than those of the average student," it should be possible to obtain his actual grades and, by comparing them with a distribution of grades, to judge whether he has answered the item truthfully. But to obtain an adequate criterion by which to judge the truthfulness of a subject's response to many other personality items is more difficult, if not impossible. By what criterion, for example, should we judge the truthfulness of a subject's response to the item: "I dream frequently about things that are better kept to myself"?

On the other hand, it is a simple matter to determine whether a subject has given a socially desirable or socially undesirable response to a personality item—the criterion provided by the SDSV of the item. It will be recalled that a socially desirable response is defined as a *true* response to an item with a socially desirable scale value or as a *false* response to an item with a socially undesirable scale value. Nothing in this definition implies that socially desirable responses are untruthful and that socially undesirable responses are truthful or vice versa.

Acquiescence Response Styles: Problems of Identification and Control[1]

Acquiescence is the variety of dimensions of individual differences in psychological assessment that cause individuals to endorse relatively many or few characteristics as self-descriptive. As such, it may be peculiar to a certain type of test or general over diverse classes of content. It may be a highly specific idiosyncracy, fleeting and illusory, or a pervasive personality disposition, broadly relevant to cognitive and social processes. I shall not appraise in detail the extensive and burgeoning literature on these and other points (but see Chapter 5, by Samuel Messick) but rather review some conceptual and methodological problems in the identification and control of acquiescence. I shall first consider a number of interpretations of acquiescence and then appraise alternative methods for controlling acquiescence variance.

1. This work was supported by NIMH Research Grant MH-08969 and the University of Western Ontario.

INTERPRETATIONS OF ACQUIESCENCE

VARIETIES OF ACQUIESCENCE

While the effects of a true-false format upon response consistency were recognized by early workers (Fritz, 1927; Lentz, 1938), the term *acquiescence* was originally used by Cronbach (1946) to denote a tendency to agree more than to disagree. Cronbach's act of labeling the tendency to agree or respond *true* to diverse content with a single term, particularly one suggesting a certain psychological characteristic, suggested to many that a single process might be expected to account for variance in a wide variety of situations. Similarly, Cronbach's choice of acquiescence has subsequently led many (for example, McGee, 1962b, 1962c and Stricker, 1963) to expect this single process to be a manifestation of a more general acquiescence or conformity construct. Actually, Cronbach's original intent, as we read it, was to employ acquiescence as a neutral descriptive term invoked to account for response variance in tendencies to agree to questionnaire or ability items, although he (Cronbach, 1950) subsequently did raise the possibility of valid variance being present in such consistent tendencies to agree or to disagree. Since evidence is now accumulating for different "species" of acquiescence rather than a simple unitary process, I will use the term here as a neutral description of a type of response consistency, allowing for the possibility of "set" (Cronbach, 1946) and "style" (Jackson and Messick, 1958, 1962b) interpretations and for varieties of acquiescence as elicited by and interacting with different types of item content and respondents.

The identification of acquiescence in a particular assessment device might take a variety of forms. For example, if a subject agreed with a set of statements and also with their opposites, we might legitimately infer acquiescence. Or, if the correlation between original statements and reversals was less than unity, or less than the correlation indicated from their respective reliabilities, the existnece of acquiescence might be inferred. Or if a random sample of items were drawn from a heterogeneous pool, and substantial response consistency was observed that could not be traced to content or other stylistic response determinants, then acquiescence might be implicated.

While acquiescence implies to many a tendency to agree rather than to disagree, its use as a description of individual differences in agreement tendencies would require only that individuals retain their relative position on an agreement-disagreement continuum. Thus, subjects in a given population might range, on a 9-point scale, from a mean score of 5 (neutral) to 9 (extremely disagree). Still, if they maintained a consistent position on this scale over heterogeneous content, the presence of acquiescence variance might be inferred. This definition of acquiescence has not always been clearly recognized (see Rorer, 1965). Some (Christie, Havel, and Seidenberg, 1958) have maintained that acquiescence was not present when average scores were in the neutral or slightly disagree category. While somewhat different and, to some extent, uncorrelated processes may be involved for consistent agreement and disagreement with an item and its opposite (Peabody, 1961; Martin, 1964), the general convention has been to consider acquiescence as a continuous dimension varying from a positive to a negative pole.

While questionnaires cast in a true-false or agree-disagree format have shown a remarkably consistent tendency to elicit acquiescence, as have difficult information tests and even contentless scales, the presence of acquiescence in these diverse situations is not necessarily an indication that the same people contribute to acquiescence in each situation (Husek, 1961; McGee, 1962b, 1962c, 1962d; Stricker, 1963). As we have already implied, it is perhaps a fault of our language and thought processes that in labeling empirical observations, we tend to impute the same processes and causal preconditions to other observations similarly identified. This has caused some confusion in the case of acquiescence. We have learned that different classes of content tend to elicit different species of acquiescence. The two species most firmly established are those elicited by aphorisms and attitude statements cast in the style of the California F scale, on the one hand, and the tendency to endorse many symptoms or characteristics in standard personality items, on the other. A number of factor analytic studies (see reviews of Damarin and Messick, 1965 and Martin, 1964) have revealed that attitude or "rational" acquiescence to F Scale-type items and endorsement of many personality items define more or less orthogonal dimensions. Furthermore, these species of acquiescence seem to be independent of acquiescence to both difficult achievement items and contentless scales. A valid distinction can even be made between the tendency to endorse many or few personality traits as self-descriptive and the tendency to respond *true* or *false* to personality items (Jackson and Messick, 1965). It would seem that content, at least within broad classes, has an important effect upon the kind and amount of acquiescence elicited. Thus, a difficult word-meaning test, or one of advanced mathematics, might elicit acquiescence in some, but not in those who possessed these abilities. An attitude scale concerned with astrology or whether familiarity breeds contempt might be of central concern to some people but of only peripheral concern to a majority, and hence elicit acquiescence. But a scale of attitudes toward Negroes, having higher salience for most people, is answered generally in terms of content, whatever the form of the statement (Prentice, 1956). Items having evaluative significance for an individual—such as, "I have black tarry looking bowel movements" or "I am afraid 1 am losing my mind"—show only small amounts of acquiescence, while items of indifferent evaluative significance often contain much acquiescence variance. In general, acquiescence will increase as a direct function of item ambiguity (Cronbach, 1950), referent ambiguity (Banta, 1961), and lack of personal relevance (Elliott, 1961), or neutral desirability levels (Jackson and Messick, 1961, 1962a, 1962b; Edwards and Diers, 1963; Stricker, 1963). Indeed, there is some evidence that these various conditions not only operate singly, but interact with each other and with aptitude in influencing acquiescent responses.

By implication, I have touched on a number of processes that might account for acquiescence to personality items. These processes would have differential relevance to different persons in the sense that an individual to whom one process was relevant would manifest one type of acquiescence, but not necessarily others. Such processes include unfamiliarity with and difficulty in understanding the language used in attitude statements, lack of knowledge where a correct answer is required, low experienced saliency for certain types of verbally elicited attitudes, and little experienced personal evaluative significance for a personality item. There is no reason to suppose that these processes need occur simultaneously, nor be intercorrelated highly, nor be all present in the same individual, nor all reflect the same personality characteristics, nor correlate with the same criteria. Indeed, it would be surprising if they did. It would be well to consider these processes and the alternative interpretations and implications of acquiescence in some detail.

ACQUIESCENCE AND CONTENT

First let us consider a fundamental distinction between responses to specific content, and responses to formal attributes of an item (Jackson and Messick, 1958, 1962b; Wiggins, 1962). A person may agree with the statement, "I believe newborn babies look very much like monkeys," either because he is very low on a nurturance dimension or because he has a general tendency to endorse a broad class of statements. More precisely, his response can be thought of as being determined by some weighted combination of these and other response determinants.

Figure 1 shows a hypothetical response distribution representing one possible combination of acquiescence and content in which each is weighted equally. Here, a respondent falling

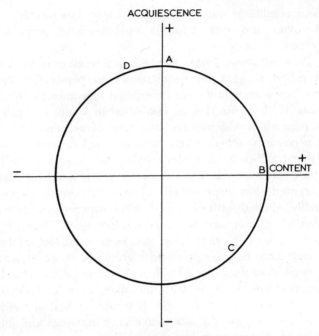

FIG. 1. Hypothetical response distribution in which acquiescence and content are weighted equally.

above the horizontal axis might be considered basically in agreement with the content of the statement, while one falling below the axis would be in basic disagreement with the statement. This does not necessarily mean that he will agree with the *item*. His agreement or disagreement to the item may also be influenced by his location on the acquiescence axis. Subject A, high on acquiescence and indifferent to content, would agree because of his general tendency to agree when the content is unimportant to him. If we took his response seriously in terms of content, we might attribute to him an attitude that he did not in fact hold. Subject B, on the other hand, would agree because he is high on the dimension represented by the statement. Since he is not strongly represented on the acquiescence dimension, his response is interpreted in terms of content.

What of C's response? It is in doubt, because tendencies to agree with the content are counterbalanced by general tendencies to disagree. If these opposing tendencies were equally weighted, as for subject C, we might expect such an item to show low test-retest stability, with the subject responding sometimes in terms of content and sometimes in terms of acquiescence. Subject D is substantially represented on the positive pole of acquiescence, but his position on the content axis would indicate that he was moderately opposed. In this case, his rather extreme acquiescence tendencies lead to a response indicating agreement with the content, but such a response would misrepresent his true position on the content dimension. Thus, the presence of acquiescence in a putative content scale will have varying effects upon different respondents. For some, it will be virtually the sole determinant of the response. For others, it will have little or no effect. For still

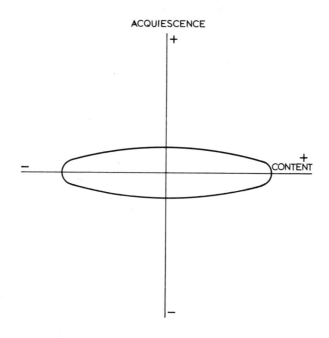

Fig. 2. Response distribution primarily determined by content.

others, the effect will be to increase unreliability or, more serious, to introduce a source of systematic error.

Other response distributions are possible. Consider, for example, this item: "Someone is trying to poison me." Although this represents a belief, in Rokeach's (1960) terms, it is a central belief, one that implies a state of affairs having some rather serious implications for a respondent. In short, such a statement is not likely to be misunderstood by the majority of respondents. Barring illiteracy or gross inattention or carelessness, subjects will respond to such a statement in terms of its content. Only minimal tendencies to acquiesce would be elicited by the item. Such a response distribution would be indicated by Figure 2. It will be seen that content represents the lion's share of the variance.

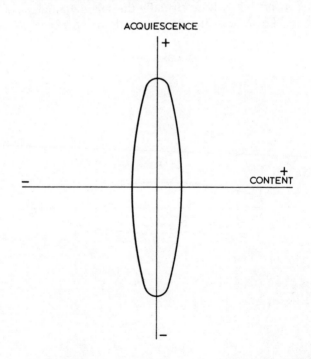

Fig. 3. Response distribution primarily determined by acquiescence.

But many questions in which the assessment specialist is interested are not so unequivocal or personally relevant. What happens when content is not salient or important to the respondent? In such a case we would have a response distribution as in Figure 3. Here acquiescence is the primary source of variance. An item having little meaning, evaluative significance, or personal relevance—such as one seeking an attitude toward a nonexistent novel—might elicit this response distribution. While items with such response distributions can be virtually eliminated with careful item writing, they are by no means rare in the attitude and personality literature. Such items, needless to say, contribute little or nothing to logical trait validity and will usually greatly complicate interpretation of total scores.

It is entirely possible that acquiescence and particular traits will be correlated to some degree. A correlation between acquiescence and low verbal ability has been observed in a number of studies (for example, Elliott, 1961; Frederiksen and Messick, 1959; Jackson and Pacine, 1961; Martin, 1964). Personality traits like impulsivity have been reported (Couch and Kenniston, 1960) to be related to acquiescence to standard personality items. This sort of situation creates real problems to the test constructor who wishes to unconfound acquiescence and trait variance. In this case, while it would be easy to find *agree* items to represent the positive pole of the content dimension, it would be very difficult to identify *disagree* items to represent the trait positively or *agree* items to represent the negative pole of the trait. Fortunately such instances are rare, but where they exist, it might be necessary to abandon the agree-disagree format altogether. A host of further possible examples might be encountered in practice, such as the case in which agreement and disagreement tendencies represent different processes or are differentially related to other traits, but the examples given should be sufficient to illustrate some of the many ways acquiescence might influence the interpretation of an individual's scores.

It is clear from the foregoing examples that if one's intent is to assess content, acquiescence is a source of confounding

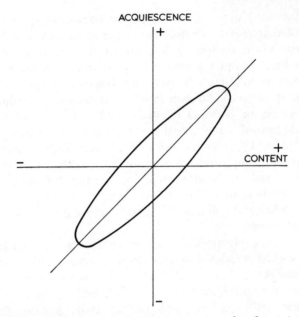

FIG. 4. Response distribution showing correlated acquiescence and content variance.

error, a source of variance that complicates the interpretation of a response to an item. The situation becomes more difficult when items are added together to yield a total score. If the content is heterogeneous and uncorrelated, the acquiescence component cumulates, while the content does not. Even though content usually outweighs a smaller acquiescence component at the item level, the situation may well be reversed at the level of the total score. While acquiescence may contribute to reliability, this is an entirely illusory and spurious property if one's goal is accurate content measurement. The danger is that spurious reliability traceable to acquiescence effects will lead the unwary investigator to conclude that he is measuring content. The literature is replete with studies in which conclusions are drawn about experimental results or correlations among tests in cavalier disregard for the very plausible hypothesis that acquiescence, rather than content, may be the primary factor.

RESPONSE SET, RESPONSE STYLE, AND CONTENT

It would be well at this point to differentiate content from response style and set. These are important distinctions conceptually as well as empirically. Polemics (see Rorer, 1965) concerning the existence of stylistic variance on personality assessment devices may hinge in part on the definition of response style used.

We (Jackson and Messick, 1962b) defined and differentiated at some length the nature of variance associated with *content* and that associated with *response style* or *set*. We pointed particularly to the interpretive complexities of response variance, which is a function of multiple determinants, as well as that arising from possible interactions between different response styles, and between the latter and content.

Variance associated with *content* was considered to refer to

> response consistencies in certain defined assessment situations which reflect a particular set of broader behavioral tendencies, relatively enduring over time, having as their basis some unitary personality trait, need state, attitudinal or belief disposition, or psychopathological syndrome . . . (p. 132)

Variance associated with *response style* was considered to have reference to

> expressive consistencies in the behavior of respondents which are relatively enduring over time, with some degree of generality beyond a particular test performance to responses both in other tests and in non-test behavior, and usually reflected in assessment situations by consistencies in response to item characteristics other than specific content. These characteristics may include the following:
> (a) Some aspect of the form or tone of item structure, such as difficulty level (Gage, Leavitt, and Stone, 1957),

positive or negative phrasing (cf. Bass, 1955; Jackson and
Messick, 1957; Chapman and Bock, 1958; Elliott, 1961),
style of wording (Jackson and Messick, 1958; Hanley, 1959;
Bass, 1959), ambiguity of specificity of meaning (Bass, 1955;
Nunnally and Husek, 1958; Stricker, 1962), and extreme
generality vs. cautious qualification (Clayton and Jackson,
1961); and

(b) Some general aspect of the connotations of the items,
such as desirability (Edwards, 1957a), deviance (Berg, 1955;
Sechrest and Jackson, 1961), controversiality (Fricke, 1956;
Hanley, 1957), communality (Wiggins, 1962a; 1962b), sub-
tlety (Edwards, 1957a; Hanley, 1957), or some perceived
difference between community and desirability, as revealed
in the MMPI Lie scale or in scales derived empirically to
detect malingering (Cofer, Chance, and Judson, 1949) or
defensiveness (Hanley, 1957). [Jackson and Messick, 1962b,
pp. 134–35. References are to articles cited in the original.]

Response sets in our terms (Jackson and Messick, 1962b,
p. 135), refer to "consistencies in response to formal item
properties that are restricted in time to a single test session
and recurrent consistencies observed only on a specific test
form."

Rorer (1965) in his review of the response style literature apparently overlooked this article and the definitions
contained therein. He proceeded to establish new definitions
of set and style in a manner that is inconsistent, arbitrary, and
misleading. Rorer proposes that the term "set" connotes a
tendency to produce a certain picture or impression of himself, or in short that "he is motivated," and distinguishes this
from "style," which "refers to a tendency to select some
response category a disproportionate amount of the time independent of the item content" (1965, pp. 133–34). Under the
terms of these definitions, Rorer would distinguish acquiescence as style, but a tendency to respond desirably would
represent a set.

Rorer states that his unique definition of set as the tendency to produce a certain picture or impression follows from
and is "consistent with usage in other areas." Rorer does not
cite what areas he has reference to, but the term "set," as

it is used in experimental psychology, has been sharply criticized (Gibson, 1941) because it admits of many different definitions and hence lacks denotative specificity. Furthermore, as Messick (1965) has pointed out, while it may be saying little to imply simply that a respondent is motivated, it is saying a great deal, probably too much, to imply that he is motivated to produce a certain picture of himself. It is dangerous to define constructs in terms of one's speculation about underlying processes. A tendency to respond desirably may be more than sheer impression management; it may represent an autistic bias in self regard (Damarin and Messick, 1965) whose motivational determinants, while perhaps recoverable in principle from developmental studies, are obscure. Furthermore, to imply that acquiescence, defined as style by Rorer, does not involve motivation to create a particular impression may be misleading. One might wish to avoid prejudging the extent to which subjects were motivated to appear "agreeable to things authoritative" (Leavitt, Hax, and Roche, 1955) or critical or negativistic or cautious under various experimental conditions, but Rorer's definition of style arbitrarily precludes these possibilities.

Rorer's definition of set emphasizes motivated strategies of creating a particular impression on an assessment device, such as the tendency to respond desirably, to fake, or to dissimulate. But what of other consistent response tendencies to connotative attributes of items, which do not necessarily fall within the domain of impression management? A number of such tendencies have been identified, particularly related to frequency of endorsement—for example, communality (Wiggins, 1962), hypercommunality (Wiggins, 1962; Martin, 1964), perceived frequency (Jackson and Singer, 1965), or deviation (Barnes, 1956; Berg, 1955)—or to general connotative attributes of item content, like perceived harmfulness (Jackson and Singer, 1965). It is not clear from Rorer's definitions of set and style what, if any, relevance they would have to such response tendencies, or whether, alternatively, a new category would have to be established to include these forms of response consistency. Rorer's definition of style as a tendency to select some response category a disproportionate amount of the time is also subject to ambiguity in interpretation. Two sets of items might both relate to the same specific content dimension, but one might be phrased in desirable terms and the other in undesirable terms. One subject, high in tendencies to describe himself in desirable terms, would answer the first set *true* and the second *false;* a second subject, low in desirability, would respond in the opposite manner. According to Rorer, subjects who respond in terms of item desirability are displaying "response set," but the subjects described in the example also meet his criterion for "response style" in that these subjects chose some response category disproportionately independent of specific content.

In summary, my preference is for retaining our earlier definitions of content and of set and style. I see little merit, and much potential confusion, if Rorer's definitions are used without careful consideration of their implications.

ACQUIESCENCE AS STYLE

Let us now consider the possibility of capitalizing on acquiescence variance to reflect individual style or personality. I have already noted that there is more than one species of acquiescence; hence, if one is interested in measuring acquiescence as style, it would be necessary to specify the context in which the measurement would take place. First I shall take this up in the context of the California F Scale, and then consider the problem more generally.

Several authors have defended the all-positive form of the California F Scale on the grounds that this was hypothesized to reflect one aspect of the authoritarian syndrome, namely authoritarian submission. According to Christie, Havel, and Seidenberg (1958), this was the position implicitly taken by the authors of *The Authoritarian Personality* (Adorno, Frenkel-Brunswik, Levinson, and Sanford, 1950). At first glance, this is appealing. Why not collapse content and style into a single total score, especially if one can show that both relate to a criterion (Gage, Leavitt, and Stone, 1957)? There are several good reasons to avoid this trap: (1) One cannot make clear ideological inferences about respondents if it can be demonstrated that they respond inconsistently to original and reversed items. (2) To the extent that content and style are imperfectly correlated, it is illogical to add them to obtain a total score. (3) The introduction of stylistic variance may also introduce correlated tendencies reflecting low verbal intelligence, low occupational and educational status, and the like. Thus, the F Scale, by virtue of its acquiescence component which correlates with measures of intellect and status, shares variance with other measures correlated with intelligence and socioeconomic status. These many relationships, often interpreted as substantive correlations between authoritarianism and personality variables, may well be a function of correlates of acquiescence, such as intelligence, rather than of content. It would be far better to separate content and style, measuring each independently, and avoid the logical confusion between ideology and mode of response.

What can we say about the more general question of the use of acquiescence measures as reflections of personality traits or style? This is an hypothesis that we (Jackson and Messick, 1958) have favored in the past, and one that has received some considerable attention in recent years. I believe that this should be an area of continuing research interest, not only for quite general measures of acquiescence but for more specific species as well. For example, one may distinguish between acquiescence to unqualified, sweeping generalizations from acquiescence to cautious, qualified statements (Clayton and Jackson, 1961; Jackson and Messick, 1958; Messick and Jackson, 1958). One may distinguish acquiescence to different types of item phrasings, to saliency, and to connotative attributes to item content, such as perceived frequency of endorsement (Jackson and Singer, 1965). Or one may separate a tendency to endorse many symptoms or characteristics as self-descriptive whether stated positively or negatively—as in responding *false* to a statement in the form: "I am not. . . ." (Jackson and Messick, 1965)—from a tendency

to respond consistently *true* or *false*. Whether the foregoing
are identified primarily in terms of acquiescence or as separate stylistic attributes is not so important as their potential
for isolating sources of response consistency independent of
specific item content.

While these and other stylistic variables may well generate interesting research hypotheses and serve as a foundation for mapping a response domain, at the present time I
do not advocate the use of measures of acquiescence as the
primary method of choice for uncovering specific personality
traits. This is not an efficient procedure. If one desires to
measure personality traits, the most reasonable approach is
to develop good direct content scales, uncontaminated with
response biases.

It is true that acquiescence may contribute to convergent
validity, as in differentiating normal subjects from schizophrenics. This variance may be employed where appropriate
for univariate prediction. But this situation is more complicated in the case of multiple classification or discriminant
validation. Here, acquiescence causes predictor variables to
be more highly correlated than they should be. Even if acquiescence style is valid, its contribution must be limited by the
fact that there are generally only two categories of response.
Hence, it would be difficult to place individuals in many more
than two categories on the basis of a simple acquiescence
dimension. This might be improved upon slightly by considering moderated relationships with other response styles or
content dimensions. For example, one might identify those
acquiescing to desirable as opposed to undesirable content.
But there is an upper limit on the discriminations that may be
made on information so derived. It is extremely doubtful that
the upper limit of this information nearly approaches the
number of meaningful dimensions of psychopathology or of
independently measurable personality traits.

Since it is very difficult to obtain reliable differences
between highly correlated predictors, particularly when the
correlation is due to response bias, the obvious solution is
to remove the source—correlated error and redundancy in

the various scales. Whatever contribution acquiescence in various scales may make to differential prediction can better be appraised independently of the confounding content. The resulting corrected scales may then make a more unique contribution to the differential prediction problem. For this reason, a major section of this chapter will evaluate methods for controlling acquiescence variance.

ACQUIESCENCE AND EVALUATIVE BIAS

I have already observed that items having little evaluative significance to a respondent may be responded to indifferently, that is, with acquiescent response style. In a series of factor analyses, Messick and I have documented a reciprocal moderating relationship between acquiescence and desirability on the MMPI. Scales with moderate levels of average-judged item desirability loaded highly on an acquiescence factor, while those at either extreme showed relatively lower loadings. More precisely, optimum placement of axes would indicate an oblique relationship. Acquiescence is slightly more strongly elicited by relatively undesirable rather than desirable items. Another way of stating this is to note that people who show positive acquiescence more frequently tend to admit more unfavorable traits and symptoms. This result is also supported by similar findings with the California Personality Inventory (Jackson, 1960).

A number of processes might account for this. For example, this might be due to a genuine acquiescence and trait correlation, as in the reported tendency of psychotics to answer more frequently in the positive direction and also to endorse more unfavorable symptoms. On the other hand, the relation might be more strictly stylistic in nature. Subjects who acquiesce might be admitting traits relatively more uncritically and, due to the preponderance of undesirable items on tests like the MMPI, might be endorsing more undesirable items. There may indeed be come tendency for acquiescence to be related substantively to a differential tendency to claim psychotic symptoms (Jackson and Messick, 1962a; Messick and Jackson, 1961a) or, stated conversely, for persons high in psychotic tendencies to prefer an agree to disagree response, as Berg and his colleagues have maintained. Such inferences are properly evaluated on item pools other than the MMPI, where psychotic (and undesirable) content is represented predominantly in the true direction.

ACQUIESCENCE AS TRAIT ENDORSEMENT
VERSUS ACQUIESCENCE AS TRUE RESPONDING

We have identified acquiescence in its general form as a tendency to endorse many characteristics as self-descriptive. Ordinarily, a *true* or *agree* response on a personality or attitude questionnaire denotes the affirmation of the trait or attitude. Hence, the tendency to endorse traits is equated with the tendency to respond true. Acquiescence has been used as a descriptive term to apply to this process, without regard to the possibility that separate processes might be operating in the tendency to endorse traits as self-descriptive versus the tendency to respond true.

Recently, Messick and I (Jackson and Messick, 1965) have hypothesized two separate processes to account for response consistency observed in factor analyses of the MMPI. In a re-analysis of intercorrelations among original and reversed MMPI scales administered to samples of males and females by Rorer (Rorer, 1963; Rorer and Goldberg, 1965a, 1965b), there was evidence to indicate the presence of each of these distinct species of acquiescence. Rorer and Goldberg report moderately high correlations between *true-* and *false*-keyed original and reversed MMPI items, as did Lichtenstein and Bryan (1965). That is, agreements to original items were correlated positively with disagreements to reversals of the same items.

When four samples of males and females administered original and reversed MMPI scales by Rorer (1963) were separately factor analyzed (Jackson and Messick, 1965), all four yielded a large factor completely separating *true-* from *false*-keyed scales. This finding would be consistent with earlier results highlighting the importance of acquiescence on the MMPI. However, when positive and negative forms of the MMPI were included in the same correlation matrix, reversed scales were represented on this large dimension with loadings very similar to the original scales. Thus, a *true*-keyed original scale loaded in the same direction as a scale comprised of reversals of the same items. What response consistency there was over original and reversed forms was traceable to the two large stylistic dimensions and not to specific factors representing content consistency in individual scales. With such consistency over *true*- and *false*-keyed scales, it might at first glance appear that acquiescence was not operating in the MMPI. People appear to respond consistently to originals and reversals, although not, as we have noted, to specific content in individual scales but to some broad factor that implicates all MMPI scales, and separates original *true*- and *false*-keyed scales completely.

The solution to what might appear to be inconsistent evidence for acquiescence is contained in our hypothesis (Jackson and Messick, 1965) that acquiescence is represented on the MMPI in two forms, the larger of which is the tendency to endorse many symptoms or traits as self-characteristic. The evidence from our factor analysis indicates that this tendency can be elicited by negative items as well as positive items. Thus, the subject who responds *true* to statements such as, "I am bothered by a lot of belching gas from my stomach," will later answer *false* to the statement, "I am not [or "it is not true that I am] bothered by a lot of belching gas from my stomach." Many of the Rorer reversed items were of this simple negative variety, rather than restatements of opposite content in more positive form. It is entirely possible for an individual to maintain a consistent tendency to endorse characteristics (whether desirable or undesirable) just so long as he is careful to pair *false* responses with negatively phrased statements. There is little reason to suppose that Rorer's literate college student subjects were not, in general, able to be sensitive to such differences.

The factor analysis of original and reversed MMPI items

also revealed a smaller additional factor, namely, the tendency to respond *true* or *false* regardless of content. Thus, *true*-keyed original items were opposed to the same items reversed in direction and keyed *false*. A consistent response to content would reqire that such scales load the factor in the same rather than the opposite direction. It is probable that this factor merged with and became indistinguishable from the larger acquiescence factor in earlier studies of the MMPI but was accentuated and separated by the type of negative reversal used.

Thus, the relative weighting of each of these two acquiescence processes will depend upon the type of item written as well as upon characteristics of the subject population. An all-positive, unidirectional item form would confound the two, while an avoidance of simple negative reversals in favor of more judicious positively stated reversals might tend to suppress the larger of the two. Anyone planning further experimental attempts to identify the respective roles of content and stylistic variance on personality inventories would be well advised to take these distinct acquiescence processes into account.

ACQUIESCENCE AND RANDOM RESPONDING

Interpretations of acquiescence usually assume that respondents read the items, although perhaps with differential success and differential thresholds for ambiguity. This interpretation is consistent with the empirical findings of lower verbal ability and presumably lower ability to process verbal abstractions on the part of acquiescers. But I should like to go one step further and identify a more extreme form of acquiescent style characterized by a failure to incorporate the subject within the desired experimental set.

My hypothesis is simply that some individuals who appear to be yielding acquiescent results—that is, those characterized by a high or low proportion of endorsements—will do so as a function of nonpurposeful random responding (Sechrest and Jackson, 1963). Even in the most carefully supervised testing sessions there will be a small percentage of individuals who respond nonpurposefully, and I have (1965) developed a scale for identifying such nonpurposeful respondents. It was found that a set of items for which the *true* or *false* alternative was highly implausible showed a surprising degree of internal consistency. This was true even though data were carefully collected and only a relatively few individuals could be classified as random responders.

Thus, under conditions where subjects are motivated to leave a testing situation, or where they are not motivated to invest the psychic energy required to read and interpret questionnaire items (Jackson, 1959), or where they wish to rebel against a testing procedure, they may engage in an act of passive noncompliance (Schafer, 1954) by responding randomly. Such random responding is rarely truly random; it more likely incorporates certain characteristic biases for responding *true* or *false*. Such patterns of responses will appear statistically similar to other species of acquiescence, although the hypothesized underlying process is different.

To take a rather extreme but not wholly unrealistic example, I have recently had occasion to review sets of personality item responses obtained under carefully supervised conditions from hospitalized psychiatric patients. A certain number of these patients, roughly 3 per cent, responded all *true* or, less frequently, all *false*, some from the very first item and some at a later point in the scale. Some of these responses were to highly implausible alternatives. Had these subjects not been eliminated from the analysis, lower scale homogeneity would have resulted for balanced content scales. Thus, considerable systematic error or possibly stylistic variance associated with random responding (Sechrest and Jackson, 1963) may emerge in the guise of acquiescence.

CONTROLLING ACQUIESCENCE BIAS

In developing sound personality and attitude measurement procedures, the problem of controlling acquiescence bias should be one step in a program designed to develop personality or attitude scales of high construct validity. As Loevinger (1957) has argued in her excellent monograph, psychological tests, if they are to faithfully represent theory, must be developed at every stage with due regard for the validational process. Therefore, attempts to control for acquiescence after a scale has been developed will be less successful than a program of test development that incorporates from the beginning a means to suppress acquiescence. But scale development that concentrates upon controlling response set variance to the exclusion of other important principles of test development, like substantive definition of variables or concern for scale homogeneity or validity, may result in scales that not only do not measure acquiescence but measure very little else. Furthermore, we have already implied that items with a high saturation of content should be less susceptible to the intrusion of acquiescence bias. Thus, one very effective means of reducing the massive effects of response set in personality assessment is the adherence to a carefully planned program of test construction of the type recommended by Loevinger. Therefore, it is important to emphasize that the particular methods outlined below for controlling acquiescence should be applied in addition to, rather than in place of, other important principles of scale development.

BALANCED SCALES

Apart from ignoring the problem of acquiescence in the forlorn hope that it may disappear of its own accord, perhaps the most frequent and intuitively appealing suggestion made for controlling its effects is to employ balanced scales. The argument runs as follows: If scales are developed with half of the items keyed *true* and half keyed *false* (or half *agree* and half *disagree*), the massive cumulative effects of acquiescence in unidirectionally keyed scales may be avoided. A general tendency to agree, for example, could not serve as a primary determinant of variance on total scores. This is thought to be so because such a tendency would balance tendencies to agree by keying half of the items *true* and half *false*. Hence, correlations with external variables can be interpreted unequivocally in terms of content or trait variance, because balancing is believed to unconfound the linear relationship between acquiescence and content.

As a first approximation to controlling acquiescence, this approach has substantial advantages over unidirectional or grossly unbalanced scales. First, it reduces spurious correlations between acquiescence and content. Second, it allows one to obtain some estimate of acquiescence either through the use of set and content formulas or by simply tallying agreements. Third, by reducing correlated method variance from a number of scales, balancing *true* and *false* keying permits a somewhat more accurate appraisal of the structure of relationships among questionnaire measures of personality traits. Similarly, since acquiescence to attitude items has been demonstrated to relate to such important variables as verbal intelligence, educational level, occupational level, and the like, balanced scales may contribute to reducing the influence of such third variables in appraising correlations with theoretically or socially important behavioral indexes.

Fourth, and perhaps most important, balanced scales have an advantage quite apart from their direct consequences in reducing acquiescence bias. Balanced scales require a more careful definition of the trait to be measured and a more thorough substantive definition (Loevinger, 1957) of the items comprising the universe sampled to construct the scale. Most attitudinal and personality traits may legitimately be conceived as bipolar, representing a particular behavioral or attitudinal disposition *and* its opposite. An orderly person has a counterpart in a singularly disorderly person. Sometimes, however, scale constructors do not bother to reflect upon the nature of the individual manifesting tendencies contrary to that represented in a high positive score or the scale. Such an approach excludes from consideration half of the potential item universe and may therefore reflect an incomplete definition of the trait or construct. For example, while positive need-autonomy items can be generated easily, their opposites would require a separation of autonomy from contrasted traits of deference, affiliation, abasement, and recognition. Thus, use of both poles of a dimension has the effect of sharpening its definition.

Attempts at defining the opposing end of a bipolar dimension are best accomplished with positive exemplars of behavior rather than denial of the original statements. Simple negations fail to qualify as truly unique items when administered in the context of the original. For example, it is doubtful that the items, "I would like to hunt lions in Africa" and "I would not like to hunt lions in Africa," represent two distinct harmavoidance items. The appearance of two such items in one scale, while contributing spuriously to statistical homogeneity, provides a biased sampling of the potential content universe. Furthermore, as our re-analysis (Jackson and Messick, 1965) of the Rorer data demonstrates, such an item reversal technique, while controlling for the "true-false" species of acquiescence, in no way controls for the tendency to attribute many or few characteristics to oneself. There are a few instances where it is difficult to write acceptable positively stated reversals (for example, hallucinatory tendencies), but whenever possible, positively stated items are much preferred to negations of the original statements.

Despite the fact that the use of balanced, bidirectional scales represents a great advance over grossly unbalanced scales, this simple expedient does not entirely resolve the problem of suppressing or unconfounding acquiescence from content variance. Certainly Block's (1965) unsupported assertion that balanced MMPI scales cannot be influenced by acquiescence variance is unwarranted. He is clearly in error in such an assumption, especially as it applies to the MMPI. There are a number of important reasons why scales balanced for the number of *true* and *false* items might still yield scores influenced by acquiescence variance. We shall consider each of these in turn.

1. Items are not uniform in acquiescence-eliciting potential.

Items and scales may not be uniform in the extent to which they elicit acquiescence for several sound reasons. Items differ in variance; an item with an endorsement frequency of 50 per cent has maximum variance, while one with a 1 per cent frequency of endorsement has less than 1/25 as much variance. Even if acquiescence variance were a constant proportion of the total variance on these two items, in absolute terms the item with the larger variance would contain more than 25 times as much acquiescence variance and potentially would correlate many times higher with an acquiescence scale than would the item with the smaller variance. This is an elementary general property of the variance of items.

Furthermore, two items with identical endorsement frequencies may have their total variance partitioned in various ways. An item saturated with particular content variance, or with desirability variance, will have correspondingly less variance remaining that may be associated with acquiescence. Items having little relevance to content or neutral in desirability would have a greater chance of eliciting acquiescence. This observation is in accord with empirical findings. Scales with mean item scale values in the moderate range of desirability and with moderate endorsement frequency levels load highly on the acquiescence factor (Jackson and Messick, 1961, 1962a, 1962b). Similarly items that are ambiguous, complicated, difficult to understand, or not salient have been observed to be related to acquiescence.

At the scale level these problems of imbalance may be compounded and exaggerated. A scale composed of ambiguous, poorly written items will elicit much acquiescence, but if the ambiguous items are differentially represented on *true-*

and *false*-keyed halves, there may be residual acquiescence variance on the total scale. A sometimes unrecognized (Block, 1965) source of acquiescence variance exists when positively worded items represent grossly psychotic processes and negatively worded items represent some more subtle negative instance of pathology.

Several of the MMPI scales, like the Paranoid Scale, are cases in point. The *true* items are unpopular and undesirable, have small variances, and elicit little acquiescence. The *false* items are more frequently endorsed, have larger variances, are of less evaluative consequence, and hence contain more acquiescence. The "balancing" of sets of such *true*- and *false*-keyed items fails to have the desired effect. One can reasonably expect an acquiescence dimension to emerge under such circumstances, as Messick's (1965) reanalysis of Block's (1965) study has demonstrated.

There is yet another problem at the scale level. Ever since Meehl's (1945) classic exposition of the dynamics of structured personality testing, so-called rational scale construction has been the object of suspicion. Empirical keying according to the responses of criterion groups was, on the other hand, the method of choice for those who aspired to be rigorous in personality measurement. Unfortunately, this method provides maximal opportunities for the emergence of acquiescence at the scale level. Ordinarily, traits represented in a criterion group are complex in their variety, interrelations, and differential weighting. Empirical keying based on a complex criterion will result in heterogeneous congeries of items. At the individual level, these items may appear to have very good quality in terms of their clarity, personal relevance, and other properties, but when heterogeneous items are grouped to form a scale, the acquiescence component, even when small at the item level, will cumulate rapidly when the items are summed.

Because content components of empirically keyed items are so often relatively uncorrelated, they will not cumulate very much. A personality scale so constructed will accumulate a good deal of excess baggage in the form of acquiescence variance. In empirical item selection, *true* and *false* items may have different validities and may be represented differentially on scales so constructed. Examples of this abound. For example, the CPI Tolerance Scale, selected on the basis of correlations with the Levinson-Sanford Anti-Semitism Scale, itself a unidirectional scale, contains only three of 32 items keyed *true*. Perhaps this situation might be corrected by empirically selecting items from large item pools and culling items disproportionately represented in the *true* or *false* category, no doubt at some cost in validity.

A more subtle problem, and one admitting no simple solution within the context of naive empirical item selection technology, is that even if systematic attempts were made to cull items on the long side—that is, by removing excess *true* or *false* items to balance the scale in terms of the total number of *true*- and *false*-keyed items—this would still not guarantee that the *true* and *false* subscales so balanced might not have been differentially selected on the basis of relative differences in their respective acquiescence or desirability components. Such a situation would be encountered in instances where the criterion might be correlated with acquiescence, or when content is moderated by acquiescence, as for example in a case in which more valid content is represented in positively stated items. I have already pointed out that discriminant validity is enhanced by a separation of acquiescence from content scales. This observation is particularly appropriate in the present context where several empirically derived scales purportedly representing different criteria may share substantial common acquiescence variance.

2. Even if two halves of a scale are perfectly balanced for total acquiescence, the presence of acquiescence on each half of the scale tends to distort the total score.

This may be illustrated by the plot of scores on a hypothetical scale consisting of a single content dimension, and in an orthogonal acquiescence dimension. This is the situation represented in Figure 5, adapted from Martin (1964). Consider two extreme subjects. One subject, A, responds entirely

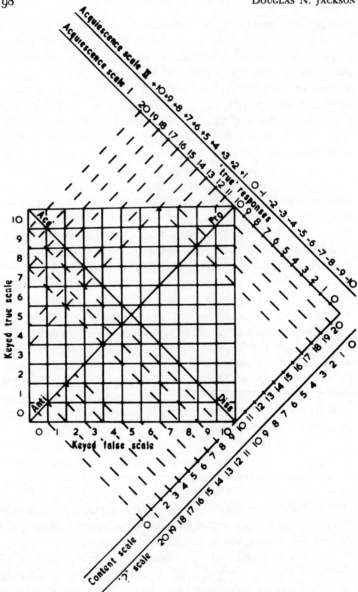

Fig. 5. Mutual constraints placed upon responses determined by acquiescence and by content. (Martin, 1964)

in terms of content. His possible score on a 20-item scale can range from 0 to 20. A second subject, B, responds entirely in terms of acquiescence. His score on this balanced score must be 10, whatever his correct placement on the underlying content dimension might be. To the extent that a subject's responses are determined by acquiescence, his range of potential scores on a balanced scale is decreased. Thus, persons high on the underlying content dimension will have their observed scale scores systematically lowered, while those low on the content dimension will receive higher scores than they should. When subjects' true content location is half the distance between zero and a maximum score, no distortion will be present if both subscales are equal in acquiescence "pull," variance, and average level of endorsement frequency. In all other instances, distortion is introduced by acquiescence.

As a further illustration of the subtle but potentially profound influence of acquiescence upon balanced scales, consider a third subject, C. Assume that he has responded to a balanced scale of sixty items containing psychopathological content. The scale, like many scales designed to assess psychopathological content, has a skewed distribution, with a mean of 10 and a standard deviation of 4. Let us assume that subject C's location on a hypothetical latent continuum of content is 6, 4 scales units and 1 standard deviation below the mean of 10. If subject C endorsed half of the items in terms of content and half in terms of acquiescent set, he would receive a score of 3, determined by content, and a score of 15, determined by set, for a total score of 18, 2 standard deviations above the mean. In this case acquiescence has shifted a subject from well within the normal range to a score far into the psychopathological area, with a shift of subject C's placement of approximately 95 percentile points.

This sort of process could easily account for misidentification of pathological processes and for significant losses in predictive power of personality scales. It is also possible that this process may account in part for empirical relationships observed between desirability and acquiescence on personality inventories, like the MMPI and the CPI, containing scales with markedly skewed distributions, pathological content, and evaluative bias. Subjects with acquiescence biases will receive scores closer to the theoretical midpoint of the scale but, relative to other subjects, in the direction of deviation and undesirability.

The above illustrations point to the obvious implausibility of a basic assumption of Block (1965), who devoted an entire monograph to an attempt to "disprove" the interpretation of the two largest factors of the MMPI (labeled Alpha and Beta by Block) in terms of stylistic response determinants. With respect to acquiescence, Block's procedure was to eliminate *true-* or *false-*keyed items from each scale until scales were balanced in terms of the number of each. He then factor analyzed the scales and showed that factor loadings for balanced scales were comparable with those from the original unbalanced scales. Block argued that since acquiescence could not operate with balanced scales, the large factor must be attributable to content. I have shown that this assumption will not ordinarily be met by scales with a good deal of psychopathological content. Messick's (1965) extended replication of Block's analyses demonstrates empirically that Block's basic assumption, and hence his argument, is incorrect. *True* and *false* subscale variances differ markedly on the MMPI, as do their average desirability (Jackson and Messick, 1962a), their reliability, and their acquiescence "pull." Furthermore, Block's evidence that the Beta factor correlated with personality traits assessed by behavior ratings can be viewed as supporting a stylistic interpretation of acquiescence (Jackson and Messick, 1958, 1962b), rather than as negative evidence for acquiescence.

3. The reciprocal moderating relationship between acquiescence and desirability complicate the problem of balancing scales for acquiescence.

In addition to the problems posed by general evaluative bias in controlling acquiescence outlined above, there is yet another problem. Even if one wanted to create scales balanced at the level of endorsement or desirability so he could better control the acquiescence eliciting potential of both halves of the balanced scale, he would find it difficult or impossible for some scales, for example a scale of delusional beliefs. Reversals of such items may sound silly, will probably not be as far in the desirable direction as the positive pole is undesirable, may have a larger variance, and hence may elicit more acquiescence. Thus, even if balanced scales were acceptable on other grounds, it would not always be possible to construct scales adequately reflecting the opposite of certain types of pathological content.

Our conclusion about the application of scales seeking to control acquiescence by employing equal numbers of *true*- and *false*-keyed items, then, is that while they do offer many substantial advantages over unidirectional or grossly unbalanced keying in suppressing acquiescence, they may not resolve all of the problems. Acquiescence imposes restraints on the variability of balanced scales and may even cause important shifts in an individual's score position. There are, furthermore, serious problems in balancing the desirability, acquiescence pull, variance, and meaningfulness of *true* and *false* sections of many pathological traits.

SEPARATE SET AND CONTENT FORMULAS

A second method for taking acquiescence variance into account is the use of various formulas, based upon a variety of rationales, for the psychometric separation of variance components or individual scores attributable to content and to set. A number of such techniques have been proposed (Helmstadter, 1957; Chapman and Bock, 1958; Messick, 1961b; Peabody, 1964; Bock, 1964; Rorer and Goldberg, 1965b). These methods provide a means whereby at least two components or scores are derivable from the same set of items, one for content and one for set. Perhaps the simplest prototype of separate content and set scores might be derived from a balanced scale with equal numbers of *true*- and *false*-keyed items. The content score would be based on the number of responses in the content-keyed direction; the acquiescent set score would simply be the number of responses of *true* to the items. Various refinements of this paradigm take into account variance of content and of set—the scaling of content—as well as attempts to maximally separate the two components. The most sophisticated model for estimating components of set and content variance is Bock's (1964) most recent model.

I shall not review the assumptions and the application of these various approaches, because I do not recommend their use in the great majority of situations for several reasons. The major objection to techniques that seek to derive set and content components from the same set of responses is that accurate estimation of components is hazardous because of the inevitable confounding of the components within a single measure. It is true that most indexes do not involve a simple linear dependence; ordinarily, set and content components need not be correlated. However, more subtle and illusive dependencies exist, such as the restrictions on variance of balanced scales caused by set described in the preceding section. The possibility of a respondent's obtaining simultaneously a maximum content *and* set score is usually not possible with scoring formulas, although it is quite conceivable that a subject's *true* scores on general acquiescence and content might both be very high or very low. By conceiving of set and content as orthogonal components, as is done in some models, one may force an independence between content and set that does not in fact exist.

In general, it is difficult to appraise the effects of the experimental dependence of set and content derived from the same set of responses. Acquiescence may interact with particular content in peculiar ways. One might question the validity of assumptions of equal valences, popularity, variances, and acquiescence, eliciting potential for items keyed in different directions. For example, some content might elicit acquiescence only in the *true* but not the *false* direction (see Jackson and Messick, 1962a). As Messick (1961a) has pointed out, models that seek to distinguish particular items answered "purposefully" from those answered in terms of set may do an injustice to the probable blending of correlated traits, defenses, and stylistic consistencies in moderating content responses. Furthermore, an identification of some particular number of items answered in terms of set in effect would base the estimate of acquiescence set on a different number of items for each respondent because of the salience of the particular content, thus affecting reliability of acquiescence measures and the magnitude of its correlates.

Our general recommendation is to use postulated indexes of content and set only with extreme caution. While their use on certain research studies may be desirable, or in any case unavoidable, their routine use in assessment has limitations. At best, they identify set and content components, but they do not generally control acquiescence nor necessarily contribute to refined estimation of content. At worst, they may require assumptions that are unrealistic in practice and may confound particular content and set in ways that are difficult to explicate.

SEPARATE SCALES FOR ACQUIESCENCE AND CONTENT

As an alternative to attempts to estimate acquiescent set and content from the same set of items, one may measure acquiescence and various content dimensions independently. Such an approach has a number of advantages: (1) acquiescence may be estimated with items deliberately selected for content heterogeneity and optimal properties for eliciting a certain type of acquiescence; (2) factor analysis and other multivariate procedures may be applied to experimentally independent scores of content and acquiescence; (3) relationships between general acquiescence and particular content and with external criteria may be estimated in a context requiring relatively straightforward assumptions; and (4) content scores may be corrected, if desired, for independently obtained acquiescence estimates.

In research studies seeking to discern relationships among personality questionnaire variables, or between personality variables and external criteria, the method of choice in separately identifying content and stylistic variance is factor analysis with oblique rotation of reference axes. Here, variance may be partitioned between set and content in a manner that permits independent appraisal of dimensions of acquiescence style and content and yet does not force orthogonality between any particular content dimension and acquiescent style, if this is not warranted by the data. Factor analysis also permits the further separation of evaluative bias in a form that does not do violence to the reciprocal moderating relationship between acquiescence and desirability. If more than one species of acquiescence is present, these may be identified in terms of separate factors, and their relationships to various criteria and content dimensions independently analyzed.

In situations in which individual assessment is the focus, or in univariate studies where content scores uncontaminated by response bias are desired, correction procedures using independently obtained set scores may be employed. If one's purpose is the simple univariate prediction of a single criterion, it is, of course, an empirical matter whether a pure content or conglomerate content and style index is superior. From the viewpoint of understanding the nature of the relation, however, it is important to identify separately the validity of set and content components. It is possible that set may have suppressor effects upon the relationship between a particular content scale and a criterion. This is potentially a very useful technique for improving the predictability of criteria, using sound psychometric reasoning and what is known concerning response styles.

The question arises of which one of the several available methods is best for statistically or experimentally eliminating acquiescence or other response set variance from predictors. The first requirement obviously is an adequate independent measure of acquiescence. A measure of acquiescence should be selected with care, with attention to optimal characteristics as these have been observed empirically. Three item characteristics are particularly important: (1) items should be heterogeneous and not linked to any particular content scale or dimension; (2) acquiescence items should be selected from the same general domain as the scale to be controlled; and (3) items should be selected from among those having a moderate level of endorsement frequency, generally in the 40 to 60 per cent range.

Perhaps the best method for insuring heterogeneity of content is to sample systematically some specified universe. For example, if a large item pool has been prepared, from which scales are then derived, items might be selected randomly from among those items in the pool having acceptable popularity levels. Restrictions might be placed upon too great a representation from certain content areas. Item analysis to select items showing the highest acquiescence saturation might appear to be a possibility, but this is ordinarily not recommended because there is the risk of also selecting substantial content consistencies. As an alternative to random sampling, stratified sampling of the item pool may be employed, selecting items from a pool of items comprised of equal numbers of items from each of a large number of content scales, as many as ten or twenty or more. Proceeding on the assumption that acquiescence is elicited more strongly by vague or indifferent items, the acquiescence scale could be selected from among items not showing high content saturation.

While the particular content of the items should be heterogeneous, it is most important that the acquiescence control items be of the same general character as the content items to be controlled. As has been indicated, there is more than one species of acquiescence. It is not reasonable to expect, for example, that acquiescence on the pathological items contained in the Maudsley Personality Inventory might be reflected in an acquiescence scale based on F Scale-type content. Eysenck's (1962) conclusion that the Maudsley scale is free from acquiescence might have been quite different had he used a more appropriate independent scale to assess acquiescence. Neither is there any great confidence in "content-less" scales for controlling acquiescence in content scales.

The second step in identifying or controlling acquiescence is to decide upon a procedure to separate this variance from that identifiable as reliable content variance. The choice of statistical means for controlling acquiescence depends upon the purposes of measurement. If this purpose is primarily individual assessment for diagnosis of counseling, it is important to employ content scales uncontaminated by response bias and a procedure that corrects raw scores for acquiescence is called for. Since acquiescence may operate differentially on *true* and *false* subscales, particularly if they are unbalanced or possess different variances, each half should be corrected separately. If such statistical correction is employed, an attempt at balancing by keying half of the items *true* and half *false* may not be necessary, especially if the content makes this difficult.

It is especially important to control for acquiescence if the purpose of the assessment is to draw inferences about respondents on the basis of content scores, or to select or assign respondents on the basis of scores purportedly representing traits or dispositions. Removing a source of variance common to many content scales, thus reducing their correlations, should sharpen inferences about correlations and improve prediction. If one's purpose is research—for example, the investigation of hypotheses regarding relationships between personality traits—a variety of different opportunities for the control of acquiescence present themselves. As I have already indicated, I favor the application of factor analysis with marker variables for acquiescence and evaluative bias. Where this is inappropriate, partial correlation may be used, particularly where both variables may contain acquiescence variance, as with two personality scales. In situations in which a personality scale is related to nontest criteria, the part correlation will be more appropriate, because it will remove only acquiescence variance associated with the predictor and not the criterion. Similarly, in experimental studies, where the emphasis is primarily upon the identification of groups varying in the content trait, analysis of covariance or partial regression techniques may be employed.

In general, techniques based upon a partial regression rationale will cause the corrected score to be uncorrelated with the score held constant, in this case acquiescence. This may be quite desirable if one is focusing upon content, but if one's aim is to investigate stylistic aspects of acquiescence, this may be an inappropriate restriction upon the possible range of acquiescence scores. Furthermore, if the relationship between a trait and acquiescence is considered primarily due to broad, pervasive stylistic determinants, rather than more circumscribed method variance, the decision to partial all of the acquiescence variance out of a trait measure may be arbitrary. In so doing, one may be removing valid variance quite relevant to the trait in question, which would have the effect of restricting the scope and representativeness of the trait measure.

Regression procedures that subtract a portion of the variance also usually attenuate reliability. If acquiescence is considered as correlated error, this may be appropriate. However, removing a portion of the variance may reduce reliability below acceptable levels, particularly if the raw trait score itself possesses only modest reliability. While partial regression procedures may be important in statistically controlling acquiescence in currently available measures, their role should be considered that of temporary expedients rather than a permanent solution. A more durable solution in my view would involve carefully developed experimental controls, introduced at the stage of test construction, rather than post hoc. It is to these that I now turn.

EXPERIMENTAL CONTROLS FOR ACQUIESCENCE

As we have seen, there is no better way to control acquiescence than by developing good items. Items written with an eye to relevance, clarity, and freedom from ambiguity have the advantage over sets of items assembled haphazardly. The choice of variables to be measured is of some consequence as well. Those having little theoretical import or tho˞˞

of little consequence to respondents may elicit a greater share of acquiescence. Items of interest and concern to respondents, also selected for representativeness and relevance by the substantive validity recommendations of Loevinger (1957), should have a greater saturation of content variance. In addition, subjecting them to item analysis with respect to a total score, in which care is exercised to control the acquiescence component as well as evaluative bias, will further increase the content saturation of the scale. Internal consistency item selection criteria is preferable to item analysis based on external criteria for several reasons. In the present context, empirical item selection in no way guarantees freedom from response set bias; quite the opposite is often true.

By following the steps outlined above, one may increase the proportion of trait variance in relation to acquiescence and other sources of irrelevant variance. A total score uncontaminated by response set variance is most important because, of course, the total score will determine the type of items selected. After the final scale has been developed, it will be fruitful to examine its correlations with acquiescence and other response sets to see how successful the attempt to suppress response biases has been.

One powerful experimental method for eliminating acquiescence bias in personality or attitude scales is to abandon the true-false or agree-disagree format altogether, using instead a forced-choice or multiple-choice procedure. There are a number of ways in which one might proceed. One might, for example, simply reverse each item and present the subject with the original or reversed pair in a forced-choice format. While this technique would eliminate acquiescence in the usual sense, the use of literal reversals might elicit differential tendencies to accept or reject statements containing negations, as encountered in the reanalysis of the Rorer data. This might be alleviated by balancing the direction of the original statements. An added problem is the repetitious nature of the second item in each pair, which would not contribute to positive rapport with respondents; and it also has the effect of increasing the time required to answer a given number of items. It does, however, tend to overdetermine responses, possibly sharpening the relevancy of the items to the scale. The main advantage of this procedure over other forced-choice formats may be that it preserves the unitary properties of the oriignal items. Thus, such an item may be written to have relevance to one and only one scale, and not more than one, as in the instance where two items from different scales are paired.

A variation of this technique is to pair one item with another item reflecting the opposite pole of the same scale (Jackson and Minton, 1963). This would not be as monotonous to respondents as responding to the same item in both positive and negative forms would be. There is a great deal to recommend in this procedure for experimentally eliminating acquiescence, especially for items in the middle range of popularity. Its greatest shortcoming is in the case of scales whose average popularity values or desirability values are extreme. While the technique will control acquiescence, it would still allow free reign to evaluative or deviant bias.

A third alternative—one that overcomes the difficulties of extreme item popularities—is to introduce an irrelevant member into each pair that has an equivalent level of desirability of endorsement frequency. This method was first recommended by Horst prior to World War II, and used extensively by Wherry and his students (Gordon, 1951). Scales with many items at extreme popularity levels may profit from this approach with an increase in variance and in reliability—in one instance (Jackson and Payne, 1963) from .81 to .96. The danger in offering respondents only a choice between two equally undesirable alternatives is that testing rapport may be destroyed. How many subjects will be satisfied choosing between: (1) "There is very little in this life that I care about" and (2) "There is something wrong with my sex organs"? One useful strategy to overcome such objections is to introduce a third statement, unscored and irrelevant to the trait being measured, but more frequently endorsed and more palatable. The respondent is instructed to indicate which statement is *most* and which is *least* characteristic of him, thus obtaining the same information the paired statements give. Scoring may be dichotomous, disregarding the rank of preference for the third statement, or it may be at three levels. The latter method yields more information, but it is more susceptible to evaluative bias. This basic paradigm may have four or more statements, each grouped in pairs on the basis of popularity or desirability.

This method has much to recommend. If care is exercised in selecting heterogeneous and irrelevant items, a content specific, statistically homogeneous, acquiescence-free scale may be constructed. Item analysis procedures may be employed for such items, but one should bear in mind that an item may prove unacceptable not because the content relevant statement is bad, but because the choice of the irrelevant member was inopportune. If time and cost are of little consequence, this procedure is the method of choice, especially if one has reason to believe that evaluative or deviant response bias is also prominently represented in the trait domain. But one inevitably pays a price for greater fidelity of measurement (Cronbach and Gleser, 1964). Administration of items in such a format requires more time, because there are twice as many statements to read. The investigator may decide that it is a price well worth paying. On the other hand, if he wishes to attempt to maximize the scope of information obtained in a limited amount of time, he may settle for another type of forced-choice procedure.

The most economical procedure, but perhaps the most troublesome statistically, is a forced-choice format in which the respondent chooses from among two or more alternatives, all of which are scored. Thus, a need endurance statement might be paired with a need achievement statement. The items may be paired on the basis of similarity in some property like desirability or popularity, or they may be paired randomly. This procedure is quite effective in eliminating acquiescence and may also reduce general evaluative bias, although there are limits in the extent to which desirable and undesirable traits may be matched. Furthermore, the pairing of items may heighten discrimination on the basis of desirability (LaPointe and Auclaire, 1961). On the other hand, such a forced-choice procedure is quite economical in that information relevant to two scales is obtained from every response. Its potential difficulties for research purposes are attributable to the dependencies between scales caused by the ipsative nature of the response. In the example above, the respondent cannot endorse both the endurance and the achievement statements, however much he would like to, but must choose one. Thus, he can obtain neither a maximum nor a minimum score on both scales simultaneously. While this built-in negative correlation may be small with a large number of scales, the loss in degrees of freedom may have serious implications for many research and prediction applications.

Part of the problem is traceable to the nature of the ipsative score, which indicates the relative position of the strength or magnitude of variables for a particular respondent. This type of score is to be distinguished from a normative score, in which different individuals may be compared with respect to the magnitude of their scores. While it is possible to develop inter-individual norms based upon ipsative scores, and it might be shown that under some circumstances a normative translation of ipsative scores so derived might correspond closely to the more usual normative scores, one should not forget that the nature of the response process is different, as are the properties of the scores.

While correlation coefficients between normative scales and external criteria may ordinarily be interpreted with impunity, the like correlations for their ipsative counterparts may be equivocal and possibly quite misleading. In a thoughtful article, Radcliffe (1963) has reviewed this problem in some depth. The average covariance between a set of ipsative scores and a normative criterion must be zero. If the variances on all of the ipsative scores are equal—a likely occurrence if items are perfectly matched for popularity—the corresponding correlations will also sum to zero. If the actual average normative correlation with a criterion were + .50, the correlations based upon ipsative estimates would average zero and, as a result, seriously underestimate validities. But each would not necessarily underestimate the normative correlation to the same degree. Thus, in the absence of detailed statistical data on the relation between scores based upon acquiescence-free normative and ipsative scales, it is generally not possible to estimate a correlation based on normative scores from one based on ipsative scores, and the latter may not be interpretable from any of the usual frames of reference. The loss of degrees of freedom in ipsative scores also tends to cause validity coefficients to be closer to zero than they would otherwise be.

These problems with ipsative scores, coupled with the fact that such scales display a degree of linear dependence, make the results of the matrix operations involved in factor analysis inappropriate, and the resulting factor patterns particularly difficult to interpret. Recently, Stricker (in press) has uncovered serious problems with the Edwards Personal Preference Inventory substantially on these grounds.

The above problems have to do with treating larger sets of test scores as a group in a research context. Certainly this is an important use for personality tests, but it not the only one. It might be possible to use individual or smaller sets of ipsative scores for research and to use an entire test composed of ipsative scores for counseling or other applied purposes. In principle, it might be possible to determine empirically the relationship between forced-choice ipsative scores and other normative scores; through such a translation, research results based on normative scales might become relevant to ipsative scales, thus permitting the use of such techniques to eliminate acquiescence and maximize information per unit cost.

OVERVIEW

In concluding this review and analysis of methods for taking account of acquiescence bias in personality measures, it might be helpful to recapitulate and to provide a few general recommendations. After introducing general problems in interpreting acquiescence, I have reviewed four general methods for controlling acquiescence bias: (1) balanced scales; (2) set and content formulas; (3) correction techniques; and (4) forced-choice scales. The first and last of these techniques are experimental, while the second and third are largely statistical. I prefer the experimental procedures for the majority of applications. Statistical techniques may be considered largely salvage operations that attempt to isolate a source of error that might better have been controlled at the stage of test construction.

While statistical procedures sometimes are based on fairly elaborate mathematical rationales, their apparent rigor in the present context may be more illusory than real, especially if one attempts to apply, for example, a correction technique whose assumptions are not clearly understood to a scale whose properties have not been analyzed. In carefully designed research studies, statistical procedures like factor analysis, partial correlation, and variance analysis have a traditional place. It may be quite appropriate to seek to partition acquiescence variance in personality scales that have been less than adequately constructed, as Bock (1964) has so carefully done. Every investigator wishing to study the nature of a personality variable cannot be expected to embark on a program of test development—although perhaps personality research would be further advanced if more did. But the use of statistical partitioning techniques in assessment should be recognized for what they are, namely, temporary, partial expedients applied to inadequately constructed tests.

The application of correction techniques in individual assessment is fraught with difficulty, given the present state of our knowledge regarding the relation and interaction between personality measures, personality traits, and response biases such as acquiescence. In making inferences about individuals on the basis of test scores, there is no adequate substitute for properly developed tests with experimental controls for acquiescence and other forms of response bias. With our present knowledge, it should be possible to develop assessment techniques having optimal properties and considerably higher construct validity than is in evidence in published techniques. If a portion of the considerable effort devoted to the task of studying the nature of personality variables using our present rather inadequate assessment devices were redirected toward fundamental research in the construction of soundly based personality measures, the long-term progress of personality theory, as well as assessment methodology, might be enhanced.

The Psychology of Acquiescence: An Interpretation of Research Evidence[1]

In recent years the literature on psychological assessment has been marked not only by an outpouring of empirical studies on response styles, but also by the periodic appearance of review articles in which various authors have attempted to pause and ponder what it all means (Blake and Mouton, 1959; Christie and Lindauer, 1963; Holtzman, 1965; Loevinger, 1959; McGee, 1962d; Messick, 1961a; Moscovici, 1963; Rorer, 1965). On the surface, research studies in this area present a morass of inconsistent and sometimes contradictory findings that, without considerable critical care, could mean all things to all people.

Research on acquiescence, for example, has been based upon a continually increasing number of instruments that purport to measure this response style. These measures, however, differ among themselves in minor (and sometimes major) ways: in the style of item phrasing, in the extremeness

1. Preparation of this review was supported by the National Institute of Mental Health, United States Public Health Service, under Research Grant M-2878. I wish to acknowledge a special debt to my colleague, Fred Damarin, for his many contributions to my thinking about response styles. I also wish to thank Lewis R. Goldberg and Leonard G. Rorer for graciously supplying the correlation coefficients that appear in Tables 4, 5, and 6.

or tentativeness of item tone, in the distribution of item desirability values, in the range of item endorsement frequencies, and in the type of item content employed. Some contain difficult information items, some social attitude items, some self-descriptive personality items, and some—like the pseudo-ESP procedure (Bass, 1957) and the phony language examination (Nunnally and Husek, 1958)—contain no item content at all. Thus, some of these tests may be contaminated with various types of content consistencies and with various other response styles, particularly desirability. These tests also differ in reliability, which further obfuscates the evaluation of correlational evidence.

Although all of these acquiescence measures have never been included in a single study, correlations among various combinations of them have been appraised. Some of the tests display moderately high intercorrelations, suggesting that they indeed measure an underlying trait; but other combinations of them just as often intercorrelate negligibly. Similarly, some of the tests sometimes exhibit significant correlations with nonquestionnaire performance measures of ability and personality, while others do not (Banta, 1961; Bass, 1956; Chapman and Campbell, 1959; Clayton and Jackson, 1961; Couch and Keniston, 1960; Dicken, 1963; Forehand, 1962; Foster, 1961; Jackson, Messick, and Solley, 1957; Jackson and Pacine, Frye and Bass, 1963; Gage and Chatterjee, 1960; Gage, Leavitt, and Stone, 1957; Gaier, Lee, and McQuitty, 1953; Husek, 1961; Jackson, Messick, and Solley, 1957; Jackson and Pacine, 1961; Kuethe, 1960; Martin, 1964; McGee, 1962b, 1962c; Moore, 1964; Quinn and Lichtenstein, 1965; Shaw, 1961; Siller and Chipman, 1963; Small and Campbell, 1960; Solomon and Klein, 1963; Stricker, 1963; Zuckerman and Eisen, 1962; Zuckerman, Norton, and Sprague, 1958).

In attempting to assimilate these findings into a coherent theory of acquiescence, should we account for some of the differences in results in terms of contaminating influences in the acquiescence measures that might have distorted the correlations? Should we account for some of the differences on the basis of subject variations, not only in terms of selection effects but also on the grounds that acquiescence may function in different ways in different types of people? Should we look for consistencies in the patterns of results for particular kinds of acquiescence measures and consider the possibility that more than one dimension of acquiescence may be operating? In keeping with the spirit of the variable under consideration, the answer to all of these questions is "yes."

All three of these strategies were recently followed by Damarin and myself (1965) in a review of research literature on acquiescence, desirable responding, and extremity responding. By emphasizing factor analytic studies primarily, they were able to take account of contaminating factors in acquiescence measures and to recognize that two distinct patterns of correlates emerged, thus suggesting that two major dimensions of acquiescence may exist. In addition, several smaller dimensions were uncovered in which acquiescence appeared to interact or blend either with a particular type of content or with another response style. Damarin and I (1965) also pointed out that much of the early thinking on acquiescence, especially by Cronbach (1950), conceived it to be related to content skills on a particular test in a nonlinear fashion. If such is the case, then some of these smaller interaction factors might have been spuriously generated by the application of linear factor analysis to a partly nonlinear domain. In light of this, a discussion of the major dimensions of acquiescence and the evidence in support of them would be more meaningful against a background of past thinking about this variable. Let us briefly consider, then, some views of the nature of acquiescence, particularly its early conceptualization as a test-taking style and the elaborations that occurred when the vicissitudes of the *Zeitgeist* placed it first in the context of authoritarianism and then in the broader context of personality questionnaires.

CONCEPTIONS OF ACQUIESCENCE

ACQUIESCENCE AND TEST PERFORMANCE

To Cronbach (1946) it seemed obvious that if a subject knew the answers to true-false achievement items, he would respond in terms of his knowledge and that if a response set were to influence test performance, it must operate on items the subject did not know. Thus, acquiescence should operate primarily on items that the subject is at a loss to answer, either because he is uninformed on the topic in question or because he is uncertain about the meaning of the items. This type of reasoning has led to the use of extremely difficult information items to measure acquiescence (Gage, Leavitt, and Stone, 1957).

On items where the answer is not known, the subject is thought to have a characteristic probability of responding *true,* that is, he is assumed to toss a loaded coin. However, in most simple ways of scoring acquiescence on true-false tests, the tendency to say *true* and the number of items not known or thought ambiguous are confounded. A subject may receive a particular score either because he displayed a high probability of rsponding *true* to a relatively small number of ambiguous items or a smaller probability of responding *true* to a greater number of ambiguous items. Thus, reliable individual differences in typical acquiescence scores do not necessarily reflect individual differences in the tendency to respond *true.*

If everyone had a relatively comparable probability level for agreement, varying only slightly around some stable value, which might turn out to be greater than .5 (Fritz, 1927), the scores might then reflect individual differences in knowledge or in the tendency to perceive items as ambiguous. Since both of these processes may operate at once, this conceptualization provides a basis for expecting two dimensions to underlie acquiescence scores—one reflecting preferred probabilities of response and one reflecting intellectual skill, particularly ability in resolving verbal ambiguity. Since the extent to which a test measures acquiescence is thus an inverse function of the subject's knowledge (and of his ability to perceive items clearly), Cronbach (1950) conjectured that scores on the test could not be represented as a linear combination of scores on a content factor and scores on an acquiescence factor, as the linear model of factor analysis would require. The possibility that scores on a true-false test are a non-linear function of content skills and of acquiescence should be kept in mind in interpreting the results of factor analytic studies.

Some attempts have also been made (at the price of various restricting assumptions) to develop scoring models to untangle the contributions of content and set by scoring acquiescence as the probability of responding *yes* on those items that are not known or clearly understood (Helmstadter, 1957; Messick, 1961b). In a model proposed by Peabody (1964), it is possible in addition to estimate two components of set separately as the "probability of agreeing" and the "weight of set," as well as to estimate the relative importance of procontent and anticontent responses.

ACQUIESCENCE, AUTHORITARIANISM, AND CONFORMITY

The role of acquiescence in personality and attitude scales became a topic of considerable research interest after the publication of *The Authoritarian Personality* (Adorno, Frankel-Brunswik, Levinson, and Sanford, 1950). The implications of this important theoretical and empirical analysis of personality were at once extensively investigated using the California F Scale of authoritarianism, a device composed of broad, sweeping attitude statements, all of which were keyed *true* (Christie and Cook, 1958; Christie and Jahoda, 1954; Titus and Hollander, 1957). Several investigators soon pointed to the confounding influence of acquiescence on the F Scale, usually by inferring its operation from asymmetries in response to original and specially written reversed items (Bass, 1955; Chapman and Bock, 1958; Chapman and Campbell, 1957, 1959; Christie, Havel, and Seidenberg, 1958; Cohn, 1953; Jackson and Messick, 1957; Jackson, Messick, and Solley, 1957; Leavitt, Hax, and Roche, 1955; Messick and Jackson, 1957, 1958; Peabody, 1961; Zuckerman, Norton, and Sprague, 1958).

Since one of the important component traits of the authoritarian personality was authoritarian submission, an effort was made to cast the psychological meaning of acquiescence in these terms and to assimilate it into the authoritarian syndrome, thereby making its operation on the F Scale not only appropriate but desirable (Gage and Chatterjee, 1960; Gage, Leavitt, and Stone, 1957; Leavitt, Hax, and Roche, 1955; Zuckerman and Eisen, 1962). Against this background, with acquiescence bearing overtones of authoritarian submission, several attempts were made to assess the validity of acquiescent response style as a personality variable by correlating acquiescence scores with behavioral measures of conformity; the results, although not perfectly consistent, were generally negative (Endler, 1961; Foster, 1961; Foster and Grigg, 1963; Frye and Bass, 1963; McGee, 1962c; Moore, 1964; Small and Campbell, 1960).

ACQUIESCENCE AND SELF-DESCRIPTION

The operation of acquiescence on personality questionnaires also received intensive study, and it soon became clear that an important elaboration could be made on previous conceptualizations of acquiescence. Not only is acquiescence unlikely to occur when the subject has specific knowledge about the answers, but it also seems unlikely to occur when some other basis for evaluating the meaning of a response, such as desirability, is available. Thus, acquiescence appears to operate mainly on scales that are relatively neutral in desirability and to decrease steadily in influence as scales become either more and more desirable or more and more undesirable

(Edwards and Diers, 1963; Jackson and Messick, 1961, 1962a). This relation may be another example of the link between acquiescence and item ambiguity, but in this case the ambiguity is not necessarily related to specific item meaning but rather to the evaluative implications of item endorsement.

The relation of acquiescent tendencies to item difficulty and ambiguity may also display a somewhat different character in the self-description of personality than it does in the expression of social attitudes. Banta (1961) found that acquiescence increased with increasing generality of the referent of attitude items. Stricker (1963) found more acquiescence on difficult than on easy-to-read attitude items, but he also found less acquiescence on difficult than on easy-to-read personality items. As Damarin and I (1965) point out, people may be more casual in their agreement with ambiguous statements that refer to abstract ideological principles or external social objects than they are with equally ambiguous statements that bear on their own character and behavior.

The psychological basis of acquiescence on personality questionnaires was investigated by Couch and Keniston (1960) in a clinical study of extreme yeasayers and naysayers. The two comparison groups in this investigation were selected on the basis of extreme tendencies to respond *yes* and *no*, respectively, to a heterogeneous, largely content-counterbalanced collection of 360 personality and attitude statements. This clinical assessment characterized the yeasayer as an impulsive, emotional, undercontrolled, stimulus-accepting extravert and the saysayer as a cautious, rational, intellectually controled, stimulus-rejecting introvert.

DIMENSIONS OF ACQUIESCENCE IN QUESTIONNAIRES

Damarin and I (1965) have recently reviewed fourteen factor analytic studies of response styles in questionnaires and classified those factors in each study that were related to acquiescence into three categories—factors that represented acquiescence measures fairly purely, factors that combined acquiescence measures with questionnaire content measures (content blends), and factors that combined acquiescence measures with measures of other response styles (style blends). (This classification appears in Table 1.)

For our purposes, there are two important points to note in Table 1: First, relatively pure acquiescence factors appeared in ten of the fourteen studies, and in four studies *two* pure acquiescence factors emerged, suggesting that at least two dimensions of acquiescence may exist. Second, in several studies measures of acquiescence also appeared on additional factors together with content scores or other response style scores. This results in part from inadequate factoring and rotation procedures and in part from the fact that many of the available acquiescence scales are not pure, but also measure to some degree other factors of content and response style. Some of these combination factors may represent genuine interactions between acquiescence and other traits, but it is also possible that some were spuriously generated by the analytic procedure in its attempt to provide a linear representation of a nonlinear domain. Additional research is required to clarify the properties of these dimensions.

Further evidence supporting the existence of two acquiescence dimensions has subsequently appeared in articles by Martin (1964) and by Quinn and Lichtenstein (1965). Both studies found a factor of acquiescence in response to self-descriptive personality items, as well as a factor primarily reflecting acquiescence to sweeping, though plausible-sounding, "common-sense" generalities.

TABLE 1. Recent Factor Studies of Acquiescence in Questionnaires *

Study References	NUMBER OF VARIABLES		Characteristics of the Study NUMBERS AND TYPES OF ACQUIESCENCE FACTORS			
	Total	Stylistic	Total	Pure	Blend	Style
Bendig (1962)	13	2	5	0	0	1
Broen & Wirt (1958)	15	4	3	0	0	2
Edwards (1963)	19	6-10	10	2	1	4
Edwards, Diers & Walker (1962)	61	1+	10	1	?	?
Edwards & Walsh (1964)	31	10	6	2	2	2
Hanley (1959)	6	6	1	1	0	0
Jackson & Messick (1961)	30	12 **	8	1	0	0
Jackson & Messick (1962) Hosp.	40	17 **	9	1	1	0
Jackson & Messick (1962) Norm.	40	17 **	11	1	1	0
Messick (1962)	26	13 **	8	2	0	0
Schutz & Foster (1963)	24	2	9	0	2	1
Solomon & Klein (1963)	9	3	2	0	0	1
Voas (1958)	8	2	4	1	0	0
Zuckerman & Norton (1961)	11	6 **	4	2	0	0

* Table 1 adapted from Damarin and Messick (1965). Some of these studies included a *true*-keyed and a *false*-keyed version of each of several scales; each such pair of *true*- and *false*-keyed subscales was counted as a separate acquiescence measure (indicated ** in the table).

A + sign indicates that some other measures included in the study may be interpretable in terms of acquiescence.
A ? indicates interpretive ambiguities arising from incomplete publication of results.

DIMENSIONS OF ACQUIESCENCE
IN BEHAVIORAL TESTS

Damarin and I (1965) also reviewed eight factor analytic studies by Cattell and his colleagues that contained measures of acquiescence along with several objective performance tests of personality. They classified all the factors related to acquiescence in these studies into three categories—major acquiescence factors (on which loadings of .30 or better occurred for two or more acquiescence tests), minor acquiescence factors (on which a loading of .30 or better occurred for only one such test), and "stylistic blend" factors (on which loadings of .30 or better appeared both for acquiescence tests and for measures of some other response style such as desirability or extremity). (This classification is given in Table 2.) It should be noted that in two of the studies (Cattell and Scheier, 1959, 1960) only one acquiescence test was included, so that no major acquiescence factor could have appeared by the criterion adopted.

As can be seen in Table 2, major or minor acquiescence factors were found in every study, and in one study (Cattell, Dubin, and Saunders, 1954a) two major acquiescence factors emerged, again suggesting that at least two basic dimensions of acquiescence may exist. As in the questionnaire studies considered earlier, the acquiescence measures included in the studies of Table 2 frequently loaded on more than one factor, suggesting that Cattell's acquiescence tests also are not pure measures of a single underlying trait but reflect other sources of variance as well. The last column of Table 2 lists the numerical labels of the acquiescence factors in each study that displayed substantial objective test correlates (that is, acquiescence factors with loadings above .30 for at least two performance tests). Eight such factors appear in Cattell's work, and an examination of their objective test correlates should provide important information about the nature of acquiescence.

TABLE 2. Factor Studies by Cattell Related to Acquiescence *

STUDY REFERENCES	NUMBER OF VARIABLES		NUMBERS AND TYPES OF FACTORS				FACTORS WITH MANY PERFORMANCE CORRELATES
	Total	Stylistic	Total	Major Acquiescence Factor	Minor Acquiescence Factor	Style Blends	
Cattell, Dubin & Saunders (1954b) C-3	117	4	17	1	0	0	F3
Cattell, Dubin & Saunders (1954a) C-4	104	3	18	2	1	0	F2,F5,F11
Cattell (1955) C-5	129	3	16	1	1	0	F3
Cattell (1955) C-6	64	2	15	0	1	1(d),1(e)	
Cattell & Gruen (1955) C-7	128	3	16	0	1	2(d,e)	
Cattell & Scheier (1959) R-2	103	1	17	.....	2	0	F6
Cattell & Scheier (1960) R-3	72	1	14	.....	1	0	F4
Cattell & Peterson (1959) R-12	81	2	20	0	2	0	F14

* Table 2 adapted from Damarin and Messick (1965). d indicates a factor combining acquiescence measures with desirability measures. e indicates a factor combining acquiescence measures with extremity measures. C-3, C-4, R-2, R-3, and so on are codes used by Cattell to identify each study.

Rather than consider all of the tests with significant loadings on each factor, however, we limited our attention to those tests that replicated their association with an acquiescence factor in more than one study. The loadings of these replicated tests on the seventeen factors in Cattell's work that implicated acquiescence to some degree are given in Table 3. It should be noted that the requirement of replication in this case is a relatively severe one, since some of these studies were based upon college students and others upon psychotics, air force cadets, and young children.

INTELLECTUALLY BASED ACQUIESCENCE

As can be seen in Table 3, factor 3 in study C-3 associates measures of acquiescence with low verbal ability, poor performance in interpreting riddles correctly, low social taste, and little logical consistency of attitude. (In the measure of social taste, subjects choose among three alternatives that have been rationally keyed for high-brow, middle-brow, and low-brow taste. In the measure of logical consistency of attitude, attitude statements are written in triads that form syllogisms, and the statements are presented to the subject in random order for his endorsement.) On this dimension acquiescence is negatively associated with verbal comprehension skills, suggesting that this type of acquiescer might have difficulty interpreting statements unambiguously. For convenience we will call this dimension "interpretive acquiescence."

Several other studies have reported negative correlations between acquiescence and measures of intellectual ability (Elliott, 1961; Forehand, 1962; Frederiksen and Messick, 1959; Jackson and Pacine, 1961; Messick and Frederiksen, 1958; Shaw, 1961). In these studies acquiescence was usually measured on some scale, such as the California F Scale or the Bass (1956) Social Acquiescence Scale, where the items were sweeping generalities and unqualified statements of general attitude or belief. This dimension may thus correspond to the type of acquiescence that Jackson and I (1958) distinguished

TABLE 3. Replicated Acquiescence Variables and Factors[*]

STUDY NUMBER AND FACTOR IN STUDY

TEST TITLE	C-3 3-	C-4 2-	C-4 -5	C-4 11+	C-5 3+	C-5 6-	C-6 3+	C-6 9-	C-6 11+	C-7 4-	C-7 6+	C-7 12+	R-2 2-	R-2 4+	R-3 14+	R-12 7+	R-12 14-
Acquiescence Markers																	
More unreflective acceptance of unqualified statements	24	-17	61	-02	26	02	07	02	10	11	36	04				Z	67
More agreement with platitudes	12		68	02	10	11				37	03	46				35	Z
More agreement with optimistic beliefs—ratio	48	40	39	35													
Much tendency to agree with optimistic beliefs—difference	29	33															
Much tendency to agree					37	62	74	63	33	67	09	49	31	53	38		
Objective Tests																	
Low verbal or verbal and numerical ability	40	25	04	-01	32	-07	-01	08	21	07	24	-19				Z	Z
Poor on riddles	47	05	21	-09						03	-10	22					
High fluency on topics																	
High speed of judgment comparing letters					46	02	-03	-17	01	06	76	10				20	Z
Fast tempo of tapping					14	-05				28	46	-02				23	Z
Fast tempo of arm circling					08	-05	-03	-08	-08							Z	23
Much impairment of reading speed by frustration	04	24	13	17	08	-04	09	30	13	-01	01	02					
Many errors in complex reaction time	02	-01	05	-02	25	00	-01	07	-01	-01	25	-11	04	30	04	Z	Z
Many slanting lines crossed in CMS								00	-03	05	14	-02	05	33	16		
Questionnaire Content Measures																	
Low social taste	82	06	30	14	22	-11	15	-08	-06								
Low ratio purposeful/non-purposeful annoyance					18	15	-01	62	06	07	24	-19					
More authority submission					26	18	48	-06	26	49	-03	44					
Questionnaire Stylistic Measures and Other Derivations																	
Little logical consistency of attitude	54	-14	-33	07	05	39				64	16	38	01	-07	-03	-33	-47
High consonant/dissonant recall ratio—corrected	20				30	53	71	14	26	47	-19	43					
More willing to confess frailties	22	-01	07	14	08	27	36	19	26	46	-11	33	01		16	Z	-25
High extremity of viewpoint					-13	-05	01	06	33								

[*] Table adapted from Damarin and Messick (1965). A leader (....) in the body of the table indicates that the variable in question has not been included in that particular factor study. A Z indicates that the exact factor loading could not be recovered from the data but that it is believed to lie between −.20 and +.20.

References for the study codes are given in Table 2. When the factor number is followed by a minus sign, the factor has been reflected.

with the term "overgeneralization," although its basis appears to lie not so much in a tendency to overgeneralize as in an inability to differentiate or particularize.

Factor 3 in study C-5 and factor 6 in study C-7 associate measures of acquiescence in varying degrees with high speed of judgment and reaction in perceptual and perceptual-motor tasks, with rapid tempo in preferred rates of movement, and to some extent with high verbal fluency. The rudiments of a similar pattern can also be found in factor 4 of study R-2 and factor 7 of sutdy R-12. This dimension is reminiscent of the Couch and Keniston (1960) clinical formulation of yea-saying, in that it appears to relate acquiescence to a temperament trait of unreflective impulsiveness. The yeasayer reacts quickly and impulsively with little reflection and probably little monitoring of performance, both on judgmental and perceptual-motor tasks and on questionnaires. The naysayer, on the other hand, is more reflective and analytical, but in the extreme he may also be handicapped in effectiveness because of an obsessively cautious and skeptical stance. This dimension will be called "impulsive acceptance."

ACQUIESCENCE, VERBAL ABILITY, AND IMPULSIVENESS

In the explication of these two possible bases for acquiescent tendencies, one of the important questions that arises concerns the specific influence of verbal ability in determining the test correlations. Although verbal intelligence appears largely unrelated to measures of the temperamentally based dimension of impulsive acceptance, there is some evidence that it bears a negative relation to measures of interpretive acquiescence (Bass, 1956; Elliott, 1961; Frederiksen and Messick, 1959; Jackson and Pacine, 1961; Messick and Frederiksen, 1958; Shaw, 1961). However, does verbal ability completely account for correlations among interpretive acquiescence measures? Or do these measures generate a separate acquiescence factor distinct from the factor of verbal comprehension, although negatively correlated with it? This acquiescence factor might than coalesce with the verbal factor, and perhaps with other traits, to form a second- or even higher-order dimension of personality organization.

Evidence on these points appears in a recent study by Kogan and myself,[2] who administered measures of intellectual ability, categorizing style, and personality to a sample of 84 males and 79 females. The personality measures included questionnaire scales of acquiescence and desirability, as well as content scales for several temperament traits. Except for the measures of acquiescence and the Rokeach (1960) Dogmatism Scale, all of the questionnaire content scales contained equal numbers of *true* and *false* items.

In the male sample, we isolated a verbal comprehension factor marked at one end by a vocabulary test with a loading of .71 and at the other end by a modified version of the California F Scale with a loading of —.45. This modified F Scale was balanced for both the number of original and reversed items and the number of extremely worded and tentatively worded items (Clayton and Jackson, 1961). No measure of acquiescence appeared on this factor, but a separate acquiescence factor emerged with loadings for several scales requiring the endorsement of generalized attitude statements— acquiescence to extreme statements on the F Scale (.80) and to tentative statements on the F Scale (.46) and the Rokeach (1960) Dogmatism Scale (.48), as well as agreement with original, extreme F Scale items (.39), reversed, extreme F Scale items (.56), and reversed, tentative F Scale items (.35). (All of the variables included in the factor analysis proper were experimentally independent; derived scores were pro-

2. Messick, S. J., and Kogan, N. *Categorizing styles and cognitive structure.* Princeton, N.J.: Educational Testing Service Research Bulletin, in preparation.

jected into the factor space by extension methods.) In addition, the Couch-Keniston (1960) Agreement Response Scale and the Fulkerson (1958) Acquiescence Scale also received moderate loadings (.44 and .34, respectively). This factor, which appears to reflect what we have called interpretive acquiescence, was found to correlate —.34 with the verbal factor and to combine with both the verbal factor and a category-width factor to produce a second-order dimension. On this second-order factor, verbal comprehension loaded .66, broad category-width .49, and interpretive acquiescence —.42.

In the same analysis, the Couch-Keniston (1960) Agreement Response Scale (ARS) also appeared on two other factors, both of which were unrelated to verbal ability. It had a marginal loading of .28 on an impulsiveness versus rigid control factor that was anchored in one direction by the Barratt (1959) Impulsiveness Scale with a loading of .49 and in the other direction by the Gough-Sanford (1952) Rigidity Scale with a loading of —.65. The Couch-Keniston (1960) Agreement Response Factor items (ARF), which were interpreted by Couch and Keniston in terms of a dimension of impulsive stimulus acceptance, also loaded .29 on this factor.

In addition, the ARS received a loading of .42 on a factor that contained the Saunders (1955) Anxiety Scale (.65), the Fulkerson (1958) Acquiescence Scale (.54), the ARF (.40), and the Stricker (1963) Desirability Scale (—.49). This factor, which appears to reflect a tendency to endorse diverse anxiety symptoms, is similar to one Jackson and I (1962a) obtained in studies of both college students and mental patients. However, in the present case it may also reflect the response style of desirability, represented in this study by only one scale.

Thus, impulsive acceptance, as measured by the Couch and Keniston items, does appear to be marginally related to a dimension of impulsiveness *vs.* rigid control, but it appears to be somewhat better related to another first-order dimension reflecting the admission of undesirable anxiety symptoms. These two first-order factors, however, were in turn found to intercorrelate .46 and to combine to form a second-order dimension that pitted impulse expression and admission of anxiety against rigidity in impulse control. The highest loading on this second-order factor was obtained by the ARF (.56), and among the salient loadings were the ARS (.47), the Fulkerson Acquiescence Scale (.38), rigidity (−.52), impulsiveness (.45), desirability (−.50), and anxiety (.47). Thus, in a pattern consistent with the above discussion of temperamental acquiescence measures appeared on this dimension, but in many heterogeneous characteristics as descriptive of the personality were found to be related to impulsiveness and the lack of rigid controls, as well as to the possibly impulsive admission of undesirable characteristics and anxiety symptoms.

In a parallel analysis of the female sample, Kogan and I again isolated a verbal comprehension factor, which was defined by a vocabulary test having a loading of .60. Again no acquiescence measures appeared on this dimensoin, but instead a separate factor emerged with loadings for the Dogmatism Scale (.52), for acquiescence to extremely worded and to tentatively worded F Scale items (.46 and .49, respectively), for the F Scale (.47), for the Fulkerson Acquiescence Scale (.38), and for a nonquestionnaire measure of uncriticalness (Frederiksen and Messick, 1959) in judging whether two alternative expressions are equivalent (.62). This factor appears to reflect a dimension of interpretive acquiescence, since it provides a direct link between the tendency to agree with generalized attitude statements and a lack of critical acumen in discerning differences in verbal meanings. It was found to correlate −.43 with the verbal factor and to load substantially on a second-order dimension along with the verbal factor and three other factors, including one related to categorizing style. Verbal comprehension loaded .55 on this second-order factor and interpretive acquiescence loaded −.66.

In this same analysis of the female sample, Kogan and I found a bipolar factor defined by the scales of impulsiveness (.72) and anxiety (.52) at one end and by rigidity (−.55) and desirability (−.52) at the other. The two Couch and Keniston (1960) scales, ARF and ARS, loaded this dimension .67 and .41, respectively. This factor, which relates measures of agreement or acceptance to impulsiveness and lack of rigid controls, is almost identical to the one that we found at the second-order in the male sample. In addition, the female sample also produced a factor linking the Fulkerson Acquiescence Scale (.59), anxiety (.64), and desirability (−.42) to measures of narrowness in categorizing and judgment.

Thus, in two different samples Kogan and I found factors relevant to temperamentally based acquiescence that related the general tendency to accept heterogeneous personality characteristics as self-descriptive to questionnaire measures of impulsiveness and lack of rigidity. Although the possibility of interactions with method consistencies cannot be discounted, these factors were not due to shared questionnaire method variance in any simple sense, since the study also included several other personality questionnaire scales that failed to load on these particular factors but did appear on other factors.

Furthermore, in both samples separate factors were found to represent verbal comprehension and interpretive acquiescence, and in both cases a substantial negative correlation was obtained between them. A second-order factor that combined interpretive acquiescence with verbal comprehension and other traits into a broad dimension of personality was also generated in each sample. It would thus appear that verbal ability does not account for all of the variance in measures of interpretive acquiescence in any direct and simple way— unless, of course, one interprets the second-order dimension strictly in terms of intellectual capacity. In that case we would be faced with the interesting result that, in females at least, acquiescence would be a better measure of stupidity than vocabulary was of intelligence.

REACTIONS TO REVERSALS:
EVIDENCE AGAINST ACQUIESCENCE?

In a consideration of research evidence *for* acquiescence it is appropriate to discuss briefly some of the research evidence *against* acquiescence. I do not mean to catalog here all ot the inconsistent and contradictory findings that have appeared in various empirical studies. Many of these are equivocal and might possibly be accounted for by variations in subject populations or variations in acquiescence measures used, particularly if one allows for the possibility that different acquiescence measures may not only contain different sources of contamination but may also reflect qualitatively different dimensions of response style. Furthermore, some examples of negative results, such as the studies that attempted to relate acquiescent response style to conformity, do not so much present evidence against acquiescence qua personality variable as they do against a particular construct interpretation of it. Rather than discuss findings of this sort, I will instead consider two attempts to demonstrate the negligibility of acquiescence in personality questionnaires—or more accurately, in the MMPI. These two attempts are of interest because they utilize methods and arguments that have a respectable history in the study of acquiescence, namely, the drawing of inferences from correlations between original and reversed statements (Lichtenstein and Bryan, 1965; Rorer and Goldberg, 1964, 1965a, 1965b).

CONSISTENCIES WITHIN ORIGINAL AND REVERSED FORMS

Lichtenstein and Bryan (1965) constructed reversed items for twelve MMPI scales and administered both the standard and the reversed scales to psychiatric patients and normal subjects. *True*-keyed and *false*-keyed subscales were considered separately, and the correlations of the sub-scales with their corresponding reversed forms were found to approximate test-retest reliabilities, especially for normal subjects. Likewise, Rorer and Goldberg (1964) constructed item reversals for the MMPI and administered both the original and the reversed forms to one group, while a control group took the standard MMPI twice. Again, the correlations of *true* and *false* subscales with their corresponding reversed forms were found to approximate the test-retest reliabilities of the original scores. In both studies it was concluded that the influence of acquiescence on the MMPI had been greatly exaggerated and, indeed, that only a negligible amount of acquiescence appeared to operate at all.

Rorer and Goldberg (1965b) attempted to estimate for several MMPI scales the proportion of response variance that could be attributed to acquiescence and found on the average that less than 5 per cent of the total variance was implicated. Jackson and Messick (1962a), on the other hand, had inferred from interrelations among *true* and *false* subscales that the second largest rotated factor on the MMPI was interpretable in terms of acquiescence. They found this factor in a college student sample to account for roughly 14 per cent of the total variance on *true* and *false* subparts of eleven frequently used clinical and validity scales and for about 18 per cent of the total variance on the forty MMPI scores included in their study. Rorer and Goldberg (1965a, 1965b) subsequently challenged this interpretation, feeling that their own more recent findings of negligible consistencies in agreeing with both original and reversed statements cast considerable doubt upon the designation of the second largest factor on the original MMPI as acquiescence.

In attempting to resolve this controversy, we should keep in mind the *relative* size of the disputed factor. Acquiescence was deemed important on the MMPI (where, incidentally, the preponderance of undesirable items happens to provide a particularly unfertile item pool in which to observe its operation) not so much because it accounted for 15 per cent of the total variance of the clinical scales, but because none of the other factors, barring desirability, accounted for nearly as much as 15 per cent of the variance.

If we are to decide whether the proportion of variance attributable to acquiescence on the MMPI is more like 15 per cent or more like 5 per cent, the inferences must be based upon data gathered under carefully controlled, comparable conditions. Unfortunately, certain differences between the two samples involved in the Rorer and Goldberg study contravene such refined estimations. To begin with, randomization procedures were not used in that study, or in the Lichtenstein and Bryan study, to assign subjects to conditions, so that obtained differences in variances between experimental and control groups should be evaluated and not necessarily attributed to random sampling fluctuation. Nor were the test-retest intervals strictly comparable in the experimental and control conditions. In the Rorer and Goldberg study, the sample that took the original MMPI followed by the reversed form was obtained at the University of Minnesota; there was a two-week interval between the two testing sessions. The sample that took the standard MMPI twice was gathered at the University of Oregon with a four-week interval between the two sessions. Thus, the test-retest reliabilities that were used as the standard against which to evaluate the correlations between original and reversed forms were based upon a longer time interval and were thereby probably systematically lower than reliabilities based upon a comparable two-week interval. Furthermore, roughly 70 per cent of the original scales had larger variances in the Minnesota sample than in the Oregon sample, so that the "criterion" test-retest reliabilities computed from the "control group" data were based upon a more restricted range than would have been appropriate for the experimental group.

Thus, although on the surface these item-reversal studies appear compelling, experimental deficiencies such as those just outlined make it difficult to assess their contribution in detail. These objections are important if we are trying to decide whether acquiescence variance on the MMPI is on the order of 5 per cent of the total or 15 per cent of the total, but they are quibbles when we consider the magnitude of the major finding of these studies, namely, the substantial correlations in the content direction between original and reversed scales. These findings warrant further scrutiny, however, since they appear to be in conflict with other evidence; in particular, the obtained high correlations between original and reversed MMPI scales do not appear to be consistent with the reported low, and sometimes negative, correlations between true and false parts of original MMPI scales.

CONSISTENCIES ACROSS ORIGINAL AND REVERSED FORMS

In three different samples, Jackson and Messick (1961, 1962a) found that correlations between true and false parts of many of the standard MMPI clinical scales were substantially lower than the scale reliabilities, and were sometimes even negative. This did not hold for *Hs*, *Pt*, and *Sc*, where sizable true-false correlations were obtained that presumably reflected consistent content responses, or desirable responding, or both. Now, if we conclude from the consistently high correlations between original and reversed forms that acquiescence is negligible on the MMPI, how can we account for the low correlations obtained between *true* and *false* parts of the original scales? Before we draw any conclusions either way, let us examine some of the correlations between original and reversed forms in more detail.

Intercorrelations among original and reversed forms of *true* and *false* subscales are presented in Table 4 separately for nine MMPI scales. Keying was reversed for reversed scales, so that all forms are keyed in the content direction. These coefficients were provided by Rorer and Goldberg. The high correlations they reported between original and reversed forms of each subscale are circled in Table 4. The three scales in the first row—*Hs*, *Pt*, and *Sc*—are the three scales that Jackson and I (1962a) found to display consistent correlations across *true* and *false* forms. This also tends to be the case here, since the uncircled correlations for each of these scales are generally substantial. For the remaining six scales in Table 4, however, the uncircled correlations are quite low and frequently negative. This holds not only for correlations between true and false parts of original scales, as Jackson and I (1962a) found, but also for correlations between *true* and *false* parts of reversed scales and, indeed, for all *true-false* comparisons. Fo reach of these six scales, then, it is apparent that more than one factor is necessary to account for the 4 x 4 matrix of intercorrelations among original and reversed forms

TABLE 4. Intercorrelations among Original and Reversed
Forms of *True* and *False* Subscales, Separately
for Each of Nine MMPI Scales *

Hs Scale	O T	O F	R T	R F
O T		61	51	47
O F	62		42	71
R T	78	50		52
R F	40	68	33	

Pt Scale	O T	O F	R T	R F
O T		52	77	35
O F	61		43	56
R T	84	57		52
R F	47	60	45	

Sc Scale	O T	O F	R T	R F
O T		44	75	31
O F	36		35	61
R T	80	36		40
R F	29	54	37	

F Scale	O T	O F	R T	R F
O T		20	58	25
O F	21		14	62
R T	59	03		26
R F	17	55	-04	

D Scale	O T	O F	R T	R F
O T		19	76	32
O F	19		20	57
R T	71	19		24
R F	21	64	15	

Hy Scale	O T	O F	R T	R F
O T		01	66	13
O F	-01		08	54
R T	65	-12		06
R F	-05	73	-15	

Pd Scale	O T	O F	R T	R F
O T		-06	76	21
O F	-02		04	56
R T	70	05		28
R F	-03	63	07	

Pa Scale	O T	O F	R T	R F
O T		-37	62	-31
O F	-37		-25	73
R T	67	-38		-28
R F	-32	68	-26	

Ma Scale	O T	O F	R T	R F
O T		-03	60	10
O F	-18		-04	72
R T	69	-15		02
R F	-11	71	-09	

* O = Original version; R = Reversed form; T = *True* items;
F = *False* items. Keying reversed for reversed scales, so that all forms
are keyed in the content direction. In each table, the correlations above
the diagonal are for males and those below the diagonal are for females.
Correlation coefficients were provided by Rorer and Goldberg, 1964.

of *true* and *false* subscales. There is also a slight tendency for
this to be the case for the scales in the first row of Table 4
as well, particularly for *Sc*.

For at least six of these scales, then, the *true* and *false*
subparts appear to be measuring different things. One pos-

sibility is that within both the original form and the reversed form, the *true*-keyed scales reflect yeasaying in addition to some other dimension of content or response style, while the *false*-keyed scales reflect naysaying in addition to this other dimension. Such a factor pattern—with each *true* and *false* scale loading in the same direction on one dimension but in opposite directions on a second (yeasaying) dimension— would appropriately produce the obtained low correlations between *true* and *false* scales within each form. However, since the same acquiescence factor would presumably operate in each scale, this interpretation also requires that the *true* parts of several scales share some common variance; in other words, not only should *true* and *false* subparts measure different things when considered scale by scale, but one of those different things should be the same in all scales.

Evidence on this point appears in Tables 5 and 6, which present for male and female subjects, respectively, the intercorrelations among *true* and *false* subparts of selected MMPI scales separately for original and reversed forms. Since these scales all contain fairly undesirable content, the pattern of correlations reveals consistencies in response to *true* scales and to *false* scales that are not completely determined by differences in desirability levels. As these tables show, there is a consistent tendency within the original form for *true* scales to correlate substantially with other *true* scales but considerably more poorly and sometimes negatively with *false* scales. Somewhat less systematically, the *false* scales also tend to correlate higher with other *false* scales than with *true* scales. Similarly, within the reversed form there is a consistent tendency for the reversed *true* scales (which are now keyed *false*) to correlate higher with other reversed *true* scales than with reversed *false* scales and, to a much lesser degree, for reversed *false* scales to correlate higher with other reversed *false* scales than with reversed *true* scales.

Jackson and I (1961, 1962a) found that such a pattern of intercorrelations among the original *true* and *false* subscales of the MMPI was accounted for in three separate samples by two major factors and several minor ones. One major factor was interpreted in terms of the tendency to respond desirably,

TABLE 5. Correlations among *True* and *False* Subparts of Selected MMPI Scales Separately for Original and Reversed Forms *

(Sample of 96 Male College Students)

		F		Hs		D		Hy		Pd		Pa		Pt		Sc		Ma		Dev	
		T	F	T	F	T	F	T	F	T	F	T	F	T	F	T	F	T	F	T	F
F	T		26	46	41	41	-07	34	-11	59	03	65	-22	58	12	68	34	52	06	68	27
	F	20		31	33	43	38	31	19	44	06	33	-04	42	38	47	56	09	-27	36	71
Hs	T	56	15		52	36	16	50	16	30	00	41	-09	40	28	52	30	40	-01	50	38
	F	48	21	61		45	33	45	38	47	17	35	-13	45	42	50	34	31	-19	47	61
D	T	53	51	47	57		24	72	-06	66	-08	51	-32	82	58	79	26	43	-31	74	52
	F	-13	23	12	22	19		17	36	07	14	09	12	09	39	10	17	-32	-20	-04	61
Hy	T	55	35	65	64	78	13		06	44	00	36	-21	64	47	62	16	41	-27	59	38
	F	-12	-02	12	34	-11	50	01		02	39	-12	49	-21	04	-13	12	-31	16	-32	33
Pd	T	72	34	39	43	62	-11	55	-17		28	61	-25	69	34	74	39	55	00	71	47
	F	-18	13	-08	00	-09	29	-10	48	-06		-03	16	-10	-08	-03	11	08	39	-05	17
Pa	T	72	21	-17	51	61	-01	60	-13	64	-17		-28	62	32	73	40	45	-10	68	34
	F	-24	-09	49	-09	-31	29	-23	64	-30	36	-37		-43	-25	-37	-02	-53	17	-56	12
Pt	T	63	34	36	55	82	-03	73	-28	74	-22	75	-43		52	85	38	58	-29	89	47
	F	28	37	56	56	54	39	50	26	43	05	38	-05	52		47	27	18	-39	43	51
Sc	T	72	43	12	62	81	01	79	-14	80	-16	78	-33	88	52		40	63	-18	88	50
	F	20	62	32	30	53	16	32	-02	46	14	23	-12	43	41	44		23	-08	37	53
Ma	T	52	17	40	26	39	-40	40	-34	64	-20	52	-44	60	18	57	22		02	76	06
	F	-15	-01	-06	-17	-32	-08	-20	36	-16	28	-22	17	-39	-24	-32	-02	-03		-24	-34
Dev	T	71	31	51	50	74	-18	65	-41	80	-23	77	-55	89	44	86	40	73	-36		38
	F	16	55	24	58	56	51	46	39	33	31	26	24	44	62	48	58	-05	-16	27	

* Correlations for the originally stated form are below the diagonal and those for the reversed form are above the diagonal. Correlation coefficients were provided by Rorer and Goldberg. Decimal points omitted.

Table 6. Correlations among *True* and *False* Subparts of Selected MMPI Scales Separately for Original and Reversed Forms *

(Sample of 125 Female College Students)

		F		Hs		D		Hy		Pd		Pa		Pt		Sc		Ma		Dev	
		T	F	T	F	T	F	T	F	T	F	T	F	T	F	T	F	T	F	T	F
F	T		-04	32	35	33	-05	34	-07	52	-01	43	-19	39	05	50	32	49	01	55	16
	F	21		08	29	34	29	22	08	29	15	19	-25	30	23	31	45	02	-21	25	56
Hs	T	65	10		33	40	12	41	-05	35	-08	24	-34	46	24	39	28	27	-09	48	29
	F	62	21	62		49	37	32	26	43	-05	40	-19	43	56	47	51	34	-27	44	61
D	T	50	30	51	54		15	54	-19	65	-04	64	-43	80	58	75	34	46	-38	76	47
	F	19	29	32	39	19		-03	29	02	29	09	-06	04	30	-02	30	-16	-09	-07	54
Hy	T	54	20	67	60	55	19		-15	42	-04	35	-30	58	28	58	25	37	-27	52	28
	F	-04	06	06	23	-23	32	-01		-12	44	-11	43	-35	14	-20	22	-26	30	-37	26
Pd	T	70	25	49	60	65	16	63	-12		07	68	-37	67	35	77	35	52	-23	74	36
	F	02	10	-08	-02	-09	35	-07	47	-02		01	09	-15	04	-03	12	-13	38	-17	18
Pa	T	59	20	47	54	68	17	51	-18	72	-13		-26	71	38	70	23	45	-17	68	28
	F	-40	-13	-25	-39	-45	-08	-29	40	-47	12	-37		-43	-14	-40	-07	-27	20	-51	-10
Pt	T	56	21	52	58	81	10	68	-33	77	-20	78	-51		45	85	28	57	-42	88	39
	F	43	36	40	65	60	42	53	05	54	03	51	-31	61		46	35	15	-32	37	51
Sc	T	65	24	49	59	72	08	68	-22	83	-06	76	-51	86	55		37	65	-32	86	41
	F	49	53	41	49	35	30	33	11	40	05	31	-09	34	38	36		27	-13	28	54
Ma	T	52	04	34	43	46	-14	46	-22	68	-14	61	-52	67	34	77	17		-09	67	04
	F	-18	-37	-19	-31	-49	-13	-24	42	-38	-34	-40	39	-52	-40	-39	-23	-18		-34	-29
Dev	T	68	19	56	62	77	04	61	-37	80	-23	79	-60	91	53	88	33	78	-50		30
	F	30	57	29	56	40	59	39	26	34	26	28	-14	35	60	32	46	01	-29	24	

* Correlations for the originally stated form are below the diagonal and those for the reversed form are above the diagonal. Correlation coefficients were provided by Rorer and Goldberg. Decimal points omitted.

140

since it was intimately associated with the judged desirability levels of the scales. The other major factor was interpreted as acquiescence, since it provided a clean separation between *true* scales and *false* scales. This separation of *true* and *false* scales cannot be attributed simply to an artifact of item overlap (Shure and Rogers, 1965), not only because this factor was larger than might be expected from overlap alone, but because care was taken in these studies to isolate factors of item overlap separately and to label them as such. In a recent factor analysis of the Rorer and Goldberg (1964) intercorrelations among reversed *true* and *false* subscales, Jackson and I (1965) similarly found two major and several minor factors. The two major factors were oriented in essentially the same manner as in the previous analysis, with one of them again separating *true* scales from *false* scales.

Thus, within the original form of the MMPI, evidence suggesting the operation of acquiescence appears in the pattern of intercorrelations among *true* and *false* subscales. Similarly, within the reversed form of the MMPI essentially the same evidence appears. In addition, however, high correlations are observed between the original and reversed forms of each scale—and this presents a problem. If these high correlations are used to discount the operation of acquiescence on the MMPI, then some other psychological basis must be found to explain not only the separate within-scale relation that *true* and *false* subparts measure different things, but also the striking between-scale consistencies that generate a factor marked by *true* scales in one direction and *false* scales in the other. By the same token, however, if the acquiescence hypothesis is retained, how can we account for the high correlations between original and reversed forms?

ACCEPTANCE AND AGREEMENT AS DIMENSIONS OF
ACQUIESCENCE

In pursuit of a solution to this problem, Jackson and I (1965) factor analyzed *true* and *false* subparts of both original and reversed MMPI scales in the same analysis. This procedure was performed separately for male and female samples. In both cases two large factors were obtained along with several smaller ones, some of which represented item overlap. After rotation, one of the large factors was found to be intimately associated with the judged desirability levels of the scales and appeared to be interpretable in terms of desirability. The other large factor provided a clear separation between original and reversed *true* scales on the one hand and original and reversed *false* scales on the other, with corresponding original and reversed scales receiving very similar loadings on the factor. Since each *true*-keyed original scale received a loading in the same direction as its reversal, which was keyed *false,* and each *false*-keyed original scale similarly loaded in the same direction as its *true*-keyed reversal, this factor can by no means be interpreted in terms of any simple tendency to agree with personality items.

This factor does not seem to be easily interpreted in terms of content, either, since it implicates many presumably diverse MMPI scales in both original and reversed forms of *true* and *false* subparts. One would expect content consistencies to be differentiated into several more specific factors. A content theory of this monolithic dimension would also have to explain the neat separation of original and reversed *true* scales from original and reversed *false* scales. In light of these difficulties, a stylistic interpretation that accounts for this separation is offered instead: This dimension represents individual consistencies in the tendency to accept many heterogeneous characteristics as descriptive of the self.[3]

Subjects scoring high on this dimension accept many characteristics as self-descriptive by responding *true* to original items and *false* to reversals. This pattern of responses generally indicates acceptance of the characteristic described in the statement, since about 80 to 85 per cent of the original

---

3. This attempt to account for the available evidence (both for the high correlations between original and reversed scales and for the internal structural properties of the original, the reversed, and the combined forms) in terms of a stylistic dimension of acceptance was formulated during conversations with Dr. Peter Bentler. His collaboration in this effort is gratefully acknowledged.

MMPI items are positively phrased and a large majority of the reversals are negatively phrased, that is, are simple negations that insert a "not" into the original statement or preface the original statement with a phrase such as, "It is not true that. . . ." It thus also follows that, within the original form of the MMPI or within the reversed form, this tendency to accept many characteristics as self-descriptive would be largely indistinguishable from (and confounded with) a simple tendency to agree or respond *true* to questionnaire items. These two tendencies would operate in the same direction on positively phrased items but in opposite directions on negatively phrased items and could therefore be unconfounded by including both positively and negatively phrased items in the same analysis.

In our factor analysis of original and reversed forms, these two response tendencies were indeed found to be differentiated. In addition to the two large factors just described, we also uncovered a smaller factor that, even in its unrotated principal axis position, tended to separate *true*-keyed scales, both original and reversed, from *false*-keyed scales. In the male sample, only three out of 25 scales with positive loadings were *false*-keyed and only four out of 27 scales with negative loadings were *true*-keyed. In the female sample, seven out of 28 scales with positive loadings were *false*-keyed and only five out of 24 scales with negative loadings were *true*-keyed. In addition, many of the misplacements fell within the hyperplane of plus or minus .10, suggesting that the separation might be made even more striking by rotation. This factor, which apparently reflects a consistent tendency to agree or respond *true* to personality items regardless of the form of phrasing, accounted for approximately 6 per cent of the total variance in the male sample and about 5 per cent of the total variance in the female sample.

Thus, two dimensions of acquiescence were distinguished in responses to original and reversed MMPI scales, one reflecting a tendency to accept many characteristics as descriptive of the self and the other reflecting a tendency to agree with or respond *true* to personality items. The acceptance tendency is reminiscent of the temperamentally based dimension of acquiescence discussed earlier, and although it would certainly be tidy if the agreement tendency were found to relate to inadequacies in verbal comprehension (as in the intellectually based dimension of acquiescence), such appraisals have little to support them at present and must await further empirical work on the generality and correlates of these MMPI dimensions.

OVERVIEW

In this chapter I have briefly reviewed evidence pertaining to the operation of acquiescent response style in psychological tests and to the possible interpretation of acquiescence as a personality variable. Acquiescence was initially conceptualized in terms of consistent individual differences in the probability of agreeing with items that subjects are at a loss to answer, either because they lack knowledge or because they are uncertain about the meaning of the item or because they cannot evaluate the desirability of the response. In addition to this agreement tendency, an acceptance tendency was empirically differentiated and conceptualized in terms of consistent individual differences in the tendency to accept many heterogeneous characteristics as descriptive of the self.

It has also been shown that at least two psychological processes of acquiescence may exist: one called "interpretive acquiescence," which is apparently a function of deficiencies in verbal comprehension, and another called "impulsive acceptance," which apparently derives from temperament characteristics of unreflective impulsiveness. Further research is required to see if the agreement tendency results primarily from interpretive difficulties and the acceptance tendency primarily from impulsiveness, or whether both intellectual and temperamental processes contribute, perhaps in different proportions, to both the agreement and the acceptance response tendencies.

Evidence has been presented for samples of both males

and females that measures of interpretive acquiescence were sufficiently distinct from measures of verbal ability to produce a separate factor. However, these two factors were found to correlate substantially negatively with each other and to combine, along with other factors, to form a second-order dimension of personality. Also found in both sexes were factors relating measures of acquiescence to impulsiveness versus rigid impulse controls and to the admission of undesirable characteristics and anxiety symptoms.

There is also some tentative indication that the operation of both types of acquiescence is more pervasive in females than in males—not because mean levels of acquiescence are higher in females, which is generally not the case, but because more variables are directly implicated for females as correlates of acquiescence. Interpretive acquiescence is directly related to nonquestionnaire measures of uncriticalness in females and is more highly correlated with verbal ability and with the second-order dimension; and a temperamental acceptance factor relating acquiescence measures to impulsiveness and the admission of anxiety appears directly in the first-order structure for females but not until the second-order for males. We thus appear to be accruing evidence that may bring us slowly around to a position long recognized in a different tradition and expressed, for example, in the folk wisdom of Oliver Wendell Holmes:

> The style's the man, so the books avow;
> The style's the woman, anyhow.[4]

4. Oliver Wendell Holmes. "How the Old Horse Won the Bet." Stanza 2.

The Deviation Hypothesis: A Broad Statement of Its Assumptions and Postulates

The Deviation Hypothesis offers a research concept and an explanation of how patterns of atypical or deviant behavior may be identified and measured. All behaviorally valid categories of deviancy are included in the explanation, not just psychopathological states. Schizophrenia, depressions, anxiety reactions, and other forms of emotional disturbance are included, together with other valid classes of deviant behavior such as mental retardation, chronic heart disease, culture patterns, safecracking, genius, any occupation characterized by distinctive response groupings, and the like. The important thing is that the deviant category of behavior must be identifiable by valid external criteria, by *responses*. A mere label connoting deviancy, like *criminal* or *executive*, is not sufficient to identify a valid class of deviant behavior, as will be shown later in this chapter. There must be a number of distinctive responses for a behaviorally meaningful category to exist. The importance of this factor cannot be overemphasized.

While the Deviation Hypothesis is intended to provide a

research framework and an explanatory concept covering the identification of all forms of deviant behavior, the primary emphasis in this chapter will be on personality assessment, since that is the topic of this entire book. A second reason is that most of the research published on the Deviation Hypothesis is in the area of personality. This research has been empirical and directed chiefly at predicting deviant behavior. Only recently have our studies begun to be more concerned with explanation than with prediction, for it was felt that the usefulness of the Deviation Hypothesis must first be empirically demonstrated in prediction studies before the necessary assumptions and postulates as a background for explanation could be investigated.

It should be noted, nevertheless, that the formulation of the hypothesis is ambitious in its scope and range, which go beyond the usual dimensions of personality assessment. In the broad sense, however, personality factors are always involved in deviant behavior, although not necessarily in the obvious or usual context. A group of armless persons, for example, would represent a deviant group clearly defined in terms of aberrant organic condition and motor responses. Yet, because members of such a deviant group cannot do certain things most people can, it seems almost certain that a large number of social and other responses would be modified, resulting in atypical personality characteristics.

The designation of the Deviation Hypothesis as a hypothesis is outmoded. As the next chapter by Adams and Butler shows, there is ample evidence that the hypothesis has been supported in a wide variety of situations (see Chapter 7) and, accordingly, deserving of a less tentative label. It could be changed to "deviation theory," but that seems to add little that is particularly meaningful. A rigid specification, like "deviation principle," would be quite inaccurate at the present time since far more evidence is needed before the provisional character of the current tag can be discarded. Thus we continue to use Deviation Hypothesis to describe our formulation.

THE DEVIATION HYPOTHESIS

In an effort to provide greater clarity the statement of
the Deviation Hypothesis that follows is somewhat modified
from an earlier version.[1] The revised statement is:

*Deviant behavior patterns are general in the sense that
those responses that are regarded as being significant for
identifying a particular category of atypicality in behavior do
not exist in isolation. Those responses that are regarded as
being significant for a particular category of deviant behavior
are associated with a number of other deviant responses that
are not regarded as being significant for that particular category of behavioral atypicality.* Note that this does not say that
where a recognized and reasonably valid category of deviant
behavior exists, such as schizophrenia, *every* response made
by members of the deviant group will be deviant. That would
be utterly absurd. The schizophrenic will have very many
responses that are quite like those of nonschizophrenics.

It is saying, however, that schizophrenia is actually a
broad pattern of deviant responses, yet only a small portion
of those responses are regarded as being significant for the
disorder. The psychodiagnostician would regard neologisms
and delusions of persecution, for example, as deviant responses
significant for schizophrenia. But he would probably be
unaware of associated deviant responses such as a variable
oral-anal temperature difference or, if aware, he would very
likely be unconcerned. Yet the deviant response pattern of
schizophrenia is considerably more general than a mere

1. The earlier version was stated as follows: "Deviant response
patterns tend to be general; hence those deviant behavior patterns
which are significant for abnormality (atypicalness) and thus regarded
as symptoms (earmarks or signs) are associated with other deviant
response patterns which are in noncritical areas of behavior and which
are not regarded as symptoms of personality aberration (nor as in-
dictators, signs, earmarks)." (Berg, 1957, p. 159; 1961, p. 335).

grouping of those particular responses that are regarded as the key or significant ones. It is believed that there is both explanatory and heuristic value in viewing schizophrenia and other classes of deviant behavior in terms of a broad pattern of deviant responses.

THE DEVIATION TRAIT

In past writings no basic trait of deviant responding has been formally postulated, although the existence of such a trait has been implied. This trait may now be defined as: "the tendency for members of a validly specified category of deviant behavior to give many kinds of responses that exceed a validly defined range of variability."

Some elaboration of this statement is necessary so that the use of certain terms is made clear. We are saying, in essence, that members of a deviant group share a number of atypical responses in the form of symptoms, signs, characteristics, etc., that are the criteria for membership; however, they also share a large number of other kinds of atypical responses that are not usually considered to be criteria for membership in the deviant group. The term *responses* is used in a very broad sense (see p. 167f, assumptions and postulates 1, 2, 3, and 4 for details).

By "a validly specified category of deviant behavior," we mean a pattern of responses that can be identified by external criteria in an operationally clean fashion. These are patterns that are *ab-normal* in the literal sense of being away from the norm, not necessarily abnormal in the sense of emotional disturbance. The professional ballet dancer and the schizophrenic are both abnormal in this context, for both exhibit certain obvious responses (or the lack of them) that set them apart from most people. In referring to "many kinds of responses" we mean the many other atypical responses that are quite remote from the response criteria for membership in a deviant group.

The meaning of "a validly defined range of variability"

is specified in statistical terms, although some other meaning could perhaps be used. Our reference is to differences in response frequency and/or strength at a given level of statistical significance (such as the .01 level of confidence) in comparison with an appropriate standard. An appropriate standard could be the responses obtained from a representative sample of the general population or, on occasion, it could be the responses of one deviant group arbitrarily designated as the standard when several special groups are being compared. For example, one might define a deviant group such as overachievers in college as those earning grade-point averages one sigma or more above expectancy based on their scholastic aptitude test scores and underachievers with grade-point averages one sigma or more below expectancy. This would represent the top and bottom 16 per cent approximately. In making our comparisons we could use either group as our anchorage point or standard.

Attention is called to the use of the singular in the statement of the Deviation Trait: "validly specified *category*." It seems probable that the plural, *categories*, will eventually be used, for there are indications that a number of the "many kinds" of atypical responses associated with the criterion deviant responses that define the group are to some extent found in several deviant behavior categories. However, current evidence on this point is limited since most research has been directed at the range and variety of deviant responses within a single category of deviant behavior. Thus, for the time being, the precaution of using the singular is observed. In this connection it is emphasized that not every response made by members of a deviant group will be deviant. Nor will all members of a deviant group manifest all deviant responses that have been identified.[2] This is true of the criterion responses that specify the deviant category as well as the other associated, noncriterion responses. These points,

_____

2. Lest it appear that undue attention is being given to these points, it may be noted that several studies that dealt critically with the Deviation Hypothesis have assumed that all responses must be deviant (Sechrest and Jackson, 1962, 1963).

along with many others related to the Deviation Hypothesis, will be expanded in the section dealing with assumptions and postulates.

The concern of the present book is with personality assessment; hence before turning to postulates and assumptions, we may review the Deviation Hypothesis in the light of personality appraisal techniques.

THE DEVIATION HYPOTHESIS AND PERSONALITY TESTING

Among other things, the Deviation Hypothesis offers an explanation for the reason positive results are often obtained in numerous studies that seek to predict behavior in one area from responses made in another area. Many thousands of such studies employ responses made to an astonishing array of stimuli used to identify, with varying degrees of success, deviant behavior categories.

The Rorschach, for example, uses inkblots as stimuli, and more than 5,000 studies concerning this test have appeared in print. The Strong Vocational Interest Blank (SVIB) and the Minnesota Multiphasic Personality Inventory (MMPI) use verbal statements as stimulus materials; each of these inventories has been the subject of over a thousand published articles. These instruments are among those in widest use, of course, but many other studies use many other stimulus forms for behavioral prediction purposes. The Thematic Apperception Test (TAT) uses pictures and the Szondi uses photographs of Hungarians, while other psychodiagnostic techniques have utilized such different things as the Archimedes Spiral Aftereffect, the autokinetic phenomenon, food preferences, mazes, abstract designs, sway suggestibility, word choices, hand preference, extreme response choice, and meaningless sounds. Elsewhere I (1961, p. 331f) review a number of these methods.

It is curious that these diverse diagnostic techniques all had some predictive value. Some worked rather well in diagnosing deviant states and some predicted only a little above chance. Yet to a slight extent, at least, even these poorer tests worked. The variety of methods, for the most part, had little or nothing in common; nevertheless, when applied to some deviant state they were better than sheer guesswork, although there were admittedly many false positive and false negative identifications. Stationary lights, whirling spirals, pencil mazes, food aversions, inkblots, photographs, and so on and on all worked as diagnostic tools, although not equally well.

What could such a potpourri of techniques have to do with deviant conditions like schizophrenia or depressions or anxiety or still other states of a nonpathological nature? When we identify schizophrenia, for example, we do so on the basis of such indicators as flattened affect, bizarre thought processes, social withdrawal, possible delusions, etc. Those are the deviant characteristics that represent our final, our ultimate interest, not responses that indicate what patients see in an inkblot or a picture or whether they like or dislike certain foods or abstract designs. Putting it another way, a patient may be legally committed to a mental hospital because of significant deviant responses like delusions, but never solely on the basis of deviant responses to inkblots, designs, and such. Yet, since we can to some extent predict one set of responses from the other, there must be some association or relationship between them. Thus we have the question of the nature of this association or implied relationship.

DEVIANT RESPONSES AND RESPONSE SETS

As will be elaborated later, it is postulated that one thing schizophrenia and other deviant states have in common with the bewildering assortment of prediction methods is that both involve deviant response sets. This is not ordinary response bias or response set. Deviant responses are those that *significantly depart from* an established response pattern, which may or may not be biased. Any response set—such as acquiescence, social desirability, or caution-incaution—may or may not be useful for producing deviant response sets. The governing factor lies in whether the response pattern of a particular category of deviant behavior is significantly different statistically from the response set. If there is no significant difference, there is no deviant response.

For example, when presented with an abstract design, 70 per cent of normal subjects may say they like it and 30 per cent may dislike it. This is response set or bias, but it is not a deviant response if a group of schizophrenics (or any other deviant group), which we are trying to distinguish from the normal group, also exhibits a 70-30 per cent distribution of *like* and *dislike* responses to the same design. While there is response set or bias in both groups, there is no significant departure of one distribution of responses from the other; hence, there is no deviant response. On the other hand, a different design may produce a 50 per cent *like* and a 50 per cent *dislike* response distribution among normal subjects. There is no bias from the normal probability standpoint in this case.

Yet, if our schizophrenics (or other deviant group) reveal a 70-30 per cent *like-dislike* response distribution to this design, we then have a deviant response that can serve with other deviant responses to distinguish the group of normals from the group of schizophrenics. This assumes that the differences in response distributions for the two groups are statistically significant at some useful level of confidence, such as the .01 or perhaps the .05 level. Thus we can define deviant responses in an operationally clean fashion by using a precise level of statistical significance in identifying them.

In identifying deviant responses, either departures from a chance or normal probability distribution or from a criterion group may be used, what are termed *absolute* and *relative* sets by Rettig, Jacobson, Despres, and Pasamanick (1958). Where departures from chance are employed, it is usually necessary to make several statistical comparisons before a deviant response can be determined.[3] That is, the response distribution of a deviant group for some particular stimulus

3. Sechrest and Jackson (1963) suggest that six sources of deviations could be used: (1) absolute deviation, (2) relative deviation, (3) statistical infrequency, (4) extremeness of traits, (5) unique structuring of traits, and (6) randomness of response.

is compared to chance expectancy. If there is a significant
difference, as noted earlier, a response set has been established
but not necessarily a deviant response. The earlier example
of a 70-30 per cent response distribution for normal and for
schizophrenic subjects is a case in point. Consequently, for
our Deviation Hypothesis studies, we have usually compared
response distributions in terms of departures from a criterion
group because it is more direct and because more deviant
responses are likely to appear, particularly when the response
distributions are not markedly different.

Let us suppose, for example, that a group of professional
sculptors and a group drawn from the general population
are being compared on the basis of whether they respond
like much, like slightly, dislike slightly, or *dislike much* to a
pattern of flashing lights. Let us further suppose that a difference of four percentage points in the response distributions
is significant at the .01 level of confidence but that a two
percentage point difference is not. As shown in our hypothesized distribution in Table 1, the *like much* and the *dislike
slightly* response options would be significant at the .01 level
when the response distribution for the general population
group is compared to that for the professional sculptors. Thus
we have identified two deviant responses. But if comparisons
are made in each case by reference to the chance distribution,
there would be no significant differences and no deviant
responses.

TABLE 1. Hypothetical Response Distribution
in Percentages

Response Option	General Population	Professional Sculptors	Chance Expectancy
Like Much	23	27	25
Like Slightly	26	24	25
Dislike Slightly	27	23	25
Dislike Much	24	26	25

It may be argued that where response distributions are
so nearly similar that significant differences can barely be eked
out, the deviant responses obtained are likely to disappear

upon cross-validation because they originally appeared by chance. This may very well be the case; however, it is equally possible that they may hold up under replication. Furthermore, the more deviant responses one has to examine, the more likely the possibility of discerning tendencies common to a number of deviant groups.

Let us imagine, for example, that we have an oval with two circles set in it so that there is a vague resemblance to staring eyes (see Figure 1). Let us also suppose that carefully defined deviant groups of bank auditors, hard-of-hearing persons, postal inspectors, paranoid schizophrenics, and secret service agents had a significant number of *dislike much* responses to this design when compared with the general population. If so, and if we found other responses similarly shared, such findings might suggest the existence of a common characteristic, possibly suspiciousness, among such disparate groups. At least, encouragement would be given for further and detailed study of such groups.

DEVIANT RESPONSES: VARIETY AND VARIABILITY

Thus far we have said relatively little about deviant response patterns in terms of the varieties of deviant responses that compose them. By way of beginning, if we look at the total population of the world, we note that many responses are shared by all living persons—all ingest food, all breathe, all sleep, and so forth. But many other responses are commonly found only among the members of certain groups and serve to distinguish them. These responses are the product, singly or in combination, of past learning, inherited structure, maturational level, or physiological and organic state and provide variability within the response repertoire of the world population. Whether such other responses form a valid category of deviant behavior will depend upon whether a suitable number of these responses can be identified in terms of a pattern or response class.

Cultural and subcultural response patterns, for example,

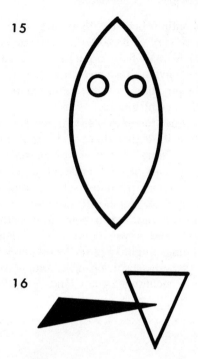

15

16

Fig. 1. Two designs used in the Perceptual Reaction Test.

are the result of past learning and, as such, could be used to identify deviant categories under appropriate conditions. Only about one person out of a thousand in the world is French; in this world sense, Frenchmen are deviant. It probably would not be difficult to select a series of stimuli to provide responses that would separate the French from the non-French with a satisfactory degree of accuracy. Language factors such as vocabulary, accent, and idioms could be used, together with items of French history, customs, and many others. Indeed, with responses to a very long series of appropriate stimuli and a lot more work, we could probably classify all of the people of the world into similar culture groupings. To do the job reasonably well, we should need to use deviant characteristics that were the product of heredity and physiology as well as learning. Epicanthal eye folds, blood types, skin color, reactions to a muezzin's call, what is done with snails or fish heads or boiled sheep eyeballs, the use of chopsticks or knife and fork, and so on are all illustrations of possible sources of deviant characteristics that might be used for this purpose.

VARIABILITY AMONG AND WITHIN RESPONSES

There is response variability, and variability within variability, and variability within variability within variability, ad infinitum. At each level of variation we can obtain deviant responses that will serve to identify response patterns for smaller and smaller groups until we can eventually specify one particular person by means of a few, unique deviant characteristics—one's fingerprints are a case in point. The expert can start with a broad pattern of fingerprint whorls and eliminate many persons; he can eliminate many more persons by the patterning of loops, still more by the size, positioning, and combinations of whorls and loops, gradually eliminating possibilities until he finally specifies one person. Central fingerprint record bureaus work in much that way. The key classification data are coded and put on tapes or cards, and progressively smaller classes are identified until, *sui generis,* the particular person is identified.

As an illustration, let us suppose that we are studying a broad pattern of responses with the aim of predicting membership of particular patterns in certain subgroups. We may begin by sampling various responses by means of a number of stimulus materials. These response samples, let us say, are obtained by probes much like hollow knitting needles that vary in length and diameter. The probes represent our psychological tests, providing samples of deviant and nondeviant responses. By using the deviant responses in an appropriate series of samples, as shown in Figure 2, we could eventually establish that a particular person was male, young adult, Asiatic, Vietnamese, psychotic, schizophrenic, paranoid type, and acutely ill. Finally, by highly individual characteristics such as fingerprints, we might identify a Vietnamese named Ding En Sik.

To do this, we should have to know something of the range and kind of deviant responses that distinguish each deviant category. Our sampling technique would have to identify a sufficient number of such responses in order for us to restrict progressively our categories. This would probably be quite simple for the first three or four categories (males, young adults, and so on) because the accepted criteria for membership are highly specific—sex organs for males, birthdate for age, and so forth. Only a rare borderline case, such as a half-caste, would give us an occasional problem for the Asiatic and Vietnamese categories. We could be even more precise with our top category, the particular person Ding En Sik, because our criteria are highly specific—that is, his fingerprints, his signature, etc. But the categories of psychosis and schizophrenia have less specific criteria, and we probably would be less accurate in our predictions. Our predictions and the criteria would both be variable.

It should be noted that even with response characteristics

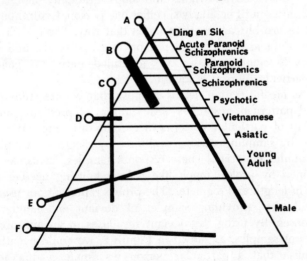

FIG. 2. General to increasing specific deviant response characteristics.

specific to one individual, there is almost certainly variability. Over periods of time, for example, the depth of fingerprint ridges may change, the distance between ridges may narrow or widen due to atrophy or exercise, size will increase with growth from infancy to adulthood, and so on. The way one writes his name is another example, for signatures on checks and other legal documents are accepted billions of times during the year as evidence that some particular person and no other was the one who signed his name. Yet variability is always present in signatures, for when confronted with two absolutely identical signatures, experts take it for granted that at least one of them is a forgery.

ARBITRARILY ESTABLISHED LIMITS OF VARIABILITY

There is always response variability and more variability, variability that does not end with responses characteristic of a single person. In this sense every response is deviant and is wholly unique if we can measure *all* of its characteristics. As a practical matter, we accept a certain latitude, a certain range of variability just as the bank teller accepts a certain amount of variation in your signature. When we group responses into classes of deviant behavior, the lines of precise demarkation are set arbitrarily and are necessarily artificial. What is normal speech, for example? Among a thousand persons regarded as speaking normally, we should probably find those who spoke rather softly, others rather loudly, some slowly, some rapidly, some with a faint lisp, others with minor blockings, and so on. The accepted variation in vocalization is fairly broad and the dividing line of normal versus abnormal vocalization is certainly not clear. Only when we encounter obvious departures from the usual range, such as the slow, tortured, labored utterances of the deeply depressed person or the staccato bursts of the hypermanic patient, is there general agreement on the label "abnormal speech pattern."

Where progress has been made in identifying deviant

states, the borderline or cut-off point has been defined in some reasonably valid operational fashion. Thus the deviant condition of alcoholic intoxication has been defined as 0.2 per cent or more of alcohol in the blood; industrial blindness has been defined as vision no better than 20/200. These are reasonably good procedures in defining deviant states. While they are far from perfect, they are considerably better than identifying schizophrenia by pooling the judgments of three or four psychologists and psychiatrists. But then, pooled judgments of experts are much better than the vague impressions of nonexperts who may use terms like "crazy" or "off base."

IDENTIFICATION OF DEVIANT GROUPS

A key problem in studying deviant behavior in any form is identification of the deviant groups. If the identification of the behavior category under investigation is quite vague, no amount of calculator pressing or computer program juggling will produce much more than frustration and negative results. Even worse is the situation in which the identification is only somewhat vague, for here the results, while inconclusive, are mixed positive and negative, and something appears to be tantalizingly present.

Should we desire to study immaturity, for example, we can start out in a number of ways. We could ask three or four knowledgeable persons to rate a group of subjects on some scale of immaturity and define our group by such ratings. On the other hand, we could also define our groups in terms of some specified criteria of chronological age and determine what responses were commonly found among children but rarely found among adults and vice versa. In all likelihood, while our raters with the vague criteria were still disputing whether some subjects were mature or immature, we should have completed our investigation. There are still other ways of defining such groups, and while further elaboration will come later, it should be clear that the identification of deviant groups by valid behavioral criteria is most essential.

VALIDLY DEFINED CATEGORIES NECESSARY

LABELS AND VALIDITY

Emphasis has been periodically given to the adjective *valid* in connection with deviant classes of behavior. While we attach descriptive labels to many patterns of behavior, the semanticists have been telling us for years that such labels are often meaningless because they lack an operational referent. As examples of labels used to indicate membership in a purportedly deviant group, consider *genius, idiot, supervisor, criminal, scientist, neurotic.* In terms of external criteria some of these labels are behaviorally valid, some are invalid, and some are vaguely in between.

Membership in the deviant behavior category of genius or idiocy can be determined in an operationally clean manner by proper administration of a standard test of intelligence. If the subject scores at IQ 140 or above, he is labeled "genius"; if he scores below IQ 25, "idiot." Some other cut-off scores could be designated, but any qualified person will know exactly what is meant by these terms. That is to say, when the subject took this standard intelligence test under the prescribed conditions for administering it, he made certain responses and avoided other responses which, when scored correctly, represented an IQ of 140 or above or below 25, as the case may be.

This does not indicate that everyone will like our definition nor that everyone will use it properly in everyday speech. Some may want a higher or lower IQ level as cut-off points. Some will persist in calling a "genius" persons talented in other areas, such as a skilled cabinetmaker or a gifted soprano. Still others may consider the standard test to be unfair in its sampling of behavior. But the all-important thing is that they do know what we mean by the deviant behavior labels *genius* and *idiocy*. In general operational terms we are stating, "If X is done (a standard intelligence test is properly administered) and Y results (a score representing an IQ of 140+), then Z is said to occur or be present (*genius,* in this example.)"

BEHAVIORALLY INVALID PATTERNS

Terms like *criminal* and *supervisor* are quite another matter, for there is no valid pattern of deviant responses that specifically identifies them. Criminals as a class have no responses that distinguish them from noncriminals except that they did something forbidden by law and were caught. But just doing something forbidden by law is not a valid pattern of deviant responses because, wittingly or unwittingly, everyone has broken some law and is therefore, in this literal sense, a criminal.

In much the same fashion the label *supervisor* (or *executive*) is meaningless for designating a pattern of responses that validly identifies a category of deviant behavior. About all that supervisors have in common is that they have something to do in organizing or directing the activities of other people. But most people do that in one capacity or another, although the label may not be used. For example, mothers supervise children, older children supervise younger children, physicians supervise patients, and so on. The label *supervisor* is far too broad to be meaningful in specific behavioral terms.

However, if we can specify the particular situation in which the criminal or supervisory behavior must occur, then it is quite likely that we can identify a pattern of deviant responses that make up a valid category of behavior. Instead of talking about criminals, for example, let us consider safecrackers, pickpockets, forgers, or strong-arm robbers. Each of these activities, while proscribed by law, probably has a number of distinctive responses that are common to the activity but uncommon among the general population as well as among other deviant groups, including practitioners of other criminal specialties. Because such requirements as skill, education, or intelligence differ, the number of deviant responses characterizing each group of specialists would differ considerably and thus produce deviant behavior categories defined with varying degrees of sharpness. To put it another way, quite a number of persons in the population could probably be successful strong-arm muggers, but very few would make good safecrackers or forgers. Many of the deviant responses that identify muggers would also be found among many nonmuggers, producing a loosely constituted deviant behavior category and not a few false positive identifications. With safecrackers and forgers our deviant category would be much sharper and the erroneous identifications would be rare. It could be argued that, with a very large number of stimuli that were also vastly different in kind, a clearly defined category of muggers could be produced. This is theoretically probable, but in practical terms the amount of labor that would be involved renders such a demonstration futile.

In much the same manner we must specify the particular situation for supervisors if we hope to identify a meaningful pattern of deviant responses that will distinguish this group. In a banking situation, for example, a supervisor of tellers typically is polite, has detailed knowledge of procedures in financial institutions, gives orders in quiet fashion to his subordinates, and so on. By contrast, the supervisor of oilfield roughnecks is physically active, may roar his orders, may often accompany orders with lurid profanity, and so on. Both are supervisors; yet it would be exceedingly unlikely that both could be fitted into a single deviant class. However, if we differentiate supervisors on the basis of who they supervise and the situation in which the supervision takes place, we should probably find a satisfactory number of deviant responses to differentiate each type of supervisor from others.

PARTIALLY VALID DEVIANT CATEGORIES

The labels *scientist* and *neurotic* for categories of deviant behavior are neither wholly invalid nor valid. The general characteristics of the members of both groups have often been described, but the specific characteristics have not. The result is a vague shifting deviant category difficult to define. There is no trouble with extreme examples—we would very probably agree that Nobel prize winner Marie Curie was a scientist and that boxing champion Joe Louis was not. Much the same may be said of neurotic reactions. The extremes offer no problem in classifying. It is the in-betweens that are troublesome. This is the reason that many investigations avoid the middle or borderline ranges entirely. Studies of academic over- and underachievement, for example, may compare the top 27 per cent with the bottom 27 per cent in grades or scholastic aptitude or, perhaps, those falling one standard deviation below and those one standard deviation above the mean. A clear definition thereby is operationally provided of the over- and underachievement categories.

The same sort of thing could be done with definitions of *scientist* and *neurotic*. *Scientist* might be defined as one possessed of the Ph.D. in certain fields such as astronomy, chemistry, or physics. There would undoubtedly be a good deal of argument, for some would want a less rigid definition of training. Others might want to add "published one or more experimental studies in professional journals" or something else. But eventually a sound definition could be worked out if it were needed. The disagreement that would first prevail would probably be much like the one that must have occurred when the ancient Norsemen used a human foot to measure length and the hand to measure height. Whose foot or whose hand was to be used? It would obviously make a difference, particularly if one were buying or selling something. We still measure in feet but define it by a less variable standard, and we will speak of a horse as so many hands high but define a hand as equal to one-third of a foot or four inches.

With respect to behavior, the problem of adequately defining deviant categories is still with us. All of us, psychologists included, typically look at the label of a category, not at the variability and type of responses behind the label. More than any other science, as Immergluck (1964) has observed, the language of psychology has borrowed heavily from the terminology of daily life. In similar fashion, while we have been quite aware of response variability, our quest for an anchorage, for a place of reference has probably led us to pay less systematic attention to variability in behavior and more attention to the label than we should have. After all, labels are comfortably unchanging while response patterns over periods of time often writhe and swell, churn and shrink like an amoeba in motion. Yet, as Immergluck also noted, "stripped of any metaphysical underpinnings, however, the concept of *variability of behavior* has a definite and useful place in the grammar of science" (1964, p. 277).

Boundaries of deviant behavior categories vary. As Figure 3 shows, the deviant behavior category is defined in terms of the degree of response variability, which may be defined by such dimensions as response intensity, duration, or frequency. This is illustrated in Figure 3 by arrows that start from no response at point A and extend to point D, the theoretically maximum limit of response range. Thus a response may be deviant because the variability is too small, as in range A to B of the diagram, or because variability is too great, as in range C to D—in other words, a handshake may be atypical because of its flaccid absence of pressure or because it is bonecrushing. The normal or nondeviant range of variability, accordingly, is the doughnut-shaped space B to C. These lines are dotted to indicate that the limits are arbitrarily set, permitting the boundaries to expand or contract as a function of the methods used to establish them.

Such expansion or contraction of the boundary lines for deviant-nondeviant behavior may occur as a result of (1) subjective criteria, (2) cultural standards, (3) response measurement techniques, or (4) the manner in which operational criteria are used.

(1) *Subjective criteria.* Different people may use personal

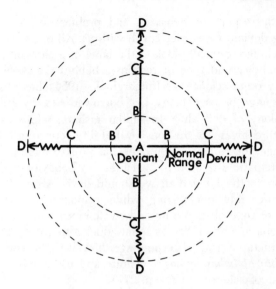

FIG. 3. Variability and deviant response boundaries.

criteria in ascertaining the deviancy or nondeviancy of responses. What is considered to be atypically loud or atypically soft speech, for example, will probably vary a good deal from person to person. Factors such as acute hearing or partial deafness will also influence individual judgments.

(2) *Cultural standards.* The latitude of the normal range will be affected by accepted cultural practices and meanings. Embracing, cheek-kissing, and dancing among men, or eating with the left hand in Moslem countries, are examples.

(3) *Response measurement techniques.* Possible errors of sampling, recording, data analysis, and so on are included here, as well as such things as confusions of stimulus, or response dimensions. For example, with auditory data, sound duration may be important but ignored, or in other instances, pitch and intensity may not be studied separately. Factors such as these can affect the establishment of demarcation lines for deviant behavior categories.

(4) *The manner in which operational criteria are used.* The deviant categories of genius could be set at IQ 140 or 150,

and idiocy at IQ 15 or 25, for example; however, different boundaries would be set in each case. In other cases there may be little or no variability at one end of the range; yet it may not be deviant. Thus, alcoholic intoxication as a deviant state can be defined as 0.2 per cent or more of alcohol in the blood, but zero amount of alcohol in the blood is still normal range. In such instances points A and B. in Figure 3 are identical. The manner in which a deviant state is defined produces such situations.

Within a particular category of deviant behavior are the responses that make it up. We face no great problem in defining these deviant responses. As noted earlier, they may be defined as those responses that depart from some established or standard distribution of responses at a predetermined level of statistical significance, usually the .01 level of confidence. Levels of greater or lesser stringency could also be used. This is a reasonably clear definition and will provide a means of identifying deviant responses, but that is only part of the story. Even when deviant responses are identified, still much more may be said about their various characteristics: how they may appear in a pattern, different values attached to them, the stimuli that evoke them, the assumptions and postulates behind them, etc. These factors of range, scope, significance, and so on are described below, admittedly with occasional minor points of overlap.

ASSUMPTIONS AND POSTULATES
OF THE DEVIATION HYPOTHESIS

1. *Deviant responses are the product, singly or in combination, of past learning, of inherited structure, maturation, or physiological and organic state.* These are the factors that make us individuals, that make us different in appearance and behavior; in short, these are the factors that provide variability.

A Swede learns to speak Swedish, which is one pattern of responses that sets him apart from non-Swedes in the world who cannot. Chromosomal factors are responsible for the hereditary differences of eye fold, skin color, and so on, which make the Swede atypical compared to native Africans or Orientals. He may be an infant, a young adult, or a very aged man, and such maturational factors of growth and decline will be associated at each stage with particular responses that distinguish him from other persons in the world who are at a different stage of development. His physiological and/or organic state may be altered permanently or temporarily—and so will certain responses—as a result of disease, amputated legs, alcohol, gout, bodily injury, drugs, and so forth. The deviant response patterns thus produced may represent a large class which includes many persons or a highly specific one which includes only a person or two.

2. *The total absence or infrequent occurrence of a response(s) that occurs commonly in a comparison group is a deviant response if it meets the requirements of our statistical definition.* The oft-encountered apathy of many schizophrenics, for example, is really a lack of responses; yet it may serve to differentiate schizophrenics from much of the general population or from hypermanic patients. These deviant responses are like those of the dog in the Sherlock Holmes story, *Silver Blaze.* He did nothing in the night time, and that, as Holmes remarked, was the curious incident.

3. *Characteristics that were produced by previous responses are also considered to be deviant responses even if relatively fixed, provided they meet the usual statistical requirements of definition.* These may be a result of occupation, such as the bump on the side of the fingertip of those who write for long periods with a pen or the enlarged and heavily calloused right hand of a blacksmith. They may also arise from some bodily defect, like the cyanosis resulting from a heart damaged long ago or exophthalmia due to a malfunctioning thyroid gland. They are due to past responses. In similar fashion, a 70-inch waistline would be the result of

many thousands of previous responses related to the ingestion of food, exercise, and so forth. Deviant characteristics may even be prenatal in origin, such as birth defects that occurred as a consequence of responses in utero to X rays, diseases, or other stimuli that disrupted the normal maturational pattern.

Such characteristics, strictly speaking, are not responses in the sense that they necessarily result from stimuli occurring at the present moment. But they exist because of past stimuli and past responses and, as such, they are included in the term deviant response. The term, admittedly, is used in a very broad sense.

4. *Deviant responses may evoke stimuli which produce other deviant responses.* Frequent and copious ingestion of food, as noted above, may be a deviant response. Such gorging is atypical and may, in turn, produce other responses such as chronic dyspepsia, which is also a deviant state. In time, the devotion to gluttony may result in an immense paunch and heavy fat deposits elsewhere on the body. The extreme corpulence may then produce deviant locomotion as represented by a manner of walking that is clearly outside the normal range.

5. *As usually measured, deviant responses will typically be found in more than one category of behavior.* Deviant responses will usually be shared by several other behavior categories that may or may not be deviant. This is a function of how deviant responses and particular deviant categories are identified.

Let us assume that we have three hypothetical, broad deviant states as depicted in Figure 4. A mental retardate (deviant intellectual state) and a hyperthyroid patient (deviant organic state) may both be highly impulsive, a response that is characteristic of several deviant emotional states. The single response of impulsivity is, accordingly, found in all three classes of deviant behavior.

While several categories may share certain deviant

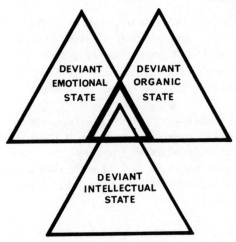

FIG. 4. Example of overlap in deviant behavior categories.

responses, not every member of these categories will necessarily manifest such responses nor will the responses necessarily be present at all times. That is, every schizophrenic
does not hallucinate and hallucinations are not continuously
present among those who do.

The overlap in Figure 4 is presented in only two dimensions and for only three deviant categories. Actually, there
are many categories, and the overlap of certain responses, like
the categories themselves, will be manifested in depth as well
as length, width, and time. In comparison, consider a truck-
load of eels; the ones on the bottom, pressed by the weight
of those above, change little in shape or position. The eels
above them shorten and lengthen, underlie and overlie each
other in their wriggling, and change in place and time. The
degree of such change will increase from bottom to top.

In similar fashion, deviant responses, whether overlapping
other categories or not, may appear to be fairly fixed or
rather changeable. Such overlap may mean that the deviant
categories have something in common with each other, something perhaps undiscovered. They may tap the same basic
condition. In other cases, the deviant responses may appear
in a number of categories as an artifact of our statistical iden-

tification. A difference in the distribution of two sets of responses at the 1 per cent level of confidence indicates high probability but not absolute certainty that the difference is valid. A much higher level of statistical significance could be used, but then many, perhaps all, potentially useful deviant responses would be lost unless one had very large groups and a very large number and types of stimuli. This aspect boils down to a question of practicality—shall we use a yardstick or a micrometer or something in between in a given situation?

In other instances, the deviant responses are shared by several categories for reasons that are well understood. The great precision with which a surgeon handles an assortment of small instruments sets him apart from most people but not necessarily from engravers or etchers, who also handle quite similar instruments with great precision.

Finally, it should be noted that the basis for comparison of responses may determine if a response is deviant in several categories or even if it is deviant at all. Argentines or Swedes typically may kick a volleyball tossed at them or they may butt it with their heads. In contrast, Americans typically will catch or bat it with their hands. Experience with national pastimes—soccer in the one case and basketball or volleyball in the other—make the difference. Thus, whether the response is deviant depends upon the comparisons made.

6. *Deviant responses may vary in frequency.* This facet of deviant responding has two aspects. The number of deviant responses will vary from category to category, although defined in the same manner, and the frequency of their appearance may vary. One class of deviant behavior may be made up of several thousand identified deviant responses while another class may have only a few dozen. In rare instances, only a single deviant response may define the category—total blindness, for example. But even such instances will have associated deviant responses.

A deviant response may be also defined in terms of its frequency. Everyone blinks his eyes, for example, but the anxiety neurotic blinks far more frequently, as Meyer, Bahrick, and Fitts (1953) showed. A tic may occur once per minute or once each hour.

7. *Deviant responses may vary in intensity.* Fever is a deviant response; it may be low grade (100° F.) or high (104° F.). A person who always shouts in ordinary conversation would be also exhibiting deviancy by means of response intensity. In many instances the response categories used can mask this characteristic. Response options, such as *like-dislike* or *agree-disagree,* compress very strong or very mild reactions into one of the two choices permitted. Since some deviant responses are deviant only because of intensity, compressed response options may conceal deviancy.

8. *Deviant responses may vary in duration.* That is, they may be permanent, like a club foot, or temporary, like drug-induced hallucinations; they may also be recurrent, like many transitory delusions.

9. *Deviant responses and the stimuli that produce them vary in breadth.* This function of the identification technique is used in ferreting out the responses.

a. The stimulus may be highly specific. A leaf falls in front of your face and you blink your eyes. Most reflexes have such specific stimuli and specific responses.

b. The stimulus may be highly specific and the response very broad. When shouted, the word *fire* is a brief change of sound waves in the air, but the response pattern may be highly complex—that is, the response is manifested in instructing people how to leave a building, telephoning the fire department, taking down fire extinguishers, and so forth. Other specific stimuli, such as the smell of smoke or a glimpse of flames, could produce similar broad response patterns. Past learning is typically involved where specific stimuli evoke a complex response series.

c. The stimuli may be very broad and the response highly specific. A person may spend a day in various pleasant activities—swimming, basking in the sun, savoring a gourmet dinner in the evening—at bedtime he simply says, "Wonderful day!" Such situations are usually due to a greatly compressed or arbitrarily established response category. This situation is typical where *like-dislike, true-false, agree-disagree,* and similar responses are specified.

d. The stimuli may be very broad and the response pattern very broad. Growing up in a certain family, living in a certain neighborhood, attending certain schools, and so forth shape behavior to such an extent that it is virtually inevitable for the scion of such a family to go to an Ivy League school and pursue a particular course of study, and then to embark on a career, perhaps in law, with a certain type of firm, with further predictable responses in his life pattern.

This example is itself wide in scope in order to emphasize the point that breadth of stimuli may be broad in the sense of extending over long periods of time and/or broad in terms of kind or variety. Obviously such factors as learning, heredity, and maturation may all be involved as stimulus sources of such breath.

10. *The sharpness with which deviant response categories are defined will depend upon the validity and preciseness that characterize the external criteria used for identification purposes.* Until less than a century ago, all severe emotional disturbances were cast into a single, gross deviant behavior category—*madness.* We now have considerably more specific categories of disturbed behavior; yet the achievement of greater precision is still much to be desired. It may be noted that one way the Deviation Hypothesis could have heuristic value would be its emphasis in a wide pattern of deviant responses, not just key symptoms, providing thereby a means of sharpening deviant behavior categories.

But to take another example, it is possible to define, fuzzily, a deviant category composed of *forgers.* The category can be somewhat more sharply drawn by dividing the category in two by means of external behavioral criteria. One group would consist of those convicted of forgery who are the "penmen," those who copy signatures with accuracy for fraudulent purposes. The other group would consist of those who specialize in passing forged checks, called "paperhangers" in the trade, who are really confidence men and usually lack a penman's skills. And it is probable that even further divisions of the forger class could be made.

11. *A variety of stimuli obtained from any sense modality may be used in producing deviant responses.* Visual stimuli are most often used, as I have indicated. (1961, p. 331ff) But auditory stimuli can be used, and there seems to be no reason why other stimuli for other sense modalities could not be similarly employed. Some would be cumbersome, such as olfactory and gustatory stimuli, because of adaptation effects and because at times they tend to linger. But in all likelihood, deviant responses could be produced.

It must be emphasized that all stimuli do not necessarily produce equally useful or an equal number of deviant responses.[4] However, by careful search and hard work, one should be able to find deviant responses for one sense modality that had equal power of discrimination as deviant responses in another sense modality. In other words, the particular item content is not important. Adams and Berg (1961c) demonstrated this by showing that certain auditory stimuli in the form of meaningless sounds were about as good as certain visual stimuli in producing deviant response sets for identifying schizophrenia. It is even possible to use affective tone as a deviant response (Adams and Berg, 1961a).

As long as deviant response sets are produced, it does

4. This point has occasionally been misunderstood. It has been assumed that I have meant such various things as that the stimulus content of test items is unnecessary or that any and all stimulus content is interchangeable with and as useful as any other. Norman (1963), for example, showed that test item content was important and then, by a strange richochet of logic, asserted that this meant that the Deviation Hypothesis was inadequate. Rorer (1965) said much the same thing, although he did state my position more fully. The interested reader will find my position on item content developed in a chapter in Bass and Berg (1959), p. 89ff). It must be acknowledged that the chapter's title, "The Unimportance of Test Item Content," may be misleading unless the material in the chapter is read in full. Perhaps a less abbreviated title should have been used.

not matter what the particular kind of stimulus is nor what sense modality is used. This does not mean, however, that all deviant response sets thus obtained will be equally useful or even applicable to a designated category of deviant behavior. They may be useful for differentiating a given deviant behavior class from others. But if they are not useful for one class, they may be useful for some other.

Stimulus ambiguity is an important factor for eliciting many forms of deviant response sets. This is particularly true of ordinary response sets as they appear in psychological tests, as Cronbach (1946, 1950) has observed. Where stimulus materials are highly structured, subjects are likely to respond on the basis of knowledge, not on the basis of set. Most Americans, for example, would respond *false* or *disagree* to the statement, "Benedict Arnold is generally regarded as one of the most popular heroes of the Revolutionary War." Since the majority of literate Americans presumably know the correct answer, there would be little opportunity for sets, like acquiescence, to appear. A small percentage of American subjects would find this item unstructured because of ignorance or confusion and respond *true* or *agree*. This would be revealing, just as it was when a famous American industrialist of great wealth but limited education testified in a courtroom that Benedict Arnold was an English novelist. But for most subjects no set could be elicited for such highly structured items. I discuss this point elsewhere (1959).

12. *The number of deviant responses and the degree to which they depart from the norm varies within a given category of deviant behavior and relates to the severity or amount of deviation.* This aspect of deviant responding relates to items 6 and 7 described earlier. When compared to normal children, for example, severely retarded children exhibited a greater frequency of deviant responses than children who are moderately retarded mentally (Cieutat, 1960). Groups of young children exhibit more deviant responses compared to adults than groups of older children (Hesterly, 1963; Hesterly and Berg, 1958).

In addition to the number of deviant responses as an indicator of severity, the duration of a deviant response or condition may at times also reflect severity. A fever of 104° F. may not mean much if it lasts only a few hours. Children often run such high fevers for short periods, as every parent knows. But a high fever that lasts for days is an indication that something serious is wrong. It should be noted that frequency and degree of departure from the norm of deviant responses are said to *relate* to severity or amount of deviation, not to be perfectly correlated. This cautious wording is used because in the case of schizophrenia, as Harris (1958) found, deviant responses to a series of abstract designs distinguished schizophrenics from normals fairly well, but severity of schizophrenia did not relate to the frequency of deviant responses. It seems probable that the validity of ratings for schizophrenia —mild, moderate, and severe—may account for his negative results, but this explanation is more speculative than established. Indeed, the category of schizophrenia may itself be faulty.

13. *Deviant responses, singly or in patterns, may have positive or negative value attached to them.* Significance or criticalness or special meaning is associated with one or more deviant responses in some instances. We are not concerned if a person strongly dislikes a particular abstract design when most people like it. But if a person runs a mile in less than four minutes or if he solemnly asserts that he is God, we may indicate positive or negative value by our applause or alarm. All three responses are deviant, but we view the latter two as significant.

Many such valued responses are culture-bound, a product of social patterns. Thus, in our society, we might send an adult away for psychiatric examination if he were eating raw worms. In certain parts of Africa, we might share his meal if we grew up in the same tribal culture. Under other conditions, deviant responses may be positive or negatively valued according to circumstances or membership in a particular deviant group. For example, a knife plunged into living human flesh may mean a surgeon or a psychopathic Jack the Ripper.

14. *The predictive accuracy obtained when identifying a deviant response pattern will depend upon the sampling method used.* Most classes of deviant behavior will involve thousands, perhaps hundreds of thousands, of responses. Even if all of them were known, which is most unlikely, it would not be feasible to examine them all. Consequently, we must resort to sampling, which can be done in a variety of ways.

Purely for illustrative purposes, let us imagine that the total response repertoire of humanity is an immense hill of wheat—several thousand carloads. Each grain of wheat represents a response that may be deviant or within the normal range. Previous experience has taught us that while each grain of wheat differs, we can accept a wide range of such differences and call them *normal.* Wheat grains differ in size, shape, color, ripeness, hardness, odor, texture, taste, and so on. In some instances, these differences may be so marked that they exceed our acceptable range of variation, and these extreme cases represent our deviant wheat. Some kinds of differences, while we are aware of them, do not concern us especially; for example, some grains may be very hard or irregular in shape, and we may merely comment on it or perhaps request a reduction in purchase price. Other deviant characteristics, however, may alarm us. Wheat grains that smell of mildew may be toxic because of fungi or mold, or very soft grains that cannot be milled may be present. To us, these are critical or significant forms of deviation, so we insist on keeping such grains apart from the others, and we refuse them. In still other instances, a portion of the grain may be unusual because of remarkable flavor, size, or other characteristics, and we may pay a premium for this grain.

Our problem is to sample our hill of wheat in order to identify any deviant portions within it. We have learned in the past that deviant wheat grains are not evenly distributed throughout the hill but are usually found in a general cluster of deviant and nondeviant grains in one section. This is largely because wheat from a particular field is dumped onto our hill in one mass. The deviant wheat may have resulted, singly or in combination, from the environment of the field (rain, sun, soil, and so on), which provided ideal or bad growing conditions; from heredity in the form of very good or very poor genetic strains; from organic or physiological changes due to disease, injury, or other causes. But whatever the reason for the deviancy, our task is to identify the deviant wheat by sampling techniques.

Our grain samplers are thin-walled tubes of various lengths and diameters that we can thrust into the hill of wheat; the sample is the grains retained in the tube when it is withdrawn. Let us assume further that our hill of wheat is divided into sections like a loaf of sliced bread and that we need a separate set of samplers for each slice because one particular set of samplers can operate only within one slice or section.

In our analogy, then, human responses in toto are represented by the grains of wheat making up our hill, and our test instruments (such as the Rorschach, MMPI, or TAT) are represented by the grain samplers. The various sense modalities employed by our test instruments as stimulus materials are represented by the slices or sections of the hill. With this example in mind, let us examine our typical practices in assessing personality and predicting deviant behavior. Nearly all tests use visual stimulus materials exclusively to sample response patterns—that is, they work within only one slice or section of our behavioral repertoire. A few tests use auditory stimuli and thus sample another different slice, but such tests are few in number. Several other tests sample still other slices by using kinesthetic or olfactory stimuli, but they are very rare indeed. Obviously, we could obtain a more complete understanding of behavior from response samples drawn from more sections, by using more sense modalities.

The problem is further complicated by the nature of our sampling instruments and our techniques of using them. To turn again to our grain sampler analogy, we may use a tube that is short, long, or in between. The tube's diameter may be narrow like a rod, wide like a drainage pipe, or somewhere in between. The tube may even have a few curves and bends in it. In handling our tubes we may thrust them in the hill of wheat from the top, from the side, or at an angle within the confines of our slice. Our technique may also include thrusting the tube in the hill for only half its length or ramming it in full-length and up to our elbows. Finally, we should note that it takes less time and is less work to use a short tube of narrow diameter *or* to thrust a long, narrow tube only part way into the hill. But fewer deviant responses will be identified with such instruments and techniques. Long, wide sampling tubes, in contrast, are cumbersome and time-consuming for sampling purposes, but they yield better samples. As indicated below, the same sort of thing may be said of psychological tests as samplers of behavior.

a. *If only a few deviant responses are sampled, prediction of a larger pattern or class of deviant behavior is likely to be quite poor.* The Archimedes Spiral Aftereffect, for example, seeks to identify organic brain damage by means of stimuli in the form of a rotating spiral (Freeman and Josey, 1949; Price and Deabler, 1955). The spiral may be rotated at several speeds and in forward or backward directions. The spiral may seem to expand, contract, or remain unchanged when rotation is stopped, thereby providing the basis for a few responses that may possibly be deviant. This is a very small range of stimuli, and few responses can result. There are bound to be many false positive and false negative identifications, particularly so when it is kept in mind that the deviant behavior category, "organic brain damage," is itself poorly delineated. The Spiral Aftereffect would be much more useful as part of a battery of stimuli. Standing alone, it is much like our short, narrow grain sampler.

b. *If a large number of deviant responses are identified, prediction of deviant behavior categories will be improved.* This is like our long, wide grain sampler tube which is more likely to include deviant grains if there are any. In this sense the MMPI is probably a better predictor than shorter inventories because it uses visual stimuli in the form of more than 500 items.

c. *Defining deviant responses in terms of a narrow range of variability will increase false negative and decrease false positive predictions. The use of a broad range of variability will decrease false negative and increase false positive predictions.* To return to our hill of wheat analogy, if we say that we will accept only grain of a certain color, size, odor, and so forth as *normal,* we shall get better grain but we shall also get less of it, because we reject a lot of perfectly good grain. On the other hand, if we are willing to accept considerable variation in grain color, size, and other characteristics, we shall get much more grain, but a larger portion of it will be substandard or poor. This would be analogous in psycho-logical testing to defining deviant responses at a .05, .01, or .001 level of statistical significance. The problem is the familiar one of establishing a practical cut-off line for a given purpose.

15. *Deviant behavior patterns sometimes include highly visible or dominant responses that may serve to obscure or overshadow other responses in the pattern that may themselves be equally or more significant.* Undue attention given to such dominant responses may serve to weaken prediction. Gibberish, a vapid expression, and an inability to understand instructions are examples of dominant responses found in the deviant class of behavior we call *idiocy.* Yet emphasis on these responses to the exclusion of other equally meaningful but less visible deviant responses has caused more than one congenitally deaf person of normal intellect to be classed as an idiot.

Hand preference is another such highly visible response that has served as a snare for the unwary, for southpaws have long been viewed as somehow different. Even in ancient times the *sinister* was the left hand, connoting deviancy, while the *dexter* was the right hand and normal. It is true that, when compared to normals, a greater incidence of left-handedness is found among mental defectives, neurotics, epileptics, and other deviant groups (Hildreth, 1949; Palmer, 1964; Wile, 1934). However, while the incidence of sinistrality is greater for such groups, it cannot be called extremely high. Furthermore, most studies have not paid much attention to the significance of degrees of handedness, and the degree of hand preference has received little attention in studies of positively valued deviant groups. Are highly creative persons often left handers? What about geniuses, great leaders, and similar outstanding people? To revert to our hill of wheat example, we may be so keenly aware of black grains that we largely ignore deviations in other characteristics of the grains that may be far more meaningful.

16. *The total pattern of deviant responses has vastly greater importance for research purposes than those deviant responses customarily singled out as the "key" or "critical" or "significant" ones.* This is a corollary of the previous item but with a special and important application. The key or significant deviant responses in schizophrenia include flattened affect, bizarre thoughts, and, at times, delusions, hallucinations, and so forth. We use these symptoms as boundary stones to delimit what we call schizophrenia. They are the deviant responses that give us pause, arouse concern, and cause alarm. But are they schizophrenia?

As should be now quite apparent, schizophrenia includes myriad other deviant responses, most of which we are unaware, and other responses we may be aware of but may lightly dismiss. In our research activities we concentrate on the key symptoms and thus become prisoners of our conceptual scheme. Like inmates marching lockstep in a circle in a prison exercise yard, we typically move in our study of schizophrenia from affect to neologism to delusion and so on around again to affect to neoglogism and on and on.

A vague, dawning awareness of the artificial boundaries impels an occasional researcher to stop the circular motion and seek meaning through some other direction. He may move backward and find something intriguing but of minor importance, like the schoolboy who discovers that *evil* in reverse spells *live.* Our researcher may then move backward *and* forward across the key symptom pattern and find meaning such as that in the palindrome, "Able was I ere I saw Elba." Or he may move up and down and find meaning as in an acrostic. He looks closely and from a distance; he arranges and rearranges—always on one corner of the table even though that corner is only a small part of the table. He zigs and zags; he indulges in gyrations, combinations, and permutations; he may eventually come up with something a bit more meaningful about schizophrenia. He may even trespass a bit beyond the self-imposed boundaries of his table corner and come up with something of importance.

THE NEED FOR A CONCEPTUAL BREAKTHROUGH

The point is, we are in need of a conceptual breakthrough, a new way of looking at schizophrenia and all other classes of deviant behavior. Such a conceptual breakthrough could undoubtedly be achieved in several ways. But I have been convinced, along with several of my coworkers, that applying the Deviation Hypothesis is one means of penetrating the "key symptom" barriers to effective research.

Deviant behavior classes should be based on deviant response sets, not merely key symptoms. The Deviation Hypothesis emphasizes that deviant behavior patterns are general in the sense that those responses regarded as significant for identifying a particular category of atypical behavior do not exist in isolation. Yet most research, by and large, has concentrated on specific, highly visible, or key portions of the pattern. This is like studying Illinois by an intensive examination of Chicago's Loop. The Loop is indeed part of Illinois but Illinois is much more than the Loop.

For some years my co-worker, E. H. Barnes, and I have felt that cleaner and more sharply defined categories of deviant behavior could be obtained from the use of broad deviant response set patterns than from phenomenological criteria narrowly focused upon a relatively small number of key responses (symptoms). This would require examination of all deviant responses that can be identified, both the critical and noncritical ones, as has been suggested earlier (Berg, 1955, 1957, 1961). We believe that such an approach would incite new explorations and provide opportunities for seeing relationships hitherto obscured.

For example, Barnes (personal communication) was

recently comparing the responses to a series of abstract designs made by normal subjects and by groups of patients diagnosed as character disorders, process, and reactive schizophrenia.[5] He noticed that, when compared to normals, the reactive schizophrenics and the character disorder patients exhibited a number of deviant responses identical for both groups, but these shared deviant responses were not found among the process schizophrenics. No overweening conclusion dare be advanced in any way for this admittedly minor observation; after all, the deviant responses examined were very few and the stimulus materials employed were exceedingly narrow in range. What is important, for illustrative purposes, is that Barnes was not looking at responses like neologisms, hallucinations, or other key symptoms. He merely noted that certain abstract designs in the Perceptual Reaction Test (Berg, Hunt, and Barnes, 1949) were disliked by many members of certain deviant groups and not by members of other groups.

This obviously has possible heuristic value in the sense that it could serve as the starting point for a breakthrough. (It could also lead to wasted effort.) Study of a sizable series of responses made to different stimuli by members of such deviant behavior categories could perhaps specify these differences. If successful, this could then lead to a reshuffling of deviant categories and an abolition of some of our present labels for deviant states.

It is within the bounds of possibility that character disorders and reactive schizophrenia are part of a larger, hitherto unsuspected pattern of deviant responses. We could also speculate on other possibilities in similar fashion. What could result from such an attack on the problem of sharply defining deviant classes of behavior would be definitions—deviant classes of behavior in terms of a broad pattern of deviant responses, not just a handful of significant ones. Conceivably, then, a number of categories of deviant behavior could be

5. Process schizophrenia takes years to develop and the symptoms are more pronounced with the passage of time. Reactive schizophrenia typically appears in a short period of time and occurs as a result of acute stress. The likelihood of recovery is considerably better for the reactive than for the process schizophrenic.

reconstituted into broader classes in some instances and narrower classes in others. New classes would probably emerge in some cases, while familiar classes would vanish. It is also conceivable that clues concerning etiology might appear by a study of broad deviant response patterns. At the very least, the likelihood for discerning common threads among a number of deviant categories of behavior would be enhanced.

RESEARCH METHODS FOR
THE DEVIATION HYPOTHESIS

THE CRITERION GROUP METHOD

A variety of approaches may be used in studying deviant response sets. The method most often used in connection with the Deviation Hypothesis, as Edwards (1959b) phrased it, is the criterion group method. This method was used by Strong (1935) in constructing the Vocational Interest Blank and by Hathaway and McKinley (1943) for the MMPI.

In using the criterion group method, both a criterion group and a deviant group are needed. The criterion group may be drawn randomly from the general population,[6] representing people in general, or it may be any other group that serves as a basis for comparison. The deviant group is a special segment of the general population that has been identified by valid external criteria, as discussed earlier in this chapter. A series of stimulus patterns of the sort described on page 151 is administered to both the criterion and the deviant groups, and the responses are separately tabulated and statistically compared. The deviant responses will be those that

6. In this connection it may be noted that the category of "normal subjects" is really a courtesy designation. A small number of clearly deviant individuals are often unwittingly included in a normal group unless special precautions are taken. The result is that categories of normal subjects are often less sharply defined than is desirable.

differentiate the two groups at some established level of significance, such as the .01 level of confidence. If a sufficient number of deviant responses are obtained, a scale may be constructed to measure the deviant behavior category, if this is desired.

The advantages of the criterion group method are convenience and a presumed awareness of the validity criteria employed for identifying the deviant and nondeviant groups. Some drudgery is involved in making the response comparisons for the groups, but, on the whole, the method is reasonably convenient. As emphasized earlier, validity criteria for defining deviant groups are often a problem. The criterion group method should require the researcher to be aware of this factor. If he defines a deviant group such as schizophrenia in terms of staff diagnostic ratings, he will know that his criteria contain a clear element of subjectivity. In contrast, he may define a deviant category like obesity as weight 25 per cent or more above the average for persons of the same age, sex, and height, thereby providing a much more objective definition. This is not to say, of course, that schizophrenia can be defined with complete objectivity at the present time or that the above definition of obesity would be acceptable to all. The intention here is merely to point out that the criterion group method should force the researcher to ponder his criteria for deviant behavior categories. Even so, errors have been made in the past and undoubtedly will be made in the future regarding such validity criteria.

The shortcomings of the criterion group method center in the nature of the criterion group composition. It is difficult to control all variables in the criterion and the deviant groups except the one relating to deviancy. In the absence of such controls, prediction will be reasonably accurate only for groups comparable to the groups used in the original study. Like factor analytic and other approaches, the criterion group method is strictly limited by what is put into the study in the form of stimulus-response materials and so forth. Berg (1961, p. 342f) and Edwards (1959b, p. 102f) offer discussions of the criterion group method.

THE GRIGG-THORPE DESIGN

In a study of the Deviation Hypothesis, Grigg and Thorpe (1960) administered items from the Gough Adjective Check List to 1400 entering freshmen at the University of Texas. They prepared a deviant response score by counting the number of times that commonly checked adjectives were *not* chosen or uncommonly checked adjectives *were* chosen. At the close of the academic year, the deviant response scores were studied for those students who reported to the Student Health Center or the University Counseling Bureau for psychiatric treatment, for personal problems, or for vocational counseling. As hypothesized, the deviant response scores were significantly higher for those students who were treated for emotional disturbances.

In the Grigg-Thorpe design, behavioral criteria for some class of deviant behavior are established in advance and the subjects assign themselves to the deviant class over a period of time. Thus, for their particular study, Grigg and Thorpe said in effect that persons who are disturbed emotionally to the extent that they will voluntarily seek treatment are deviant and, in terms of the Deviation Hypothesis, should exhibit a significantly high frequency of deviant responses on the Gough Adjective Check List. This is a clear statement of behavioral criteria. In addition to this advantage, it is also feasible to define other deviant behavior categories and permit subjects to assign themselves, as was done in the case of those seeking treatment.

Several disadvantages to the Grigg-Thorpe design may be mentioned. One is that a very large pool of subjects is required to obtain significant results. This is necessary to compensate for subjects who may meet the established criteria for membership in a deviant class of behavior but who are not identified because of the technique used. Some subjects in the Grigg-Thorpe study may have sought private professional treatment or may have worried along without formal treatment. These subjects would not appear at one of the University of Texas clinics and, accordingly, would not be included in the study. This would not affect the validity criteria for those subjects who actually did appear at the clinics and were identified as deviant, but it does mean that the deviant group studied was much smaller than it would have been had all cases been identifiable.

Another disadvantage, while not crucial, is the time lag that often must occur while subjects assign themselves to a deviant behavior category. This is not merely the idle period between obtaining deviant response scores and actual study of the deviant group. More important is the possibility that the time period may be so long that behavioral characteristics may change in some instances. In the Grigg-Thorpe study, for example, some subjects may have revealed only a few deviant responses well within the normal range at the time of testing, but by the end of the academic year the stress of college life may have caused them to seek treatment. Their deviant response scores may have increased, but this would not be known. Then, too, other cases may be missed because treatment was sought *after* the end of the established time limit. Despite the cumbersomeness of a large number of subjects and the possible disadvantage of the time lag, the Grigg-Thorpe design provides many attractive research features for the study of deviant behavior.

FACTOR ANALYTIC METHODS

Factor analytic approaches have often been suggested to those working with deviant response sets. These techniques are quite feasible. However, one problem involves accurately naming the deviant response class meaningfully when the factors have been isolated, and a second is that the particular factor technique used often governs what may be found. Adams (1960b) factor analyzed data from several deviant response classes and obtained four factors that he called *general variability, acquiescence, negativism,* and *hostility expression.* His findings lent strong support to the idea of using deviant response sets for measuring personality characteristics.

A provocative approach was suggested by Bass (1957) in his iterative inverse factor analytic procedure. He proposed that persons and items be interchanged to provide a rapid method of clustering persons according to their patterns of responses to the items. Since the items may be quite heterogeneous in form and content, Bass's technique would allow the use of many expressions of deviant response sets obtained from stimuli of several sense modalities. It would be quite possible to isolate deviant response classes by this technique; however, knowing what they represented would be exceedingly difficult, if not virtually impossible, in many cases.

In order to apply the iterative inverse factor procedure effectively, it is necessary to know all the significant personal characteristics of the subjects used in the study, if the factors are to be named accurately. This would be a simple matter for some factors but not for others. It would be easy to identify subjects clustered on the basis of males versus females, advanced age versus youth, and so on, since such personal characteristics could be readily determined. But other clusterings might represent alcoholism or irritability or ulcers or high sociability, and such characteristics might not be known. Such personal characteristics could conceivably be ascertained for a large group of persons, but, to say the least, it would often be exceedingly difficult to do so.

At the present time the criterion group method appears simpler, less time consuming, and more specific in the identification of deviant response patterns if valid criteria are used. For the present stage of deviant response set research, factor analytical techniques will probably be most useful when combined with other investigative procedures. But eventually, it is hoped, a means will be found for conveniently identifying a large number of personal characteristics of subjects. Then the most promising of all techniques is likely to be the iterative inverse factor analytic approach.

RESEARCH OF THE FUTURE

In the future, new research approaches will undoubtedly be used to study deviant behavior, and present designs will be elegantly reshaped. But the pressing need of the future, as it is in the present, is the identification of a large number of response measures that can be used for the study of deviant response sets. It seems likely that the most significant response measures will be those found inside the body, such as changes in blood chemistry, in physiological relationships, and in tissues and internal organs. While it may be a long time before the significance of such internal responses for overt behavior is fully understood, it seems probable that the key is inside the organism proper. After all, responses involving marks on a paper to indicate *true* or *disagree* or vocalizations or muscular movements are essentially external and rather remote from the basic internal source. Behind externally observed behavior like social dominance, for example, are cellular changes in neural and other tissues produced by past learning and endocrine and other physiological factors. A full understanding of such processes will enable us to explain, not merely to predict, deviant behavior.

Upon reflection, it seems reasonable to forecast that a theory of personality can eventually be developed by the use of deviant response sets in various patterns and combinations, and that, from such a theory, the laws and principles of personality can be established. This is perhaps far in the future, but we may note that thirty years ago Stagner (1937, p. 117) equated the concept of "set" with personality traits.

Currently, we are forced to work with ill-defined categories of behavior in most instances. However, it seems feasible that when valid categories are established for many areas of deviant behavior, progress in developing a system of laws of personality will be rapid. This will take many new response measures and will require detailed understanding of response variability for individual responses and for response patterns. That is why such emphasis is placed on *deviant* response sets. Because some variability is found even in highly individual characteristics and responses (fingerprints, for example), every response is deviant within a certain range. It is this range of variability that gives us individuality at one level and membership in broader categories at another.

SUMMARY

The Deviation Hypothesis states that deviant behavior patterns are general in the sense that those responses that are regarded as being significant for identifying a particular category of atypicality in behavior do not exist in isolation. Those responses that are regarded as being significant for a particular category of deviant behavior are associated with a number of other deviant responses that are not regarded as being significant for that particular category of behavioral atypicality. Thus the dominant or significant responses that are commonly used to designate a class of deviant behavior are accompanied by a large number of other responses to which little or no attention is paid. These other responses explain why a large variety of stimulus materials obtained from a number of sense modalities can be used to predict deviant behavior by means of psychological tests. This is a reflection of the "Deviation Trait," which may be defined as "the tendency for members of a valid specified category of deviant behavior to give many kinds of other responses that exceed a validly defined range of variability." A number of assumptions and postulates are associated with the Deviation Hypothesis as a research concept and explanation for the identification and measurement of deviant behavior.

SEVEN / HENRY E. ADAMS AND
JOEL R. BUTLER

The Deviation
Hypothesis: A Review
of the Evidence

This chapter is an attempt to assess the data relevant to
Berg's Deviation Hypothesis (1955, 1957) and to provide for
the following evaluations: (1) the *accuracy* of the hypothesis
in terms of its reliability and validity, (2) its *psychological
relevance*, (3) *generality*, or the extent to which the hypothesis enters into other, broader behavioral responses classes,
and (4) *utility*, or the extent to which the hypothesis is used
either in theory or application. This last evaluative aspect in
reality is the primary justification for the hypothesis. With
these four evaluative questions to serve as guides by which
we may determine the character of the evidence, we will attempt a review of the rationale and of the experimental
results of the Deviation Hypothesis.

The idea of a pattern of responses that is characteristic
of and yet distinguishes man from his fellows is not new.
Certainly the "life style" of Alfred Adler's (1927) theory
fitted such a concept, and, while such a notion was broader
than the Deviation Hypothesis, it was much less subject to
experimental analysis. On the other hand, the Deviation
Hypothesis seeks to encompass such conceptions as Cronbach's (1946) response set, which is defined as "a tendency
causing a person consistently to give different responses to
test items that he would when the same content is presented
in different form," or "response styles," as they are termed by

Jackson and Messick (1958). Social desirability responses (Edwards, 1957a) or such response biases as acquiescence and extremeness would also fit in the statement of the Deviation Hypothesis.

At any rate, the concepts, or perhaps the problems, of set or *Einstellung*, dispositions, attitudes, bias responses, readiness, response preference, response systems, systematic error, and the like have long been prominent in psychological research and theory. In general, they have served to aid in the prediction and generalization in SR and RR relationships. It was recognized early that such individual differences in response habits might well introduce a systematic error particularly in studies of perception (George, 1917). Principles in perception and in cognition (Gardner, Holzman, Klein, Linton, and Spence, 1959) have been studied as stylistic tendencies in cognitive behavior with the results summarized by Gardner and his associates (1959) and termed *cognitive controls*. An excellent review of these stylistic tendencies as found in the MMPI is supplied by Wiggins (1962). Gloye (1964) has a briefer but straightforward commentary on the same problem. In Wiggins and Rumrill (1959) special attention is given to the Social Desirability Variable. (*See* Chapters 2 and 3 by Edwards.)

It has been suggested that these consistencies in cognitive organization may possibly account for the manifestation of response set (Jackson and Messick, 1958). While Forehand (1962) was unable to show the relationship between response styles and the general stylistic tendencies of perception and cognition because of his limited sampling of cognitive behavior, he did demonstrate, however, that the extreme response tendencies in one instrument were significantly related to similarly defined tendencies in another instrument. In the same study, Forehand evidenced restraint in generalizing the concept of acquiescence as a common trait to describe response tendencies and held that acquiescence as well as response perseveration may be studied as constructs but only as they specifically relate to a given test.

In a review of the measurement of deviant behavior by

means of deviant response sets, Berg (1959) set forth the relationship of set and human behavior when choice behavior is compared to the normal probability distribution (Berg and Rapaport, 1954; Goodfellow, 1940; Lorge, 1937; Robinson, 1933; Ross and Kohl, 1948; Singer and Young, 1941). Berg makes the point that a wide array of evidence indicates that response biases are quite stable and doubtless occur in psychological tests as well as other areas of responding. Quite likely such biases affect the validity and reliability of tests as well as constitute a problem in classification of an individual's total behavior pattern.

The tendency to respond with a consistent set includes various ways of behaving such as gambling, acquiescence, evasiveness, caution-incaution, criticalness, and indecision (Bass, 1955; Chapman and Campbell, 1957; Cohn, 1952; Cronbach, 1946, 1950; Fredericksen and Messick, 1958; Guilford, 1954; Howard and Diesenhaus, 1965; Jackson, Messick, and Solley, 1957; Rubin-Rabson, 1954; Shelley, 1955). Indeed, deviant response sets appear to be limited only by the varying stimulus patterns that allow for their produciton. The stimuli to which deviant response patterns have been evoked are widely diverse and include the Rorschach, Thematic Apperception Test (TAT), Minnesota Multiphasic Personality Inventory (MMPI), Perceptual Reaction Test (PRT), the autokinetic phenomenon, the Archimedes Spiral Aftereffect, embedded figures, tilting rooms, the amount of body sway, and food aversions (Berg and Collier, 1953; Eysenck, 1947; Freeman and Josey, 1949; Lewis and Taylor, 1955; Rechtschaffen and Mednick, 1955; Voth, 1947; Wallen, 1945, 1948; Witkin, 1959; Witkin, Lewis, Hertzman, Machover, Meissner, and Wapner, 1954). In fact, it appears that almost anything to which a response can be made can evoke a deviant response.

Berg (see p. 148) has reformulated the Deviation Hypothesis as follows:

Deviant behavior patterns are general in the sense that those responses that are regarded as being significant for identifying a particular category of atypicality in behavior do not exist in isolation. Those responses that are regarded as being significant for a particular category of deviant behavior are associated with a number of other deviant responses that are not regarded as being significant for that particular category of behavior atypicality.

This does not mean that those people who behave differently in some area of functioning that is important to themselves and to society (critical behavior) will behave differently or deviantly in all relatively less important areas of functioning (noncritical). Such variation in behavior should be accepted as fact since all persons, no matter what their actions, habits, or customs, in their overall behavioral patterns will always exhibit more similarities than differences. In effect, at any one given time, more nondeviant responses are being made by individuals irrespective of their group membership, whether deviant or nondeviant. Thus, by sheer force of number and classification, a great area of normal functioning exists, in which all physical and personality behaviors will show a relatedness in the response norm. Man will always be more like his fellows than unlike them in the *total* response repertoire. Accordingly, the range of related nondeviant behavior is much wider in scope and more general than the deviant response patterns, and no manner of deviancy except death can totally and completely place an individual outside this normal range. Thus, the statement that deviant behavior patterns are general in no way attempts to divorce man from all of that which is normal or nondeviant, as many interpretations of this statement would seem to indicate (Sechrest and Jackson, 1962). Deviant behavior in a crucial area does not produce deviancy in all other areas of behavior, as Sechrest and Jackson indicated.

RESULTS OF STUDIES CONCERNING
THE DEVIATION HYPOTHESIS

One of the initial approaches to the Deviation Hypothesis was to attempt to determine whether deviant responses could be used for assessment purposes. The first few studies dealt with variables that were clearly and obviously deviant.

SCHIZOPHRENIA AND PSYCHOSIS

Barnes (1955) was one of the early investigators to use deviant responses in developing scales for assessing psychosis. He used the Perceptual Reaction Test (PRT) that had been developed by Berg, Hunt, and Barnes (1949). (*See* Figure 1 in Chapter 6.) This test is composed of sixty abstract designs that were constructed with ruler and compass and has four options for each design: *like much, like slightly, dislike slightly,* and *dislike much.* The majority of the studies investigating the Deviation Hypothesis have used the PRT.

Barnes used the criterion group method described by Edwards (1959b) to develop his scales. His criterion groups were 500 normal males and 350 normal females; the schizophrenic patients were 99 males and 68 females. The male and female data were analyzed separately. He also used the Katzell (1951) item cross-validation technique, which requires splitting the groups and cross-validating one upon the other—essentially a dual cross-validation. With this technique he was able to develop a reliable and reasonably valid schizophrenia scale, among others. The significant point here, of course, is not the development of a scale, for such scales have been in existence for decades. The significant thing is that using a test that takes about seven minutes to administer on the average, Barnes developed a suitable scale by using only deviant responses.

Harris (1958), in a further investigation of the *Sigma* or schizophrenia scale developed by Barnes, attempted to determine whether frequency of deviant responses occurring in the *Sigma* Scale were related to the severity of the schizophrenic reaction. The idea was that the more severe schizophrenic reactions would be accompanied by a larger number of deviant responses than would accompany the milder forms. But when schizophrenics were placed in categories of *mild, moderate,* and *severe,* the deviant response frequency did not relate to severity. The failure to discriminate between degrees of severity of schizophrenia may be because it is relatively difficult to determine severity of the schizophrenic disorder. For example, it is likely that the schizophrenic who is hallucinating will be rated severe, while the quiet withdrawn patient may perhaps be rated moderate or mild. However, active hallucinating on the part of the individual may be a function of an acute disorder that remits rapidly, while the withdrawn schizophrenic may remain withdrawn and hospitalized for the remainder of his life. It is significant, however, that the scales developed by Barnes discriminated quite well between normals and schizophrenics in Harris's study, thus representing an independent cross-validation. A later study by Spruill (1963) indicated that the reliability of this scale was .96. Further, the PRT scales, when compared by Spruill with the MMPI, seemed to discriminate about as well.

Investigation of the Deviation Hypothesis with the PRT has not been strictly limited to the development of scales for measuring schizophrenia. For example, Hesterly and Berg (1958) hypothesized that normal young children should be significantly different from normal adults on the basis of deviant response characteristics as measured by the PRT, because of the difference in maturation. If this were correct, they further hypothesized that since adult schizophrenics who are often characterized as immature should resemble children more than normal adults in their response patterns. They found that this hypothesis was supported with three different age groups of 8, 10, and 12 years. The younger children tended to be more significantly different from normal adults in terms of deviant response frequency than the older children were. With increasing age there was a decreased frequency of deviant responses that distinguished adults from children.

However, when the younger children were compared with adult schizophrenics, it was found that the deviant response patterns were quite similar. Further, the degree of similarity between adult schizophrenics and children decreased when comparison was made to the older children. Hesterly (1963) explored the immaturity pattern further and found that the deviant response patterns of young children and elderly adults were quite similar.[1] In fact, he found that the young children and the aged adults (those over 60) resembled each other more than the adults in the age range from 20 to 60. He felt that this may have been a reflection of the generally held notion that older individuals tend to enter a "second childhood."

Adams and Berg (1961a) hypothesized that certain deviant groups appeared to have stable response preferences that are associated with a characteristic affective tone under certain circumstances. For example, some groups of subjects show a preponderance of responses such as *true* or *like* while others exhibit opposite tendencies with preferences for *false, dislike,* and so forth. They found on the PRT that normals tended to select nearly as many positive options as negative options but that schizophrenics, both male and female, showed a marked preference for positive affective responses. They also found that neurotics tended to select more positive affective options (that is, *like much*) on the PRT than normals, while individuals with character disorders tended to prefer the negative options (that is, *dislike much*) In a similar, earlier study Barnes (1956), has shown that atypical true answers on the MMPI are associated with psychotic states, while atypical false answers are usually associated with neurotic states.

Adams and Berg (1961b) also attempted to assess quali-

1. Van de Castle (1965) lent some support to Hesterly's findings in his development of a Perceptual Maturity Scale.

tative deviant responses. Qualitative deviant responses are those responses that cannot readily be scored in a quantitative manner but that are believed to have diagnostic significance. On the PRT, Adams and Berg found that about 35 per cent of psychotic patients embellished their test booklets, omitted responses, or checked several options when the instructions required only one selection. Only about 1 per cent of a large group of normal subjects exhibited such behavior. Barnes (1955) had initially, in his doctoral dissertation, called attention to this tendency on the part of patients to embellish their test booklets. Stone and Margoshes (1965) found much the same thing in a study of verbal embellishments in MMPI responses. In this connection one may wonder whether embellishing one's body by tatoos may not be indicative of possible emotional disturbances. A study by Yamamotu, Seeman, and Lester (1963) would suggest this to be the case.

Barnes (1955) also developed a scale called *Delta* (both female and male scales) that reflected general behavioral disturbance. He compared the PRT responses of a normal population to the responses of patients hospitalized for a wide variety of emotional disturbances. He also developed the *Psi* Scale (male and female scales) for assessing psychotic states. A *Chi* Scale was developed for identifying character disorder but only for male patients. Bradford and Adams (1964) later developed a scale for character disorders in female patients. It should be noted that Spruill (1963) found that the *Delta, Psi,* and *Sigma* scales were highly correlated, but this high correlation is understandable since they are all measuring forms of psychotic reactions.

A novel feature of the PRT was a diagnostic sharpener scale developed by Barnes called *Psi Chi,* which allowed subjects who scored high on both psychotic and character disorder scales to be differentiated in terms of character disorder or psychoses. Berg and Adams (1965) developed a similar diagnostic differentiating scale that distinguished fairly well between groups of mental retardates and schizophrenics.

NEUROSIS

Following the lead offered by the Hesterly (1963) study, Roitzsch and Berg (1959) studied the response patterns of normal and adult neurotics on the hypothesis that neurotics were immature but to a lesser degree than schizophrenics. As they saw the problem, the response pattern of neurotics would be similar to children at the adolescent level. They found that both the adolescents and neurotics could be discriminated from normals, but the neurotics were quite similar to the adolescents on the basis of deviant response patterns.

Using Barnes's general approach, Bradford and Adams (1964) developed deviant response scales for measuring depression. Again the deviant response scales were found to be quite reliable, discriminating quite well between normal and depressed subjects.

Studies of psychopathology utilizing deviant responses have not been limited to adults. House (1960), for example, used the criterion group method to compare the responses of a large group of disturbed children whose ages ranged from 7 through 15 years with a group of normal children who were matched for age, sex, intellectual level, and approximate socioeconomic status. He found that the PRT would discriminate between these groups and that scales for measuring emotional disturbances in children could be developed. However, it should be noted that he failed to cross-validate these scales.

MENTAL RETARDATION

Since Hesterly and Berg (1958), as well as Roitzsch and Berg (1959), have indicated that deviant responses can be employed to reflect behavioral immaturity, it seems reasonable to expect that deviant responses could also be used in assessing mental deficiency. Cieutat (1960) administered the

PRT to over 400 mentally retarded subjects whose ages ranged from 16 to 67 and found that, when their responses were compared to responses of normal adults, the majority of the options on the PRT would differentiate normals from mentally retarded individuals. She constructed an *Iota* Scale that reflected mental retardation. She also found that as the deviant response frequency increased on the *Iota* Scale, the degree of retardation increased. Cieutat next attempted to determine whether mental retardates differed from schizophrenics in their deviant response pattern and found that they did.

As noted earlier, Berg and Adams (1965) later constructed a diagnostic sharpener scale intended to differentiate between schizophrenic and mentally retarded groups. Vegas, Frye, and Adams (1963) further explored Cieutat's *Iota* Scale by determining its validity for normal children. They hypothesized that with normal children there should be a negative relationship between chronological age and scores on the *Iota* Scale. In other words, normal children who were quite young should obtain high scores on the *Iota* Scale, but as their mental age increased, their scores on the *Iota* Scale should become lower. This study confirmed the hypothesis. Hence, the *Iota* Scale may be measuring something similar to mental age.

SENESCENCE

It has been noted previously that deviant responses appear to be useful in the appraisal of immaturity as defined by chronological age. An allied problem is whether senescence is also characterized by deviant behavior that is associated with identifiable deviant response patterns. With this in mind, Hawkins (1960) selected a group of individuals from 60 to 79 years of age who were still quite energetically pursuing their careers and compared them with a group of males from 19 to 24 years of age who were matched for education and approximate socioeconomic background. These older individuals were not typical oldsters. They averaged three years of college, and many held such important positions as school board president, bank official, and merchant.

The PRT did not discriminate between these two groups —the youthful and the aged—when they were compared. Further, the two groups did not differ significantly on a measure of statistical rigidity developed by Adams (1960a) on the PRT. It is rather important to note that the behavior of the oldsters did not show deviancy nor was deviancy reflected on scales designed to measure deviant responses. It is of passing interest that the measure of statistical rigidity for these individuals predicted performance on a learning task— that is, paired associate learning of moderate difficulty—better than intelligence test scores did.

In contrast to these subjects who were physically, socially, and vocationally quite active, Boozer (1961) used elderly subjects who were much more typical of the aged population. She administered the PRT to over 2000 subjects, of which 602 were from 60 to 97 years of age. The remaining subjects were used as controls. The aged subjects were divided into three groups: (1) the normally aging individuals who were members of Golden Age Clubs and senior citizens groups, somewhat akin to the age sample collected by Hawkins; (2) resident patients in a state mental hospital who exhibited a few symptoms of senility; and (3) people who were living in homes for the aged, the majority of whom were infirm and required nursing care.

Boozer found no significant difference in the three groups that could be identified by deviant responses. However, the elderly individuals differed quite markedly from the normal control groups from 20 to 60 years of age. She constructed a scale for aging called *Alpha*. This scale was checked for similarity to the *Sigma* Scale and the *Delta* Scale (the schizophrenic and the hospitalized mental patients scales) and was found to be distinctly different in pattern from these Barnes scales.

CHRONIC PHYSICAL DISEASE

It has been occasionally suggested that certain serious diseases are associated with certain personality characteristics. As a result of chronic illness, these personality characteristics may represent a change or alteration in the personality pattern or, of course, the disease may produce such changes. A number of studies have examined the possibility that the physiological aberration is associated with psychological aberration, which in turn may be reflected by deviant response patterns.

For example, Engen (1959) administered the PRT to a large number of tuberculosis patients and found that certain PRT responses would discriminate both male and female TB patients from groups of matched normal individuals. Further, he found that male patients who had been diagnosed as far advanced in tuberculosis revealed a significantly larger number of deviant responses when compared to moderate cases, although he did not find this trend among the female patients. The pattern of responses of the tuberculosis patients did not seem to be similar to the pattern of responses of schizophrenic patients.

Using a somewhat similar design, Berg (1962) administered the PRT to 125 cardiac patients and compared the responses to those obtained from normal subjects. He also found that deviant response patterns discriminated between the cardiac and the normal groups. When the cardiac patients were scored on the PRT Masculinity-Femininity Scales, the cardiac males scored at the same level as normal males. However, the cardiac females scored significantly in the masculine direction. Berg has speculated that it may be within the bounds of possibility that females who exhibit response patterns that are more characteristic of males than of females may perhaps be more prone to heart disorder.

ITEM CONTENT

A corollary of the earlier statement of the Deviation Hypothesis is the statement by Berg (1955, 1957, 1959) that particular item content is not important. While not related to the Deviation Hypothesis as such, this dismissal of item content has been sharply challenged (Rorer, 1965; Sechrest and Jackson, 1962). Perhaps Berg was unclear in his statement. A more cautious or appropriate statement might be that item content is largely unessential in measuring deviant behavior, since any number and variety of stimuli can be used for this purpose. This notion was first tested by Adams and Berg (1961c) who used ambiguous auditory stimuli. This stimuli ranged from simple chords to clicks and other noises. The response categories to these tones were those used with the PRT—that is, *like much, like slightly, dislike slightly,* and *dislike much.* When normal and schizophrenic subjects were compared on this auditory test, it was found that the auditory test discriminated between the two groups almost as well as the PRT. In a somewhat similar study, Lindeman and Adams (1963) used light flashes of very short duration to which subjects used response options that were identical to the PRT. Using groups of schizophrenic and normal patients, Lindeman and Adams found that the light flash test would discriminate between these two groups about as well as the PRT.

Klipple (1964) attempted to determine whether the meaningfulness of the abstract designs used in the PRT was related to item discrimination in schizophrenic and normal individuals. Her hypothesis was that the less meaningful the abstract designs in terms of number of associations to it, the more the designs should discriminate between the groups. However, this hypothesis was not supported because there did not seem to be any significant direct relationship between item discriminability and meaningfulness. These results might be due to the fact that most of the items are rather ambiguous and, therefore, have little inherent meaningfulness.

However, Weingold, Adams, and Wittman (1963) investigated the possibility that protruding objects on the PRT might be perceived as male sex symbols and receptacle-type designs perceived as female sex symbols. They had the sixty PRT figures reproduced on 3x5 cards and required male and female schizophrenics to sort them into bins marked "male," "female," and "neutral." They found that the majority of the cards were either accepted as neutral or sorted randomly. There was a rather interesting tendency among schizophrenic males to perceive receptacle-type designs of the PRT as female symbols and for schizophrenic females to perceive protruding objects as male sex symbols, although they did not perceive the symbolic representation of their own sex.

Stricker (1963), in a study concerning response style at the item level, reports a lack of relationship between item location and content. This suggests that many of the changes in test scores that have been observed may occur because of changes in response style tendencies rather than content.

Rorer (1965) conducted a rather interesting personal assessment of the Deviation Hypothesis and item content. He seemed to reason that, since everyone is apparently agreed that "contentless" tests do not exist and individuals are not responding to a particular response alternative, therefore deviant response scales must be content scales. Further, he claimed that replications of earlier studies (he did not specify which studies) have not held up. Since he did not quote any of these replicated studies, it is rather difficult to know how to evaluate his statement. It would appear that his conclusions were drawn from Sechrest and Jackson (1962), who found that deviant response scales were not highly intercorrelated. This is not surprising since psychosis and genius both represent deviant behavior, but the hypothesis that they are causally related has been long discarded. Further, the traits that have been measured by deviant response patterns are complex and multidimensional. The most pertinent question about a scale measuring schizophrenia, for example, is whether it discriminates schizophrenic and other groups, not how closely it is related to another scale purporting to measure schizophrenia.

OTHER APPROACHES

A rigorous test of the Deviation Hypothesis has been conducted by Grigg and Thorpe (1960), who did not utilize the criterion group method. Instead, they used a modified Gough Adjective Check List and prepared a list of the most commonly and uncommonly selected adjectives. This revised checklist was given to freshmen entering the University of Texas. Deviant responses were measured by counting the number of times a commonly selected adjective was not checked and the number of times an uncommonly selected adjective was checked by the subjects.

At the end of the year, Grigg and Thorpe compared the deviant response scores for those students who had reported to the student health center or to the university counseling bureau for psychiatric help, for personal adjustment, or for vocational counseling, and with 150 randomly selected non-client controls. They hypothesized that the nonclient controls and the vocational counseling group would have significantly fewer deviant responses than the psychiatric treatment and personal adjustment counseling group, and found support for this hypothesis. In a later study Grigg (1963) compared the frequency of deviant responding for 97 subjects who prepared ego-involved and nonego-involved ratings, and concluded that either ego- or nonego-involved tasks can be used to elicit deviant responses.

While Grigg and Thorpe (1960) demonstrated that a high and positive relationship existed between deviant responses as determined by the checking of certain adjectives and the need for treatment (thus strongly supporting the generality of deviant responses between noncritical and critical areas of behavior), their experiment raised the question of whether types of deviant responses within noncritical areas were related. Elder, Butler, and Adams (1963) sought to answer this question by hypothesizing that the variable that would determine whether deviations in either critical or noncritical areas were related would be the similarity of the behavior or responses exhibited. They proposed that the relationship between deviant responses in noncritical areas would be determined by the similarity of the deviant responses. They further proposed to determine the similarity of deviant responses in tests by the actual physical similarity of the response categories or options and the pattern of responses.

They used two sets or scales in their study, the PRT and the Grigg and Thorpe modification of the Gough Adjective Check List. The results indicated that the type of response categories available to the person is possibly more important in determining and predicting the relationship between deviant response scales than the criterion groups that are used in developing the scales. That is, the similarity of available response choices—for example, two tests both using *true-false* answer options—is more important in accounting for the degree of relationship between the deviant response scales than a similarity of groups used to develop the scales.

This study concluded that the different measures or scales of personality variation are not always measuring the same source of variance in the criterion group. By utilizing different types of deviant response scales, additional variance may be tapped, thereby increasing the validity of the personality assessment.

In a somewhat different approach, Bullock (1960) found that in brief operant discrimination tasks psychiatric patients were less likely to reach established performance criterion. He indicated that his investigation provided preliminary support for Berg's contention that the Deviation Hypothesis could be extended to conditioned responses. Using extreme position response sets, Soueif (1958) found that social groups with higher tension levels revealed less tolerance for ambiguity than groups with lower levels of tension, in terms of extreme responses. He considered his results to be in harmony with the findings of Berg and Collier (1953).

Zuckerman, Oppenheimer, and Gershowitz (1965) also used extreme response sets as they occurred on the PRT in a study of actors and teachers, with actors and actresses scoring significantly higher than teachers. Singh and Rettig (1962) used American students, Indian students residing in the

United States, and Indian students residing in India for a cross-cultural study of absolute response sets. They reported that Indian students, irrespective of language and country, when compared with the Americans, significantly preferred the responses that were less indicative of anxiety.

Kreidt and Dawson (1961) used the Gordon Personal Inventory to predict clerical job performance and found it valuable in predicting job success because, ironically, it permitted response sets to influence the scores. They interpreted their findings as supporting Berg's viewpoint. In this broad context, the study by O'Donovan (1965) is of interest regarding the significance of rating extremity and pathology. He offers a series of sensible, testable propositions for studying the problem of extreme positions sets in relation to meaningfulness and pathology.

A study that did not utilize the criterion group method was that of Adams (1960b). He operationally defined seven personality characteristics in terms of PRT response patterns: (1) *statistical rigidity,* based upon the variation of selection of option choice; (2) *acquiescence,* based on the frequency the option like much was selected; (3) *negativism,* based upon the frequency dislike much was chosen; (4) *perseveration,* based upon the tendency to repeat the previous options choice; (5) *affect constancy,* based upon the maintenance of a particular emotional tone (that is, *like* or *dislike*) in selecting options; (6) *affect shifts,* based upon changes from one extreme of option choices to the other; and (7) *affect ratio,* based upon the square root of the ratio of acquiescence to negativism.

He then used five different groups of subjects, half of each group was male and half female: normal children, normal adolescents, normal adults, schizophrenic adults, and neurotic adults. It was found that the various groups differed in the pattern of personality characteristics that they exhibited, and that some groups were similar in terms of certain of the personality characteristics. This study lends support to the idea that deviant responses can also be utilized for the measurement of personality characteristics.

A final point on predictive validity of scales using the

criterion group method and deviant response technique was made by Spruill (1963), who compared all of the PRT scales with the various MMPI scales. She found that, in terms of reliability and discrimination among various pathological groups, the PRT was similar to but slightly less effective than the MMPI in predictive validity, but that both used together were better than either used alone for the identification of individuals belonging to pathological groups.

SUMMARY

A review of the evidence provided by a large number of studies concerned with Berg's Deviation Hypothesis specifically or response set generally, all things considered, clearly lends support for the hypothesis. In terms of psychological relevance, accuracy, and generality in application as well as usefulness, the available data indicate the concept is a viable one. In terms of the numerous studies it has generated, it is also obviously provocative. Because the concept is ambitious in the range of behavior it seeks to cover, despite the amount of published data, many other studies are necessary to explore and map its behavioral boundaries and internal relationships.

The Set to Respond in Personality Assessment: A Review of Reviews

An item is an item; a person is a person. When a person is asked to interact with an item by responding to it in a prescribed way, his behavior toward the item can be measured and scored. And if he is asked to respond to more than one item on a given occasion, or to more than one item on more than one occasion, his behavior toward the items can also be measured and scored. When the behavior of numerous persons is thus elicited, scored, and analyzed, there are conditions under which idiosyncratic kinds of behavior are more rather than less likely to occur. That formally and empirically diffuse proposition, which rests on the assumption of person-item interaction, is what seems to knit together otherwise disparate contributions to this book. A proper title for the area of investigation so delimited, one infers, is "response set in personality assessment."

For the person who likes to read summary chapters before deciding whether to plunge into a main text, further generally descriptive remarks are in order. Some things the book is not. For instance, it is neither broadly encompassing of nor any kind of cookbook on the measurement of human performance, nor is it more than tangentially concerned with attitude formation and change, nor does it even tell us very much, substantively, about human personality. The authors do have important things to say about an important methodological problem in the study of human differences and about the construction and use of instruments—in this case largely paper-and-pencil tests—to measure and analyze such differences.

As already suggested the problem is to determine whether there is warrant for assuming that human idiosyncracy exists and can be measured in amount, and, if so, how the idiosyncracy is to be defined and measured. One becomes aware that idiosyncracy may be postulated to exist in the person, in the item, or in their interaction. To a lesser extent, one is made aware that idiosyncratic behavior may be determined by the time and the place of test-making. And if one is not too much intimidated by the thought of multiple interactions —for example, among persons, items, times, and places—one is allowed even to entertain the belief that idiosyncratic behavior may have several determinants. To a much lesser extent, one is helped to understand that idiosyncratic behavior may have biosocial and cultural determinants, as well as its own biogenesis. Irwin A. Berg is almost alone among the contributors in giving emphasis to these—a reflection of his own insatiable and far-ranging curiosity about behavior.

In his historical review of psychological research, on the phenomenon of "response set" generally and more specifically on its relation to human personality, Richard K. McGee presents an orientation to what follows in the book. He makes it obvious that problems of defining "response set" are recurrent and unsolved, and he urges a moratorium on data collection to afford opportunity for more systematic observation and inference about what is at hand. By what one infers to be a deliberate sin of omission on McGee's part, his otherwise excellent review has little to say about situationally induced, experimentally manipulated "set." Although a great deal of contemporary social psychological research, stemming from such pioneer work as that of Lewin and his associates on "social climate" and that of Sherif and Asch on "social judgment," centers on that kind of investigation, McGee and his fellow contributors are not much interested in it. One infers the fusion of psychometric and experimental data collection and analysis to have been too large a task for the present contributors to have attempted, in any event. Though one may experience some personal disappointment on this score, it must be conceded that McGee and others in this book have argued well what they have argued.

Such deliberate exclusion is not at all one-sided; consider, for example, McGuire's very recent review of research on "attitudes and opinions," in which among 252 cited references there is almost no overlap with the extensive literature reviewed in this book. "We," says McGuire in regal conclusion, "are filled with unease at the large number of *noble-isolates that we were compelled to ignore* . . . because of our *decision to concentrate in depth on the controversial issues* . . . we acted on a working hypothesis that . . . *where the heat is,* there will also be found the light for the next step forward" (p. 504; italics not in original).[1]

As an invited "in-house" reviewer in the present case, I can but hope that the outside reviewer will subordinate his own parochialism to the task of understanding what this book is about. If the issue of experimental definition and manipulation of variables versus their psychometric definition and measurement has not been resolved here, neither does it seem to have been met particularly well elsewhere.[2]

Meanwhile, what McGee clearly recognizes in historical perspective, a tendency for students of "response set" to ride off in many directions of inquiry, is well illustrated by the other contributors, who have provided broad statements and reviews of evidence in three major areas of investigation: "social desirability,' "acquiescence sets," and just plain "deviance." These discussions introduce another analytic category to the methodology of assessing "response set," namely, that of the investigator as playwright and producer of what is to

1. *See* W. J. McGuire "Attitudes and opinions." *In* P. R. Farnsworth, Olga McNemar, and Q. McNemar (Eds.), *Annual Review of Psychology*, 1966, *17*, 475–514.
2. An exception that may prove the rule is to be found in D. W. Fiske and S. R. Madde (Eds.), *Functions of Varied Experience* (Homewood, Ill.: Dorsey Press, 1961).

be seen and interpreted by an audience of his scientific peers. Precisely because of the contributors' preoccupation with "response set" and the fact that they have so frequently opted to challenge each others' empirical findings and interpretations, one has opportunity to see for himself just how important spectator as well as participant definitions of the situation can be in shaping accounts of psychological research. One may become as fascinated (as I obviously have) with the "response sets" of the reviewers as in the subject matter reviewed.

What becomes startlingly apparent in this process is that, in addition to the original persons whose interactions with items have produced data to be analyzed, there are always other persons to be considered in any assessment of what has taken place. These others—from the original investigators to their successive reviewers—will all have a hand in creating the kind of scholarly fiction that one ultimately encounters in textbooks. In the scientific community, as in other settings where aggregate behavior is organized to get things done, "uncertainty absorption" increases as one moves further and further from original observation, and one may expect spectator "response sets" to be as determining of what appears in the lecture hall or in print as those of original participants.[3]

Among the idiosyncratic viewpoints presented in this book, that of Allen L. Edwards appears to me to express the most orderly, lucid, and logical progression of thought. The logical and empirical "fit" of Edwards's propositions about the construct that he calls "social desirability" is impressive, and he does not hesitate to acknowledge when he has found himself to be in error. Yet he seems to argue quite persuasively for the lack of utility of his construct in "serious life" arenas, such as when behavior is to be intepreted clinically. What does it all mean then? One may hope that Edwards will be able to say more about the scientific as well as the social

3. See J. G. March and H. A. Simon, *Organizations* (New York: Wiley, 1958); also R. Rosenthal, "On the social psychology of the psychological experiment," *American Scientist*, 1963, *51*, 268–83. An expanded argument along these lines may be found in H. B. Pepinsky, K. E. Weick, and J. W. Riner, *Primer for Productivity* (Columbus: Ohio State University Research Foundation, 1965).

usefulness of a demonstrably clear psychology of social desirability.

Douglas N. Jackson's chapter on "acquiescence sets" tells us a good deal about how a multivariate analyst thinks. He is predisposed to accept a response as dependent on numerous (to be specified) contingencies. In apparent contradiction of Edwards, Jackson argues for the development of "good direct content scales," from which the "contamination" of "response bias" has been removed. One gathers (and I agree, intuitively) that there is no substitute for careful test development in the first place; *a posteriori* correction or partitioning techniques are largely "clean-up" operations, where it is likely that an irremediable mess has already been made.

Jackson's long-time research partner, Samuel J. Messick, illustrates in his companion chapter what a careful hypothetico-deductive search can contribute to the psychometrician's knowledge about personality assessment. Aided by a considerable computer technology, Messick is able to analyze his own and others' data and to suggest, provocatively, that there may be several kinds of "acquiescent" responses, for example, "interpretive" as opposed to "impulsive" or "agreeing" as opposed to "acceptant." While both Jackson and Messick are highly critical of previous research on "acquiescence sets," Messick seems the more reluctant to discard the construct at this time.

In his lengthy discussion of the "deviation hypothesis," his most comprehensive statement to date, Irwin A. Berg makes the initial assumption that an organism responds qua organism to its environment. If one peeps at part of a human organism's behavior, therefore, one should expect other kinds of behavior to be consistent with what has been observed, particularly if one has picked out salient characteristics that place the organism in a membership class and by virtue of which it can be clearly distinguished from nonmembers of that class.

Berg is careful to point out, however, that what is significant is always significant in someone's view. Particularly if a pathological deviance is clearly manifest, the salience of the deviance is great, and, following Berg's hypothesis, non-salient attributes will also operate to distinguish the members of a pathological class from nonmembers. Berg's hypothesis, in retrospect, does offer some justification for thousands of tedious studies involving the relation of individual and group tests to each other or to some criterion.

As in most of the argument presented in this book, one finds in Berg's "assumptions and postulates" a curious mixture of *ad hoc* and a priori reasoning. It is not yet clear, either, by what rule or rules the investigator is to select one criterion of deviancy over another. Reluctantly, it must be inferred that an important rule is expediency. Nevertheless, Berg has made a laudable attempt to attain a concept of "deviance." In later revision of his expository statement, it is to be hoped that his present mixture of "assumptions and postulates" can be replaced by a set that includes these as more explicitly identified subsets and an equally clear identification and separation of definitions, propositions of relationship, and procedural admonishments, all of which are now lumped together.

Essentially, Berg's argument, as it stands, is a methodological guide to the study of deviance, and he is to be commended for making his argument vulnerable to critical review. In a way that can be made more explicit than it is now, the important and voluminous research that he has generated and guided and interpreted provides an important bridge between the ideas and methods of psychological research and those of a social and cultural anthropology.

The chapter by Henry E. Adams and Joel R. Butler, which reviews some of the considerable evidence amassed in relation to the "deviation hypothesis," testifies to the importance of the concept in generating and helping to make sense out of an enormous yield of data. The reference citations, which are found here and in the other chapters of this book, become highly useful in helping to point up the particular kinds of response bias that help an investigator to shape and to interpret the results of research inquiry as categorical instances of "response sets." And Adams and Butler do establish for the reader the warrant for assuming that any measured response is the result of person-item interaction, with meaningful variance attributable to both.

If the "state of the art" in the study of response sets is no less complicated by problems of definition and measurement than it was prior to the publication of this book, it is because a seemingly undiminished supply of evidence has raised more questions than it has answered. A high-speed computer technology has exacerbated rather than reduced these problems. The temptation to gather, analyze, and publish data of this sort is abetted by recourse to ever more rapid data processing and the greater premium that our society accords to results as compared to the means of attaining them. For that reason McGee's admonition to be thoughtful about what is known is not likely to be heeded. Yet this kind of symposium occasions a pause, at least, to review what is going on. On a like occasion, when "mathematical methods in small group processes" were reviewed, Moore and Anderson made this interesting comment: "We would still advise a person interested in the human condition to read Durrell's *Alexandria Quartet* . . ." (p. 237).[4]

Like the *Alexandria Quartet's* four volumes, each chapter in this book tells a different story about a situation in which many characters reappear. With McGee, however, one is impelled to believe that "response set" as a staging apparatus is here to stay.

4. *See* O. K. Moore and A. R. Anderson, "Some puzzling aspects of social interaction." *In* Joan Criswell, H. Solomon, and P. Suppes (Eds.), *Mathematical Methods in Small Group Processes* (Stanford: Stanford University Press, 1962), pp. 232–49.

Bibliography

ADAMS, H. E. Statistical rigidity in schizophrenic and normal groups measured with auditory and visual stimuli. *Psychol. Rep.*, 1960, 7, 119–122. (a)

————. Deviant responses in the measurement of personality characteristics. Unpublished Ph.D. dissertation, Louisiana State University, 1960. (b)

————, and BERG, I. A. Affective tone of test option choice as a deviant response. *Psychol. Rep.*, 1961, 8, 79–85. (a)

————, ————. Schizophrenia and the frequency of qualitative deviant responses. *Psychol. Rep.*, 1961, 8, 123–126. (b)

————, ————. Schizophrenia and deviant response sets produced by auditory and visual test content. *J. Psychol.*, 1961. 51, 393–398. (c)

ADAMSON, R. E. Functional fixedness as related to problem-solving. *J. exp. Psychol.*, 1952, 44, 288–291.

ADLER, A. *The practice and theory of individual psychology.* New York: Harcourt, 1927.

ADORNO, T. W., FRENKEL-BRUNSWIK, ELSE, LEVINSON, D. J., and SANFORD, R. N. *The authoritarian personality.* New York: Harper, 1950.

ALLPORT, G. W. Attitudes. In C. Murchison (Ed.), *A handbook of social psychology.* Worcester: Clark University Press, 1935. Pp. 798–844.

————. *Personality: A psychology interpretation.* New York: Holt, 1937.

————. *Theories of perception and the concept of structure.* New York: John Wiley, 1955.

ANGELL, J. R. Review of studies in philosophy and psychology. *J. Phil. Psychol. sci. Meth.*, 1906, 3, 637–643.

BANDURA, A., and WALTERS, R. H. *Social learning and personality development*. New York: Holt, Rinehart, 1963.

BANTA, T. J. Social attitudes and response styles. *Educ. psychol. Measmt*, 1961, 21, 543–557.

BARNES, E. H. The relationship of biased test responses to psychopathology. *J. abnorm. soc. Psychol.*, 1955, 51, 286–290.

———. Response bias and the MMPI. *J. consult Psychol.*, 1956, 20, 371–374.

BARRATT, E. S. Anxiety and impulsiveness related to psychomotor efficiency. *Percept. mot. Skills*, 1959, 9, 191–198.

BASS, B. M. Authoritarianism or acquiescence? *J. abnorm. soc. Psychol.*, 1955, 51, 616–623.

———. Development and evaluation of a scale for measuring social acquiescence. *J. abnorm. soc. Psychol.*, 1956, 53, 296, 299.

———. Undiscriminated operant acquiescence. *Educ. psychol. Measmt*, 1957, 17, 83–85. (a)

———. Iterative inverse factor analysis—a rapid method for clustering persons. *Psychometrika*, 1957, 22 105–107. (b)

———, and BERG, I. A. (Eds.). *Objective approaches to personality assessment*. New York: Van Nostrand, 1959.

BENDIG, A. W. A factor analysis of "social desirability," "defensiveness," "lie," and "acquiescence" scales. *J. gen. Psychol.*, 1962, 66, 129–136.

BERG, I. A. Response bias and personality: The deviation hypothesis. *J. Psychol.*, 1955, 40, 62–72.

———. Deviant responses and deviant people: The formulation of the deviation hypothesis. *J. counsel. Psychol.*, 1957, 4, 154–161.

———. The unimportance of test item content. In B. M. Bass and I. A. Berg (Eds.), *Objective approaches to personality assessment*. New York: Van Nostrand, 1959. Pp. 83–99.

———. Measuring deviant behavior by means of deviant response sets. In I. A. Berg and B. M. Bass (Eds.), *Conformity and deviation*. New York: Harper, 1961. Pp. 328–379.

———. Deviant response patterns among cardiac patients. *Psychol. Rep.*, 1962, 11, 628.

———. The generality of deviant behavior. Presidential address, delivered at Southeastern Psychological Assn. meeting, Miami Beach, 1963.

————, and ADAMS, H. E. Differentiating mental defect from schizophrenia on the basis of deviant response sets. *Amer. J. ment. Defic.*, 1965, *70*, 16–20.

————, and BASS, B. M. (Eds.). *Conformity and deviation.* New York: Harper, 1961.

————, and COLLIER, J. S. Personality and group differences in extreme response sets. *Educ. psychol. Measmt*, 1953, *13*, 164–169.

————, HUNT, W. A., and BARNES, E. H. The perceptual reaction test. Evanston, Ill.: Irwin A. Berg, 1949.

————, and RAPPORT, G M. Response bias in an unstructured questionnaire. *J. Psychol.*, 1954, *38*, 475–481.

BLAKE, R. R., and MOUTON, JANE S. Personality. *Annu. Rev. Psychol.*, 1959, *10*, 203–232.

————, and RAMSEY, G. V. (Eds.). *Perception—an approach to personality.* New York: Ronald, 1951.

BLOCK, J. Unconfounding meaning, acquiescence, and social desirability in the MMPI. Unpublished manuscript, May 1962.

————. *The challenge of response sets.* New York: Appleton-Century-Crofts, 1965.

BOCK, R. D. Components of variance due to content and acquiescence in the *Hy* and *Pt* scales of the MMPI. Chapel Hill, N.C.: Psychometric Laboratory Research Memorandum No. 21, 1964.

BOOZER, D. G. Response sets as indicators of senescence and of psychopathology in old age. Unpublished Ph.D. dissertation, Louisiana State University, 1961.

BORING, E. G. *A history of experimental psychology.* (2nd ed.) New York: Appleton-Century-Crofts, 1950.

BRADFORD, JUNE T., and ADAMS, H. E. Deviant responses as indicators of depression and character disorder. *Psychol. Rep.*, 1964, *14*, 235–238.

BROEN, W. E., JR., and WIRT, R. D. Varieties of response sets. *J. consult. Psychol.*, 1958, *22*, 237–240.

BRUNER, J. S., and GOODMAN, C. D. Value and need as organizing factors in perception. *J. abnorm. soc. Psychol.*, 1947, *42*, 33–44.

————, and KRECH, D. *Perception and personality: A symposium.* Durham: Duke University Press, 1950.

————, and POSTMAN, L. Symbolic value as an organizing factor in perception. *J. soc. Psychol.*, 1948, *27*, 203–208.

BUGELSKI, B. R. *The psychology of learning.* New York: Holt, 1956.

BULLOCK, D. H. Performances of psychiatric patients in a brief operant discrimination test. *Psychol. Record,* 1960, 83–93.

CATTELL, R. B. Psychiatric screening of flying personnel. Personality structure in objective tests—a study of 1,000 Air Force students in basic pilot training. Project No. 21-0202-0007, Report No. 9. Air University, USAF School of Aviation Medicine, Randolph Field, Texas, June 1955.

———, DUBIN, S. S., and SAUNDERS, D. R. Personality structure in psychotics by factorization of objective clinical tests. *J. ment. Sci.,* 1954, *100,* 154–176. (a)

———, ———, ———. Verification of hypothesized factors in one hundred and fifteen objective personality test designs. *Psychometrika,* 1954, *19,* 209–230. (b)

———, and GRUEN, W. The primary personality factors in 11-year-old children, by objective tests. *J. Pers.,* 1955, *23,* 460–478.

———, and PETERSON, D. R. Personality structure in four and five year olds in terms of objective tests. *J. clin. Psychol.,* 1959, *15,* 355–369.

———, and SCHEIER, I. H. Extension of meaning of objective test personality factors: Especially into anxiety, neuroticism, questionnaire, and physical factors. *J. gen. Psychol.,* 1959, *61,* 287–315.

———, ———. Stimuli related to stress, neuroticism, excitation, and anxiety response pattern: Illustrating a new multivariate experimental design. *J. abnorm. soc. Psychol.,* 1960, *60,* 195–204.

———, and WENIG, P. W. Dynamic and cognitive factors controlling misperception. *J. abnorm. soc. Psychol.,* 1953, *47,* 797–809.

CHAPMAN, L. J., and BOCK, R. D. Components of variance due to acquiescence and content in the F scale measure of authoritarianism. *Psychol. Bull.,* 1958, *55,* 328–333.

———, and CAMPBELL, D. T. Response set in the F scale. *J. abnorm. soc. Psychol.,* 1957, *54,* 129–132.

———, ———. The effect of acquiescence response set upon relationships among the F scale, ethnocentrism, and intelligence. *Sociometry,* 1959, *22,* 153–161.

CHRISTIE, R., and COOK, PEGGY. A guide to published literature relating to the authoritarian personality through 1956. *J. Psychol.*, 1958, 45, 171–199.

———, HAVEL, JOAN, and SEIDENBERG, B. Is the F scale irreversible? *J. abnorm. soc. Psychol.*, 1958, 56, 143–159.

———, and JAHODA, MARIE (Eds.). *Studies in the scope and method of "The authoritarian personality": Continuities in social research.* Glencoe, Ill.: The Free Press, 1954.

———, and LINDAUER, FLORENCE. Personality structure. *Annu. Rev. Psychol.*, 1963, 14, 201–230.

CIEUTAT, L. G. Deviant responses as a function of mental deficiency. Unpublished Ph.D. dissertation, Louisiana State University, 1960.

CLAYTON, MARTHA B., and JACKSON, D. N. Equivalence range, acquiescence and overgeneralization. *Educ. psychol. Measmt,* 1961, 21, 371–382.

COHN, T. S. Is the F scale indirect? *J. abnorm. soc. Psychol.*, 1952, 47, 185–192.

———. The relationship of the F scale to a response set to answer positively. *Amer. Psychologist*, 1953, 8, 335. (Abstract)

COUCH, A., and KENISTON, K. Yeasayers and naysayers: Agreeing response set as a personality variable. *J. abnorm. soc. Psychol.*, 1960, 60, 151–174.

———, ———. Agreeing response set and social desirability. *J. abnorm. soc. Psychol.*, 1961, 62, 175–179.

COWEN, E. L., and BUDIN, W. The social desirability of trait-descriptive terms: A comparison of 17 samples. *J. soc. Psychol.*, 1964, 63, 281–293.

———, DAVOL, S. H., REIMANIS, G., and STILLER, A. The social desirability of trait descriptive terms: Two geriatric samples. *J. soc. Psychol.*, 1962, 56, 217–225.

———, and FRANKEL, GAIL. The social desirability of trait-descriptive terms: Applciation to a French sample. *J. soc. Psychol.*, 1964, 63, 233–239.

———, STAIMAN, M. G., and WOLITZKY, D. L. The social desirability of trait descriptive terms: Applications to a schizophrenic sample. *J. soc. Psychol.*, 1961, 54, 37–45.

———, and STRICKER, G. The social desirability of trait descriptive terms: A sample of sexual offenders. *J. soc. Psychol.*, 1963, 59, 307–315.

———, and TONGAS, P. The social desirability of trait descriptive terms: Applications to a self-concept inventory. *J. consult. Psychol.*, 1959, 23, 361–365.

CRONBACH, L. J. Response set and test validity. *Educ. psychol. Measmt*, 1946, *6*, 475–494.

———. Further evidence on response sets and test design. *Educ. psychol. Measmt*, 1950, *10*, 3–31.

———, and GLESER, GOLDINE. *Psychological tests and personal decisions*. (2nd ed.) Urbana: University of Illinois Press, 1964.

CROWNE, D. P., and MARLOWE, D. A new scale of social desirability independent of psychopathology. *J. consult. Psychol.*, 1960, *24*, 349–354.

CRUSE, D. B. Socially desirable responses in relation to grade level. *Child Develpm.*, 1963, *34*, 777–789.

DAHLSTROM, W. G., and WELSH, G. S. *An MMPI handbook*. Minneapolis: University of Minnesota Press, 1960.

DAMARIN, F., and MESSICK, S. Response styles as personality variables: A theoretical integration of multivariate research. Princeton, N.J.: Educational Testing Service Research Bulletin 65-10, 1965.

DASHIELL, J. F. A neglected fourth dimension to psychological research. *Psychol. Rev.*, 1940, *47*, 289–305.

DAVIS, R. C. Set and muscular tension. *Indiana University Science Ser. No. 10*. Bloomington: Indiana University Press, 1940.

DICKEN, C. Good impression, social desirability, and acquiescence as suppressor variables. *Educ. psychol. Measmt*, 1963, *23*, 699–720.

EDWARDS, A. L. The relationship between the judged desirability of a trait and the probability that the trait will be endorsed. *J. appl. Psychol.*, 1953, *37*, 90–93.

———. *The social desirability variable in personality assessment and research*. New York: Dryden, 1957. (a)

———. *Techniques of attitude scale construction*. New York: Appleton-Century-Crofts, 1957. (b)

———. Social desirability and the description of others. *J. abnorm. soc. Psychol.*, 1959, *59*, 434–436. (a)

———. Social desirability and personality test construction. In B. M. Bass and I. A. Berg (Eds.), *Objective approaches to personality assessment*. New York: Van Nostrand, 1959. Pp. 100–118. (b)

———. Social desirability or acquiescence in the MMPI? A case study with the SD scale. *J. abnorm. soc. Psychol.*, 1961, *63*, 351–359.

————. Social desirability and expected means on MMPI scales. *Educ. psychol. Measmt*, 1962, *22*, 71–76.

————. A factor analysis of experimental social desirability and response set scales. *J. appl. Psychol.*, 1963, *47*, 308–316.

————. Prediction of mean scores on MMPI scales. *J. consult. Psychol.*, 1964, *28*, 183–185.

————, and DIERS, CAROL J. Social desirability and the factorial interpretation of the MMPI. *Educ. psychol. Measmt*, 1962, *22*, 501–509.

————, ————. Neutral items as a measure of acquiescence. *Educ. psychol. Measmt*, 1963, *23*, 687–698.

————, ————, and WALKER, J. N. Response sets and factor loadings on sixty-one personality scales. *J. appl. Psychol.*, 1962, *46*, 220–225.

————, and WALKER, J. N. A short form of the MMPI: The SD scale. *Psychol. Rep.*, 1961, *8*, 485–486. (a)

————, ————. A note on the Couch and Keniston measure of agreement response set. *J. abnorm. soc. Psychol.*, 1961, *62*, 173–174. (b)

————, and WALSH, J. A. Relationships between various psychometric properties of personality items. *Educ. psychol. Measmt*, 1963, *23*, 227–238.

————, ————. Response sets in standard and experimental personality scales. *Amer. educ. Res. J.*, 1964, *1*, 52–61.

————, ————, and DIERS, CAROL J. The relationship between social desirability and internal consistency of personality scales. *J. appl. Psychol.*, 1963, *47*, 255–259.

ELDER, S. T., BUTLER, J. R., and ADAMS, H. E. Generality of deviant responses in critical and noncritical areas of behavior. *Psychol. Rep.*, 1963, *13*, 915–920.

ELLIOTT, LOIS L. Effects of item construction and respondent aptitude on response acquiescence. *Educ. psychol. Measmt*, 1961, *21*, 405–415.

ENDLER, N. S. Conformity analyzed and related to personality. *J. soc. Psychol.*, 1961, *53*, 271–283.

ENGEN, E. P. Response set of pulmonary tuberculosis patients. Unpublished Ph.D. dissertation, Louisiana State University, 1959.

EYSENCK, H. J. *Dimensions of personality*. London: Kegan Paul, 1947.

————. Response set, authoritarianism, and personality questionnaires. *British J. soc. clin. Psychol.*, 1962, *1*, 20–24.

FOREHAND, G. A. Relationships among response sets and cognitive behaviors. *Educ. psychol. Measmt,* 1962, 22, 287–302.

FOSTER, R. J. Acquiescent response set as a measure of acquiescence. *J. abnorm. soc. Psychol.,* 1961, 63, 155–160.

———, and GRIGG, A. E. Acquiescent response set as a measure of acquiescence: Further evidence. *J. abnorm. soc. Psychol.,* 1963, 67, 304–306.

FREDERIKSEN, N., and MESSICK, S. J. Response set as a measure of personality. Office of Naval Research, Contract ONR-694(00), Project Designation NR 151-113, Educational Testing Service, Princeton, New Jersey: 1958.

———, ———. Response set as a measure of personality. *Educ. psychol. Measmt,* 1959, 19, 137–157.

FREEMAN, E., and JOSEY, W. E. Quantitative visual index to memory impairment. *Arch. neurol. Psychiat.,* 1949, 62, 794–796.

FREEMAN, G. L. *The energetics of human behavior.* Ithaca, N.Y.: Cornell University Press, 1948.

FRITZ, M. F. Guessing in a true-false test. *J. educ. Psychol.,* 1927, 18, 558–561.

FRYE, R. L., and BASS, B. M. Behavior in a group related to tested social acquiescence. *J. soc. Psychol.,* 1963, 61, 263–266.

FULKERSON, S. C. An acquiescence key for the MMPI. *USAF School of Aviation Medicine Report,* No. 58-71, July 1958.

GAGE, N. L., and CHATTERJEE, B. B. The psychological meaning of acquiescence set: Further evidence. *J. abnorm. soc. Psychol.,* 1960, 60, 280–283.

———, LEAVITT, G. S., and STONE, S. C. The psychological meaning of acquiescence set for authoritarianism. *J. abnorm. soc. Psychol.,* 1957, 55, 98–103.

GAIER, E. L., LEE, MARILYN C., and McQUITTY, L. L. Response patterns in a test of logical inference. *Educ. psychol. Measmt,* 1953, 13, 550–567.

GARDNER, R. W., HOLZMAN, P. S., KLEIN, G. S., LINTON, HARRIET B., and SPENCE, D. P. Cognitive controls: A study of individual consistencies in cognitive behavior. *Psychol. Issues,* 1959, 1, No. 4.

GEORGE, S. S. Attitude in relation to the psychophysical judgment. *Amer. J. Psych.,* 28, 1–37, 1917.

GIBSON, E. J., and McCARVEY, H. R. Further studies on thought and reasoning. *Psychol. Bull.,* 1937, 34, 327–350.

GIBSON, J. J. A critical review of the concept of set in contemporary experimental psychology. *Psychol. Bull.*, 1941, *38*, 781–817.

GLOYE, E. E. A note on the distinction between social desirability and acquiescent response styles as sources of variance in the MMPI. *J. counsel. Psychol.*, 1964, *11*, 180–184.

GOLDBERG, L. R., and RORER, L. G. Test-retest item statistics for original and reversed MMPI items. Oregon Research Institute Monograph, 1963, 3.

GOODFELLOW, L. D. The human element in probability. *J. gen. Psychol.*, 1940, *33*, 201–205.

GORDON, L. V. Validation of forced-choice and questionnaire methods of personality measurement. *J. appl. Psychol.*, 1951, *35*, 407–412.

GOUGH, H. G., and SANFORD, R. N. Rigidity as a psychological variable. Berkeley: University of California, Institute of Personality Assessment and Research, 1952. (Unpublished manuscript.)

GRIGG, A. E. Comparison of deviant responses of self descriptive and non-self descriptive judgments. *Psychol. Rep.*, 1963, *13*, 282.

————, and THORPE, J. S. Deviant responses in college adjustment clients: A test of Berg's Deviation Hypothesis. *J. consult. Psychol.*, 1960, *24*, 92–94.

GUILFORD, J. P. Psychometric methods. (2nd ed.) New York: McGraw-Hill, 1954. (a)

————. The validation of an "indecision" score for predicting proficiency of foremen. *J. appl. Psychol.*, 1954, *38*, 224–226. (b)

HANLEY, C. Social desirability and responses to items from three MMPI scales: *D, Sc*, and *K. J. appl. Psychol.*, 1956, *40*, 324–328.

————. Responses to the wording of personality test items. *J. consult. Psychol.*, 1959, *23*, 261–265.

HARLOW, H. F. The formation of learning sets. *Psychol. Rev.*, 1949, *56*, 51–56.

HARRIS, J. L. Deviant response frequency in relation to severity of schizophrenic reaction. Unpublished M.A. thesis, Louisiana State University, 1958.

HATHAWAY, S. R., and McKINLEY, J. C. A multiphasic personality schedule (Minnesota): I. Construction of the schedule. *J. Psychol.*, 1940, *10*, 249–254.

———, ———. *The Minnesota Multiphasic Personality Inventory.* (Manual). New York: Psychological Corp., 1943.

HAWKINS, W. A. Deviant responses, response variability, and paired associate learning. Unpublished Ph.D. dissertation, Louisiana State University, 1960.

HEFFERLINE, R. F. Learning theory and clinical psychology—an eventual symbiosis? In A. J. Bachrach (Ed.), *Experimental foundations of clinical psychology.* New York: Basic Books, 1962.

HELMSTADTER, G. C. Proceedures for obtaining separate set and content components of a test score. *Psychometrika,* 1957, *22,* 381–393.

HESTERLY, S. O. Deviant response patterns as a function of chronological age. *J. consult. Psychol.,* 1963, *27,* 210–214.

———, and BERG, I. A. Deviant responses as indicators of immaturity and schizophrenia. *J. consult. Psychol.,* 1958, *22,* 389–393.

HILDEN, A. H. *Universe of personal concepts.* Webster Groves, Missouri (628 Clark Avenue): Author, 1954.

———. Q-sort correlation: Stability and random choice of statements. *J. consult. Psychol.,* 1958, *22,* 45–50.

HILDRETH, G. The development and training of hand dominance. Part I. *J. genet. Psychol.,* 1949, *75,* 197–220.

HILGARD, E. R. *Theories of learning.* (2nd ed.) New York: Appleton-Century-Crofts, 1956.

HOLTZMAN, W. H. Personality structure. *Annu. Rev. Psychol.,* 1965, *16,* 119–156.

HOUSE, C. W. Response bias as a measure of emotional disturbance in children. Unpublished Ph.D. dissertation, Louisiana State University, 1960.

HOWARD, K. I., and DIESENHAUS, H. I. Intra-individual variability, response set, and response uniqueness in a personality questionnaire. *J. clin. Psychol.,* 1965, *21,* 392–396.

HULL, C. L. *A behavior system.* New Haven: Yale University Press, 1952.

HUSEK, T. R. Acquiescence as a response set and as a personality characteristic. *Educ. psychol. Measmt,* 1961, *21,* 295–307.

IMMERGLUCK, L. Determinism-freedom in contemporary psychology: An ancient problem revisited. *Amer. Psychologist,* 1964, *19,* 270–281.

IWAWAKI, S., and COWEN, E. L. The social desirability of trait-descriptive terms: Applications to a Japanese sample. *J. soc. Psychol.*, 1964, *63*, 199–205.

JACKSON, D. N. Independence and resistance to perceptual field forces. *J. abnorm. soc. Psychol.*, 1958, *56*, 279–281.

———. Cognitive energy level, response acquiescence, and authoritarianism. *J. soc. Psychol.*, 1959, *49*, 65–69.

———. Stylistic response determinants in the California Psychological Inventory. *Educ. psychol. Measmt*, 1960, *10*, 339–346.

———. The development and evaluation of the Personality Research Form. University of Western Ontario Research Bulletin, 1965.

———, and MESSICK, S. J. A note on "ethno-centrism" and acquiescent response sets. *J. abnorm. soc. Psychol.*, 1957, *54*, 132–134.

———, ———. Content and style in personality assessment. *Psychol. Bull.*, 1958, *55*, 243–252.

———, ———. Acquiescence and desirability as response determinants on the MMPI. *Educ. psychol. Measmt*, 1961, *21*, 771–790.

———, ———. Response styles on the MMPI: Comparison of clinical and normal samples. *J. abnorm. soc. Psychol.*, 1962, *65*, 285–299. (a)

———, ———. Response styles and the assessment of psychopathology. In S. J. Messick and J. Ross (Eds.), *Measurement in Personality and Cognition.* New York: John Wiley, 1962. (b) Acquiescence: The nonvanishing variance component. *Amer. Psychologist*, 1965, *20*, 498. (Abstract)

———, ———, and Solley, C. M. How "rigid" is the "authoritarian"? *J. abnorm. soc. Psychol.*, 1957, *54*, 137–140.

———, and Minton, H. L. A forced adjective preference scale for personality assessment. *Psychol. Reports*, 1963, *12*, 515–520.

———, and PACINE, L. Response styles and academic achievement. *Educ. psychol. Measmt*, 1961, *21*, 1015–1028.

———, and PAYNE, I. R. Personality scale for shallow affect. *Psychol. Reports*, 1963, *13*, 687–698.

———, and SINGER, J. E. Items, judgments, and persons. University of Western Ontario Research Bulletin, 1965.

KATZELL, R. A. Cross-validation of item analyses. *Educ. psychol. Measmt*, 1951, *11*, 16–22.

KENNY, D. T. The influence of social desirability on discrepancy measures between real self and ideal self. *J. consult. Psychol.*, 1956, *20*, 315–318.

KLEIN, E. B., and SOLOMON, L. F. Game playing correlates of response set among schizophrenics. Paper read at American Psychological Assn. meeting, New York, 1961.

KLETT, C. J. The social desirability stereotype in a hospital population. *J. consult. Psychol.*, 1957, *21*, 419–421.

———, and YAUKEY, D. W. A cross-cultural comparison of judgments of social desirability. *J. soc. Psychol.*, 1959, *49*, 19–26.

KLIPPLE, SUZANNE J. The effect of stimulus meaning in the elicitation of response bias. Unpublished M.A. thesis, Louisiana State University, 1964.

KREIDT, P. H., and DAWSON, R. I. Response set and the prediction of clerical job performance. *J. appl. Psychol.*, 1961, *45*, 175–178.

KUETHE, J. L. Acquiescent response set and the psychasthenia scale: An analysis via the Aussage experiment. *J. abnorm. soc. Psychol.*, 1960, *61*, 319–322.

LaPOINTE, R. E., and AUCLAIRE, G. A. The use of social desirability in forced-choice methodology. *Amer. Psychologist*, 1961, *16*, 446. (Abstract)

LEAVITT, H. J., HAX, H., and ROCHE, J. H. "Authoritarianism" and agreement with things authoritative. *J. Psychol.*, 1955, *40*, 215–221.

LENTZ, T. F. Acquiescence as a factor in the measurement of personality. *Psychol. Bull.*, 1938, *35*, 659. (Abstract)

LEVINE, R., CHEIN, I., and MURPHY, G. The relationship of the intensity of a need to the amount of perceptual distortion. *J. Psychol.*, 1942, *13*, 283–293.

LEWIS, H. B., and FRANKLIN, M. An experimental study of the role of the ego in work: II. The significance of task-orientation in work. *J. exp. Psychol.*, 1944, *34*, 195–215.

LEWIS, N. A., and TAYLOR, J. A. Anxiety and extreme response preferences. *Educ. psychol. Measmt*, 1955, *15*, 111–116.

LICHTENSTEIN, E., and BRYAN, J. H. Acquiescence and the MMPI: An item reversal approach. *J. abnorm. Psychol.*, 1965, *70*, 290–293.

LINDEMAN, H. H., and ADAMS, H. E. Deviant responses to ambiguous visual stimulus patterns. *Psychol. Rec.*, 1963, *13*, 73–77.

LINDQUIST, E. F. *Design and analysis of experiments in psychology and education.* Boston: Houghton-Mifflin, 1953.

Loevinger, Jane. Objective tests as instruments of psychology theory. *Psychol. Reports*, 1957, *3*, 635–694. (*Monograph Supplement 9*)

————. Theory and techniques of assessment. *Annu. Rev. Psychol.*, 1959, *10*, 287–316.

LORGE, I. Gen-like: Halo or reality? *Psychol. Bull.*, 1937, *34*, 545–546.

LÖVAAS, O. I. Social desirability ratings of personality variables by Norwegian and American college students. *J. abnorm. soc. Psychol.*, 1958, *57*, 124–125.

LUCHINS, A. S. Mechanization in problem-solving. *Psychol. Monogr.*, 1942, *54*, No. 6.

MACCORQUODALE, K., and MEEHL, P. E. EDWARD C. TOLMAN. In W. K. Estes, *et al. Modern learning theory.* New York: Appleton-Century-Crofts, 1954.

McGEE, R. K. The relationship between response style and personality variables: Acquiescence and social orientation. Unpublished Ph.D. dissertation, Vanderbilt University, 1961.

————. Additional data on the acquiescence myth. Paper read at Midwestern Psychological Assn. meeting, Louisville, 1962. (a)

————. The relationship between response style and personality variables: I. The measurement of response acquiescence. *J. abnorm. soc. Psychol.*, 1962, *64*, 229–233. (b)

————. The relationship between response style and personality variables: II. The prediction of independent conformity behavior. *J. abnorm. soc. Psychol.*, 1962, *65*, 347–351. (c)

————. Response style as a personality variable: By what criterion? *Psychol. Bull.*, 1962, *59*, 284–295. (d)

————, and Komorita, S. S. Further studies on acquiescence and personality. *Moccasin Bend Research Bulletin*, 1963, No. 1.

————, and LAND, S. L. An analysis of the stimulus acceptance vs. stimulus rejection explanation of the acquiescence response set. Paper read at Midwestern Psychological Assn. meeting, Chicago, 1963.

McGEOCH, J. A. *The psychology of human learning.* New York: Longmans, Green, 1942.

McGINNIES, E. Emotionality and perceptual defense. *Psychol. Rev.*, 1949, *56*, 244–251.

MAIER, N. R. F. An aspect of human reasoning. *British J. Psychol.*, 1933, *24*, 144–155.

MARLOWE, D., and CROWNE, D. F. Social desirability and response to perceived situational demands. *J. consult. Psychol.*, 1961, *25*, 109–115.

MARTIN, J. Acquiescence response styles as conformity and deviation. Unpublished Ph.D. dissertation, University of Western Australia, 1964. (a)

———. Acquiescence—measurement and theory. *British J. soc. clin. Psychol.*, 1964, *3*, 216–225. (b)

MEEHL, P. E. The dynamics of "structured" personality tests. *J. clin. Psychol.*, 1945, *1*, 296–303.

MESSICK, S. J. Personality structure. *Annu. Rev. Psychol.*, 1961, *12*, 93–128. (a)

———. Separate set and content scores for personality and attitude scales. *Educ. psychol. Measmt*, 1961, *21*, 915–923. (b)

———. Response style and content measures from personality inventories. *Educ. psychol. Measmt*, 1962, *22*, 41–56.

———. Psychology and methodology of response styles. Paper read at Western Psychological Assn. meeting, Honolulu, Hawaii, 1965.

———, and FREDERIKSEN, N. Ability, acquiescence, and "authoritarianism." *Psychol. Reports*, 1958, *4*, 687–697.

———, and JACKSON, D. N. Authoritarianism or acquiescence in Bass's data. *J. abnorm. soc. Psychol.*, 1957, *54*, 424–426.

———, ———. The measurement of authoritarian attitudes. *Educ. psychol. Measmt*, 1958, *18*, 241–253.

———, ———. Acquiescence and the factorial interpretation of the MMPI. *Psychol. Bull.*, 1961, *58*, 299–304. (a)

———, ———. Desirability scale values and dispersions for MMPI items. *Psychol. Rep.*, 1961, *8*, 409–414. (b)

MEYER, D. R., BAHRICK, H. P., and FITTS, P. M. Incentive, anxiety and the human eyeblink. *J. exp. Psychol.*, 1953, *45*, 183–187.

MOORE, ROSEMARIE K. Susceptibility to hypnosis and susceptibility to social influence. *J. abnorm. soc. Psychol.*, 1964, *68*, 282–294.

MOSCOVICI, S. Attitudes and opinions. *Annu. Rev. Psychol.*, 1963, *14*, 231–260.

NORMAN, W. T. The relative importance of test item content. *J. consult. Psychol.*, 1963, *27*, 166–174.

NUNNALLY, J. C., and HUSEK, T. B. The phony language examination: An approach to the measurement of response bias. *Educ. psychol. Measmt*, 1958, *18*, 275–282.

O'DONOVAN, D. Rating extremity. *Psychol. Rev.*, 1965, *72*, 358–372.

PALMER, R. D. Development of a differentiated handedness. *Psychol. Bull.*, 1964, *62*, 257–272.

PEABODY, D. Attitude, content, and agreement set in scales of authoritarianism, dogmatism, anti-Semitism, and economic conservatism. *J. abnorm. soc. Psychol.*, 1961, *63*, 1–11.

———. Models for estimating content and set components in attitude and personality scales. *Educ. psychol. Measmt*, 1964, *24*, 255–269.

POSTMAN, L., BRUNER, J. S. and McGINNIES, E. Personal values as selective factors in perception. *J. abnorm. soc. Psychol.*, 1948, *43*, 142–154.

PRATT, C. C. Repetition, motivation and recall. *British J. Psychol.*, 1936, *26*, 425–429.

PRENTICE, N. M. The comparability of positive and negative items in scales of ethnic prejudice. *J. abnorm. soc. Psychol.*, 1956, *52*, 420–421.

PRICE, A. C., and DEABLER, H. L. Diagnosis for organicity by means of spiral aftereffect. *J. consult. Psychol.*, 1955, *19*, 299–302.

PROSHANSKY, H. M., and MURPHY, G. The effects of reward and punishment on perception. *J. Psychol.*, 1942, *13*, 295–305.

QUINN, R. P. Personality, conformity, and the extraneous third variable—acquiescence response set. Paper read at American Psychological Assn. meeting, Philadelphia, 1963.

———, and LICHTENSTEIN, E. Convergent and discriminant validities of acquiescence measures. *J. gen. Psychol.*, 1965, *73*, 93–104.

RADCLIFFE, J. A. Some properties of ipsative score matrices and their relevance for some current interest tests. *Australian J. Psychol*, 1963, *15*, 1–11.

RAZRAN, G. H. S. Attitudinal control of human conditioning. *J. Psychol.*, 1936, *2*, 327–337.

RECHTSHAFFEN, A., and MEDNICK, S. A. The autokinetic word technique. *J. abnorm. soc. Psychol.*, 1955, *51*, 346.

REESE, H. W. Discrimination learning set in rhesus monkeys. *Psychol. Bull.*, 1964, *61*, 321–340.

RENNER, K. E. The idiographic case study: Its place in theories of personality and psychopathology. Unpublished manuscript, 1964.

RETHLINGSHAFER, D. *Motivation as related to personality.* New York: McGraw-Hill, 1963.

RETTIG, S., Jacobson, F. N., DESPRES, L., and PASAMANICK, B. Rating response set as a function of objective status criteria. *Sociometry*, 1958, *21*, 281–291.

ROBINSON, E. S. The psychology of public education. *Amer. J. Pub. Hlth.*, 1933, *23*, 1–125.

ROHRER, J. H., and SHERIF, M. (Eds.) *Social psychology at the crossroads.* New York: Harper, 1951.

ROITZSCH, J. C., and BERG, I. A. Deviant responses as indicators of immaturity and neuroticism. *J. clin. Psychol.*, 1959, *15*, 417–419.

ROKEACH, M. *The open and closed mind.* New York: Basic Books, 1960.

RORER, L. G. The function of item content in MMPI responses. Unpublished Ph.D. dissertation, University of Minnesota, 1963. (a)

————. The great response-style myth. *Oregon Research Institute Research Monograph*, 1963, *3*, No. 6. (b)

————. The great response-style myth. *Psychol. Bull.*, 1965, *63*, 129–156.

————, and GOLDBERG, L. R. Acquiescence in the MMPI? *Oregon Research Institute Research Bulletin*, 1964, *4*, No. 1. (a)

————, ————. Acquiescence and the vanishing variance com-*Oregon Research Institute Research Bulletin*, 1964, *4*, No. 1. (b)

————, ————. On the negligibility of acquiescence response variance. *Amer. Psychol.*, 1964, *19*, 493–494. (Abstract) (c)

————, ————. Acquiescence on the MMPI? *Educ. psychol. Measmt*, 1965, *25*, 801–817. (a)

————, ————. Acquiescence and the vanishing variance component. *J. appl. Psychol.*, 1965, *49*, 422–430. (b)

ROSENHAN, D. Hypnosis, conformity, and acquiescence. Paper read at American Psychological Assn. meeting, Philadelphia, 1963.

ROSENTHAL, D., LAWLOR, W. G., ZAHN, T. P., and SHAKOW, D. The relationship of some aspects of mental set to degree of schizophrenic disorganization, *J. Pers.*, 1960, *28*, 26–38.

ROSS, S., and KOHL, D. M. Perceptual factors in number choices. *J. gen. Psychol.*, 1948, *39*, 39–47.

RUBIN-RABSON, G. Correlates of the noncommittal test-item response, *J. clin. Psychol.*, 1954, *10*, 93–95.

SAUNDERS, D. R. Some preliminary interpretive material for the PRI. Research Memorandum 55-15. Princeton, N.J.: Educational Testing Service, 1955.

SCHAFER, R. *Psychoanalytic interpretation in Rorschach testing.* New York: Grune and Stratton, 1954.

————, and MURPHY, G. The role of autism in visual figure-ground relationship. *J. exp. Psychol.*, 1943, 32, 335–343.

SCHLOSBERG, H. An investigation of certain factors related to the ease of conditioning. *J. gen. Psychol.*, 1932, 7, 328–342.

SCHUTZ, R. E., and FOSTER, R. J. A factor analytic study of acquiescent and extreme response set. *Educ. psychol. Measmt.*, 1963, 23, 435–447.

SECHREST, L., and JACKSON, D. N. The generality of deviant response tendencies. *J. consult. Psychol.*, 1962, 26, 395–401.

————, ————. Deviant response tendencies: Their measurement and interpretation. *Educ. psychol. Measmt*, 1963, 23, 33–53.

SELLS, S. B. The atmosphere effect. *Arch. Psychol.*, N. Y., 1936, 29, No. 200.

SHAKOW, D. Some psychological aspects of schizophrenia. In *Feelings and emotions*, the Mooseheart symposium, 1950, Ch. 31, 283–290.

SHAW, M. E. Some correlates of social acquiescence. *J. soc. Psychol.*, 1961, 55, 133–141.

SHELLEY, H. P. Response set and the California Attitude Scale. *Educ. psychol. Measmt*, 1955, 16, 63–67.

SHERIF, M. *The psychology of social norms.* New York: Harper, 1936.

SHERRINGTON, G. S. *The integrative action of the nervous system.* New Haven: Yale University Press, 1952.

SHURE, G. H., and ROGERS, M. S. Note of caution on the factor analysis of the MMPI. *Psychol. Bull.*, 1965, 63, 14–18.

SILLER, J., and CHIPMAN, A. Response set paralysis: Implications for measurement and control. *J. consult. Psychol.*, 1963, 27, 432–438.

SINGER, W. B., and YOUNG, P. T. Studies in affective reactions: III. The specificity of affective reactions. *J. genet. Psychol.*, 1941, 24, 327–341.

SINGH, P. N., and RETTIG, S. Cross-cultural differences in habitual response preferences as an index of anxiety. *J. soc. Psychol.*, 1962, 58, 9–15.

SMALL, D. O., and CAMPBELL, D. T. The effect of acquiescence response-set upon the relationship of the F scale and conformity. *Sociometry*, 1960, 23, 69–71.

SMITH, S., and GUTHRIE, E. R. *General psychology in terms of behavior.* New York: Appleton-Century-Crofts, 1921.

SOLOMON, L. F., and KLEIN, E. B. A comparison of response set tendencies in a normal and schizophrenic sample. Paper read at Eastern Psychological Assn. meeting, Philadelphia, 1961.

————, ————. The relationship between agreeing response set and social desirability. *J. abnorm. soc. Psychol.*, 1963, *66*, 176–178.

SOUEIF, M. I. Extreme response sets as a measure of intolerance of ambiguity. *British J. Psychol.*, 1958, *49*, 329–334.

SPERRY, R. W. On the neural basis of the conditioned response. *British J. Animal Behav.*, 1955, *3*, 41–44.

SPRUILL, JEAN. Concurrent and empirical validity of the Perceptual Reaction Test. Unpublished M.A. thesis, Louisiana State University, 1963.

STAGNER, R. *Psychology of personality.* New York: McGraw-Hill, 1937.

————. *Psychology of personality.* (2nd ed.) New York: McGraw-Hill, 1948.

STONE, L. A., and MARGOSHES, A. Verbal embellishment responses on the MMPI. *J. clin. Psychol.*, 1965, *21*, 278–279.

STRICKER, L. J. Acquiescence and social desirability response styles, item characteristics, and conformity. *Psychol. Reports*, 1963, *12*, 319–341. (*Monograph Supplement* 2–12.)

————. A review of the Edwards Personal Preference Schedule. In O. K. Buros (Ed.), *The sixth mental measurements yearbook.* Highland Park, N. J.: The Gryphon Press, 1966.

STRONG, E. K., JR. *Manual for Vocational Interest Blank for Men.* Stanford: Stanford University Press, 1935.

STRUENING, E. L., and SPILKA, B. The structure of social desirability as measured by the Edwards and Marlowe-Crowne scales. Paper read at American Psychological Assn. meeting, Los Angeles, 1964.

TAYLOR, J. B. Social desirability and MMPI performance: The individual case. *J. consult. Psychol.*, 1959, *23*, 514–517.

THORNDIKE, E. L. *The psychology of learning.* New York: Teachers College, 1913.

TITUS, H. E., and HOLLANDER, E. P. The California F scale in psychological research: 1950–1955. *Psychol. Bull.*, 1957, *54*, 47–64.

TOLMAN, E. C. Theories of learning. In F. A. Moss (Ed.), *Comparative psychology.* New York: Prentice-Hall, 1934.

TORGERSON, W. S. *Theory and methods of scaling.* New York: Wiley, 1958.

VAN DE CASTLE, R. L. Development and validation of a Perceptual
Maturity Scale using figure preferences. *J. consult. Psychol.,*
1965, *29,* 314–319.

VEGAS, OLGA V., FRYE, R. L., and ADAMS, H. E. Validation of
the Iota scale of the Perceptual Reaction Test. *Percept. mot.
Skills,* 1963, *17,* 242.

VOAS, R. B. Relationships among three types of response sets.
Pensacola, Fla.: U.S. Naval School of Aviation Medicine,
Report No. 15, 1958.

VOTH, A. C. An experimental study of mental patients through the
autokinetic phenomenon. *Amer. J. Psychiat.,* 1947, *103,* 793–
805.

WALLEN, R. W. Food aversions of normal and neurotic males.
J. abnorm. soc. Psychol., 1945, *40,* 77–81.

———. Food aversions and behavior disorders. *J. consult. Psychol.,*
1948, *12,* 310–312.

WEINGOLD, H. P., ADAMS, H. E., and WITTMAN, F. Sexual sym-
bolism, abstract designs, and the PRT. *Psychol. Rep.,* 1963,
13, 90.

WIGGINS, J. S. Strategic method, and stylistic variance in the
MMPI. *Psychol. Bull.,* 1962, *59,* 224–242.

———, and RUMRILL, C. Social desirability in the MMPI and
Welsh's factor scales A and R. *J. consult. Psychol.,* 1959, *23,*
100–106.

WILE, T. S. *Handedness: right and left.* Boston: Lothrop, Lee, and
Shepard, 1934.

WITKIN, H. A. The perception of the upright. *Scient. Amer.,* 1959,
200, 50–56.

———, LEWIS, H. B., HERTZMAN, M., MACHOVER, K., MEISSNER,
P. B., and WAPNER, S. *Personality through perception.* New
York: Harper, 1954.

WOODWORTH, R. S. Imageless thought. *J. Phil. Psychol. sci. Meth.,*
1906, *3,* 701–708.

———. Situation and goal-set. *Amer. J. Psychol.,* 1937, *50,* 130–
140.

YAMAMOTU, J., SEEMAN, W., and LESTER, B. K. The tattooed man.
J. nerv. ment. Dis., 1963, *136,* 365–367.

ZAX, M., COWEN, E. L., and PETER, SISTER MARY. A comparative
study of novice nuns and college females using the response
set approach. *J. abnorm. soc. Psychol.,* 1963, *66,* 369–375.

———, ———, BUDIN, W., and BIGGS, C. F. The social desirability of trait descriptive terms: Applications to an alcoholic sample. *J. soc. Psychol.*, 1962, 56, 21–27.

ZEIGARNIK, B. Uber das Behalten von erledigten und unerledigten Handlungern. *Psychologische Forschung*, 1927, 9, 1–85.

ZUCKERMAN, M., and EISEN, BARBARA. Relationship of acquiescence response set to authoritarianism and dependency. *Psychol. Rep.*, 1962, 10, 95–102.

———, and NORTON, J. Response set and content factors in the California F Scale and the parental attitude research instrument. *J. soc. Psychol.*, 1961, 53, 199–210.

———, ———, and SPRAGUE, D. S. Acquiescence and extreme sets and their role in tests of authoritarianism and parental attitude. *Psychiat. Res. Rep.*, 1958, 10, 28–45.

———, OPPENHEIMER, C., and GERSHOWITZ, D. Acquiescence and extremes response sets of actors and teachers. *Psychol. Rep.*, 1965, 16, 168–170.

Index